# MODERN SOCIAL WORK PRACTICE

To
Elizabeth, Emma, Richard
Adam, Amy, Sara

# MODERN SOCIAL WORK PRACTICE

## Teaching and Learning in Practice Settings

MARK DOEL and STEVEN M. SHARDLOW

Interactive workbook
combines learning with
Exercises which can
be undertaken with
Practice Assessors
Links into the NOS 2002

ASHGATE

Published by
Ashgate Publishing Limited
Gower House
Croft Road
Aldershot
Hampshire GU11 3HR
England

Ashgate Publishing Company
Suite 420
101 Cherry Street
Burlington, VT 05401-4405
USA

Ashgate website: http://www.ashgate.com

**British Library Cataloguing in Publication Data**
Doel, Mark
    Modern social work practice : teaching and learning in
    practice settings. – 3$^{rd}$ ed.
    1.Social work education 2.Social services – Problems,
    exercises, etc. 3.Social case work – Problems, exercises,
    etc. 4.Social workers – In-service training
    I.Title II.Shardlow, Steven, 1952- III.Doel, Mark. New
    social work practice
    361.3'2'0683

**Library of Congress Cataloging-in-Publication Data**
Doel, Mark.
    Modern social work practice : teaching and learning in practice settings / by Mark
Doel and Steven M. Shardlow. - 3$^{rd}$ ed.
        p. cm.
    Includes bibliographical references and index.
    ISBN 0-7546-4120-1 (hardback) - ISBN 0-7546-4121-X (pbk.)
  1. Social work education. 2. Social service--Problems, exercises, etc. 3. Social
casework--Problems, exercises, etc. 4. Social workers--In-service training. I.
Shardlow, Steven, 1952- II. Title.

    HV11.D64 2005
    361.3'2'0683--dc22

2004021202

ISBN 0 7546 4120 1 (Hbk)
ISBN 0 7546 4121 X (Pbk)

Reprinted 2006

Typeset by Tradespools, Frome, Somerset
Printed and bound in Great Britain by MPG Books Ltd., Bodmin, Cornwall

# Contents

# List of figures and tables

## Figures

## Tables

# Acknowledgements

We would like to thank Jessica Kingsley Publishers for allowing us to use an adapted version of the Glossary from *Learning to Practise Social Work: international approaches*, edited by Shardlow, S.M. and Doel, M. (2002). Acknowledgement is also due to Kevin Kallaugher for allowing us to reprint his cartoon (p. 204).

Finally, we would like to take this opportunity to thank all those people who have helped to develop the materials in this book. We hope that the materials will be well-used and further refined, so that we can all continue to learn about good social work practice.

# Introduction

This book is about social work practice, with a particular focus on teaching and learning social work in practice settings. We hope that readers will find it a useful and entertaining guide to becoming a social worker. Its first appearance as *Social Work Practice* was in 1993, published by Gower in a workbook format. We updated and revised this in 1998 to produce *The New Social Work Practice*. This current incarnation, *Modern Social Work Practice*, follows the same pattern as its parent and grandparent, though it has been rewritten to take account of the fast-changing world of social work practice.

As the authors, we cannot presume exactly who you, our reader, is. If you are a student of social work you may be using this book independently to support your learning or, more likely, with a person who is guiding your learning in the agency setting. If you are the person who has responsibility for helping a student learn about social work, you may be a practitioner, manager, service user or carer. Your location may be a statutory agency, such as a social services department, a voluntary, not-for-profit organization, a private agency, a user-led agency or, indeed, a place in which social work is not a prime activity. Whatever the site for the student's practice learning, it is important to remember that your task is to help the student learn about social work, not to train them to do your job. In other words, the specific work in which you are engaged is but one example of practice. Your perspective as the student's guide or teacher is immensely valuable, but it should be set in the broader context.

Helping students to move from the specific of your location to the general of social work practice, and back to different specifics (not just yours), is a demanding skill. You may not be wearing the 'L' plates, but this is going to be a learning experience for you, too, no matter how experienced you are.

## Modern social work practice: *the more things change ...?*

The opportunity to rewrite and update a book of this kind is also an occasion to make a statement of what constitutes 'modern social work practice'. What should social workers know? How should they be able to 'do' it? The modern curriculum for social work reflects current political as well as professional and service user concerns, and it has been an interesting exercise to decide what changes to make in the book's coverage. Indeed, if the lifespan of the qualifications in social work in the United Kingdom is an indicator, we can see that the pace of change is increasing, with the Certificate of Qualification in Social Work (CQSW) surviving for over twenty years and the Diploma in Social Work (DipSW) for barely ten. At this rate, we could expect the new social work award in the UK (the undergraduate degree) to withstand a mere five years!

The content of practice learning for social work arises, of course, from the expectations of government, employers and regulators, as well as from those who practise social work and those who use it. Occupational standards set by employers' organizations, such as TOPSS in England (TOPSS, 2002), the requirements of government departments, such as the Department of Health (DH, 2002), statements from higher education bodies such as the Quality Assurance Agency (QAA, 2002), and professional codes of practice, such as those of the GSCC (2002a) and the respective care councils for Northern Ireland, Scotland and Wales, all shape the final curriculum for social work education and training.

Social work is a highly contextual form of practice; in particular, the organizations in which social work is practised have a significant impact on the shape of that practice. Currently, these organizations are experiencing an extraordinary rate of change, and the highly fluid and unpredictable organizational context can sap practitioners' and managers' energies. In addition, at a political level, the expectation of speedy, observable improvements is a further pressure, especially since, in reality, the horizons for change on this scale are far-reaching.

Yet, amidst the whirlwinds of change, there is much that endures. We might transform our wardrobe with increasing frequency, but the body beneath hardly alters. One constant is the mission of social work to combat social injustice and oppression by working with people who are at the margins of society, and the commitment of practitioners to that mission. Almost a century ago, Clement Attlee (1920) claimed that social workers will always be agitators. Of course, we cannot expect to receive thanks for our ability to remind the wider society of the effects of inequality and poverty. No change there. Competent social work practice continues to depend on an unusually broad, and often contested, repertoire of knowledge, values and skills – not just in direct work with individuals, families, groups and communities, but also in negotiating complex organizations. Capable social workers continue to need qualities that help them cope with dilemma and doubt on a daily basis, and to maintain their intellectual curiosity.

In these circumstances, it is crucial that we find ways of making social work attractive to those who are not yet committed. In a careers choice survey of more than 1000 students conducted by the Careers Research Advisory Committee in 2003, 17 out of 100 students favoured management as a career choice, 13 chose banking and financial services, and 12 sales and marketing. Careers in the public sector were the least popular, with only 3 out of 100, and just 1 out of 100 choosing 'social healthcare' (*Times Higher Educational Supplement*, 13 June 2003). Any literature which captures the imagination of possible practitioners is to be welcomed. We hope this book will be a contribution to the mission to explain social work to a wider constituency.

It is not surprising that there is an enduring anxiety in the profession about its survival. However, contrary to some of the grim audits on offer (for example, Jones, 2001), there is a strong case to be made that social work's values are being absorbed by other professions; for example, the occupational therapy described in *Occupational Therapy Without Borders* (Kronenberg *et al.*, 2004) is surely social work by another name? Indeed, social work values, such as celebrating diversity and difference, are increasingly those of the wider society.

So, whatever the current wardrobe of occupational standards, the fundamentals change only very slowly. Indeed, in those aspects of life where real change would be most welcome (poverty and structural discrimination, for example) the pace of change is imperceptible. Service users continue to experience poverty, injustice and distress – and many continue to survive these experiences with resourcefulness and determination. It is important to remember these constants in the midst of the frenetic activity which is sometimes mistaken for purposefulness.

Speaking in 1981 at an inauguration ceremony at Birmingham Polytechnic (now the University of Central England), Dame Eileen Younghusband reviewed several decades of social work education, training and practice. In addition to looking back over several decades, she also looked forward to the year 2001:

> There will be some things which won't change. What really matters, in the last resort, what people in perplexity, sorrow or disgrace really want is commitment to them as people – staying on the job, being 'for them', being understanding and determined to help them, and having the imagination, the knowledge, the confidence and the resources to do so. It is that, more than anything else, that I hope will be alive and active in the year 2001.

Her vision for the year 2001 is just as true for the year 2021 and beyond.

# Modern practice learning

> The new social work qualification has been introduced to ensure that the training of social work students will result in higher standards of service delivery to the people who will rely on them in times of need, and ensure that graduates are confident and competent to practise on qualification. We have always made it clear that the emphasis of training must be on practice and the practical relevance of theory. This means that students need a plentiful and varied supply of good opportunities to practise and learn safely. The success of the new qualification depends on this. (Stephen Ladyman, Parliamentary Under Secretary of State for Community, Foreword to Practice Learning Taskforce, *First Annual Report*, 2004)

> In theory there is no difference between theory and practice, but in practice there is. (Anon)

There is no doubt that the place of practice teaching and practice learning in social work has been transformed over the last two decades. Students themselves have long reported favourably about their placements, and this message has been heard in the arrangements for social work education, as indicated by Stephen Ladyman's statement (above) and by the increased resources available to practice learning. For example, the Practice Learning Taskforce (PLTF), which was established to increase the opportunities for practice learning in England and Wales, disbursed £400 000 to support seventy-two regional development projects in a five-month period up to March 2003 (PLTF, 2004: 5).

There are early indications that the arrangements for practice learning in the new social work award in the UK will offer a broader range of sites for students' learning (Kearney, 2003). Many programmes are taking the opportunity of an increase in the number of days in practice learning to introduce a range of opportunities, often at three or even four separate sites.[1] The hope is that students will experience 'non-traditional' learning, sometimes in sites which are not specifically social work, and from a broad range of teachers, which will include service users and carers. This is a tremendous opportunity and one which other professional groups are likely to follow with keen interest. In the field of occupational therapy, for example, Fieldhouse (2003) has noted the opportunity for developing practice by *learning from service users*, in this instance via the impact of a gardening group on the mental health, well-being and social networking of the group members.

The emphasis on practice learning follows the successful evolution of 'student supervision' to 'practice teaching' over the last few decades. In both its conceptualization and its application, practice learning has been transformed, with the role of the practice teacher now firmly established as that of a teacher and mentor, not just an experienced role model. The opportunities for continuing professional development for practitioners (via the Practice Teaching Award in the UK) have consolidated these changes, even if they have not been able to prevent a haemorrhage of practice teachers into social work management. There is relatively little on offer for managers, by way of education and training, so we should not be surprised that practice teaching courses have been seen as a valuable foundation for staff supervision.

Modern practice learning is, therefore, at an exciting stage of development, with the expansion into new learning sites and the potential for students to develop new and different services. However, we should not underestimate the challenge of increasing the numbers of opportunities and sites for practice learning, with shortfalls in England calculated in June 2004 as running at anything up to a requirement for a 140 per cent increase in provision by 2006–7 (PLTF website). We must also ensure that the practice community learns from these experiences, since we still know too little about what actually occurs in the detail of practice tutorials[2] or about the suitability of different kinds of arrangement for practice teaching and learning. The Practice Learning Taskforce noted in its 2004 *Annual Report* (p. 9) that 'there is no common agreement between agencies, particularly Local Authorities, regarding which staff are suitably qualified or experienced to take on the practice assessor/teacher role'.

---

[1] We use the term 'site' to describe the place where practice learning takes place; this is different from 'practice learning opportunity' which may not necessarily be a physical location.

[2] Our preferred name for 'student supervision session', though we use both terms in this book.

It will also be important to be vigilant that the emphasis on the practical relevance of theory does not lead to the *thinking* aspects of social work being eclipsed by the *doing* aspects. As one student commented about theory-less practice, 'it's like an airfix kit without the instruction book'. We hope this book provides both the kit and the instructions.

These themes continue to be explored in greater detail throughout the book, and especially in the introduction to Part I.

## The content, structure and purpose of the book

*Modern Social Work Practice* builds on features from *Social Work Practice* and *The New Social Work Practice*. The four parts remain in place: Foundations of Practice; Direct Practice; Agency Practice; and Themes of Practice. Taken together these parts define a curriculum for practice learning. However, the Introductions to each of the four parts reflect the changing context of practice: new opportunities for practice learning; interprofessional learning and practice; creative and procedural practice; and evidence-based practice.

We have also introduced new topics which reflect developments in social work practice, such as Whistleblowing and Working with Risk. That is not to suggest that these are new concerns; the complex dilemmas of what to do when faced with questionable practices and the need to be aware of, and balance, risks are hardly novel. However, they are attracting increased attention, as evidenced in the occupational standards for social work (TOPSS, 2002) and the Benchmark Statement for social work (QAA, 2002).

### Activities

Readers of *Social Work Practice* and *The New Social Work Practice* have commented favourably on the technique of having one substantial activity to introduce the theme of a chapter, and this approach has been maintained for *Modern Social Work Practice*. Most of the activities are new to this book, and each is introduced with its purpose, a suggested method to use it and ideas for variations on this method. In addition, we give consideration to how students from other related professions could use the activity, either together with social work students or independently, and we link the theme of the chapter to occupational standards for social work. These standards underpin the new social work award in England and Wales, though they have wider relevance to the role and tasks of social workers.

Although individual activities can be used on a one-off basis, it is better to become acquainted with the whole beforehand, and to return to activities at different stages in the student's learning. The topics in Parts I, II and III are in no strict chronological order, and the themes in Part IV run through the whole of social work practice. A knowledge of the whole curriculum for general practice will help when searching for the right activity for the occasion. A 'teachable moment' happens when the learner is particularly receptive to the teaching, and a well-timed activity can help these moments to occur.

The activities which introduce each chapter in this book are designed to help participants to explore issues in practice as well as enhance technical skills. They develop an ability to learn, which we believe is a necessary condition to develop a competence to practise. Work-based supervisors, practice teachers and assessors need to make links between the learning which takes place via these activities and the student's direct practice with people using the agency's services.

Sometimes it is helpful to translate an activity into circumstances which reflect the particular practice setting. This has its value. However, it is also true that it is easier to 'think outside the box' if you are not actually in it! In other words, new kinds of situation are less likely to rely on established patterns of thinking and doing. We return to this theme later in the section on simulated learning.

The activities can be used to assess students' practice learning as well as to develop it. In particular, revisiting an activity towards the end of a period of practice learning is a good way of measuring changes in the understanding of practice. However, participants should always be clear about the purpose of any activity and what uses may be made of it.

Following each activity are two sections – one about teaching and the other about learning, and each related to the theme of the chapter. The teaching notes consider likely opportunities for the topic of the chapter and explore the topic in greater detail. The learning notes conclude with a section about issues of assessment in the topic under consideration, with pointers to further reading. Although each set of notes addresses the reader as the teacher and the student respectively, you will nevertheless find it helpful to read both sets of notes, whatever your role, since there is considerable overlap between teaching and learning. However, just occasionally there is a suggestion in the guidance for the activity that you do not read the notes until *after* the activity has been completed.

## Terminology

Developments in practice have their parallels in changes in terminology. The term 'service user' has superseded 'client'. The name used to describe the person who facilitates the student's learning in practice settings and assesses their ability has also seen changes. This person was for many years known as the student supervisor (field instructor in North America). Towards the end of the 1980s 'student supervisor' was replaced with the term 'practice teacher' in a move which reflected the increasing importance of the educational function of supervision with students, and to differentiate it from staff supervision. (In North America, practice teacher is a term already in use, but it describes a person who teaches social work practice in the college setting.)

With the introduction of a new social work award in the UK, there have been some references to 'practice assessors', presumably as a desire to emphasize the assessment function in this role. This change has not been embraced by the field, with some suspicion that the educational aspects of the role are devalued by this new term, and it is too early to know whether the term will gain currency. Even so, new arrangements for practice learning will challenge us to reconsider who might take on the role of 'practice teacher', with students likely to experience some day-to-day supervision with people who are not social workers, including service users and carers. This book is written with these new developments in mind.

We have included a glossary towards the end of the book, as a guide to terminology and acronyms (pages 265–274).

# Learning

## ... and participation

The kind of activity-based learning advocated in this book is participative in a number of ways. Practice teachers and practice learners are undergoing a similar process, whilst recognizing their different roles. The teacher is not a repository of knowledge who fills the student's empty vessel, but rather a person with considerable experience who is prepared to look at practice critically and reflectively. This applies to the teacher's own practice as well as the student's. Activity-based learning acknowledges that students bring knowledge, beliefs, values and skills which will have a vital impact on their practice and, perhaps even more crucial, on their ability to learn practice.

Those who use these activities must, therefore, be prepared to be open about their own practice and experience. Learning flourishes in a creative and energetic climate, but conjuring up this environment in a busy day is not easy. The activities can add spice to student learning and staff development, and we would be surprised if they did not have an impact on everyone's practice, whether 'teacher' or 'learner'.

In summary, the activities are participative in two ways: as a method of learning which is engaging and active, but also as a process in which all participants (whether they are styled teachers or learners) are learning.

## ... and simulation

There are different ways of learning. *Learning by doing* is one, and it has been used heavily by student supervisors in the past. The student experiences direct practice with people and learns 'on the job', with some preparation beforehand and discussion afterwards with the supervisor. Although the student gets an authentic experience of the coalface, this method of learning tends to perpetuate existing practices – good and bad – and often fails to highlight the learning which may have taken place. When learning opportunities come solely via direct practice experience it is difficult to pace them in a way that can match the individual student's needs and abilities.

*Live teaching* in the same room uses direct practice with people as a learning opportunity. The practice teacher can give direct feedback to students about their work, and this has an immediate impact on the students' practice in a way that is not possible when the practice teacher is absent. The advantages of such immediate feedback are clear, but the presence of the practice teacher has to be carefully managed.

Another way of learning, illustrated by the activities in this book, is by using materials which *simulate practice situations*. These can be very close approximations to practice, like flight simulations used to train pilots, or activities which, by their very distance from direct practice, help to cast it in a new light. Sometimes an interesting mix of distance and proximity can be achieved by using metaphors, and a number of activities in the book are based on metaphor.

We have described the advantages of using these kinds of teaching materials elsewhere (Doel and Shardlow, 1996). Simulated practice is a relatively safe environment for learning because the pace of action can be controlled and the consequences of taking risks are not serious. In these circumstances, the learner can feel free to experiment and be open to new approaches. The learner can also take the time to reflect on the issues which underlie the practice, especially the assumptions and values which might otherwise remain hidden or unchecked. The practice teacher can regulate the degree of challenge facing the student, so that it is sufficiently stretching to break new ground, but not so demanding that it breaks the student's confidence. Activities which simulate or represent aspects of social work practice can accelerate learning by encouraging risk taking.

Opportunities for learning in practice settings remain scarce, so there are economic as well as educational pressures to consider how opportunities for simulated learning might be constructed independent of the practice learning site. However, activities such as the ones in this book are no substitute for direct practice. Direct practice is essential to put the learning from simulation into action, to test it out and to experience a sense of imminence and of responsibility (Doel and Shardlow, 1996).

One of the best-known examples of a successful simulacrum is the London Underground map. This design icon has helped millions of people to navigate a large city, and its success lies in its ability to distort the places it portrays, both in terms of relative distance and position. The powers-that-be initially complained that it was an inaccurate and misleading guide to London's real complexities. However, we – the travelling public – know the diagram's success to lie in its emphasis on connections and linkages, because it provides a mental map of the city – and one that works.

The Underground map is an excellent analogy for the difference between social work practice 'on the ground' and the ability to present that practice in an accessible manner. The task of the teacher of practice is to create a design based on confidence that an element of distortion can help learning rather than hinder it, because the missing parts and the chaotic aspects can be fitted into the student's mental map sooner or later, once the basic linkages have been absorbed.

To illustrate this point, we can choose to present the contents of this book in the conventional linear fashion (see pages v–xii) or as an Underground-style design (see below).

Which do you find the more illuminating – the sequential presentation or the design? Some will prefer the former, others the latter. Some might be attracted to the idea of the design, but find its execution wanting (for instance, the reliance on grey

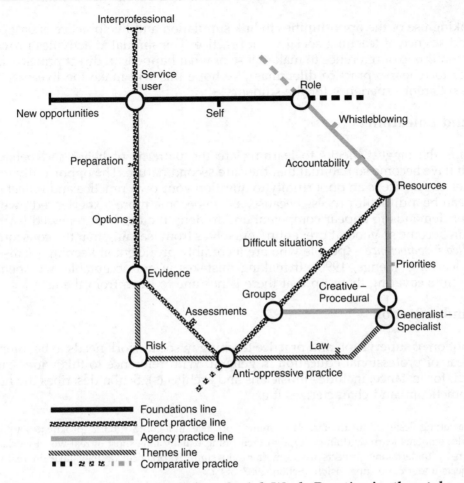

Figure I.1 **The contents of *Modern Social Work Practice* in the style of the London Underground**

shading rather than colour is too obscure). Ask yourself why you are more attracted to one format than another.

It is important to reflect on your own response to these different approaches because, collectively, they mirror the different responses to styles of learning social work practice. The search for variety is a vital ingredient of effective teaching and learning. The topics in this book, and their attendant activities, should provide a lively and diverse experience, but it is necessary to use them alongside other methods as well, such as live teaching. It also helps to think of different arrangements for the practice learning: one-to-one, small groups and so on. In addition to gaining an understanding of preferred approaches to learning, it is useful to broaden these preferences. Students should not cut themselves off from certain kinds of learning experience.

Making use of the opportunities to link simulation and live practice is part of the art and science of teaching social work practice. The simulated activities provide a common frame of reference to make sense of what happens in direct practice, and a chance to rehearse practice dilemmas. We hope this will make the live practice a more coherent experience for the student.

## ... and unlearning

Perhaps the biggest blocks to learning are the patterns of belief and behaviour which have become so habitual that they are second nature. The opportunity to be a teacher of practice is an opportunity to question your own practice and reflect on it. This can be a difficult process because, as we become more 'experienced', we face greater demands to appear competent and to deny the need for renewed learning. We can become so good at preventing ourselves from learning that the consequence is *skilled incompetence* – 'people who are incredibly proficient at keeping themselves from learning' (Senge, 1990). If making mistakes is not acceptable, we spend so much time covering them up that there is no time to learn from them.

## ... and reflection

The notion of supervision and practice teaching in social work needs to be informed by ideas of professional education in general. With reference to this wider canvas (which, for instance, includes musicians and architects), Schön describes the notion of a practicum, and characterizes it as:

> ... a setting designed for the task of learning a practice. In a context that approximates a practice world, students learn by doing, although their doing usually falls short of real-world work. They learn by undertaking projects that simulate and simplify practice; or they take on real-world projects under close supervision. (Schön, 1987: 37)

The view that existing professional knowledge cannot fit every case and that not every problem has a right answer leads Schön to the notion of reflection-in-action, by which 'students must develop new rules and methods of their own'. It relates to a central tenet of social work education – the concept of the transferability of knowledge; in other words, learning is not about experiencing every possible contingency (clearly an impossibility), but about making links and connections from one situation to another, and by creating a greater whole out of the sum of the parts.

Practice learning for professional education transcends both the learning site and the educational establishment, but must not become divorced from them. Schön goes even further, suggesting that 'in order to be credible and legitimate, a practicum must become a world with its own culture, including its own language, norms and rituals. Otherwise, it may be overwhelmed by the academic and professional cultures that surround it' (Schön, 1987: 170). This moves a long way from the notion of professional education as an apprenticeship, in which supervision is primarily concerned with regulating the student's behaviour to fit the requirements of work tasks. In this vision of practice learning, the student enters a distinct world created for the purpose of learning reflective practice. This is essential in order to establish professional practitioners as opposed to skilled technicians.

Crucially, supervision which nurtures the reflective student guarantees a future for the reflective practitioner.

## In conclusion

In *Modern Social Work Practice* we aim to provide a comprehensive guide for all those engaged in teaching and learning social work practice, an aid to understanding and doing social work in the context both of the new curriculum and the new health and social care landscape. The methods we use are similar to those employed in *Social Work Practice* (Doel and Shardlow, 1993) and *The New Social Work Practice* (Doel and Shardlow, 1998), using activities to introduce each separate theme.

There are already texts which are specifically tailored to the new social work in the UK, such as Parker and Bradley's excellent series, *Transforming Social Work Practice*, which is designed to help students to understand the various components of the curriculum and we make reference to other books in each chapter as appropriate. *Modern Social Work Practice* differs in its specific focus on the learning which takes place in the practice learning site, and in its aim to include all of those who are likely to be involved in this endeavour – students, teachers, assessors, users and carers – in active, participatory learning.

Your comments have been very helpful in our work to transform *The New Social Work Practice* into *Modern Social Work Practice*. Please let us know how you have used this book and, should we feel inspired to revisit this yet again in another five or so years, what aspects we should keep and what you would advise we change.

Mark Doel,
Centre for Health and Social Care
  Research,
Sheffield Hallam University,
Collegiate Crescent Campus,
Sheffield S10 2BP
email: m.doel@shu.ac.uk

Steven M. Shardlow,
Salford Centre for Social Work
  Research,
University of Salford,
Allerton Building,
Frederick Street,
Salford M6 6PU
email: s.m.shardlow@salford.ac.uk

# Visit our website

We have set up a website to complement the book. At the time of publication the website contains materials that have been previously published by us but have not been included in the present book. These materials include additional activities that practice teachers and students may wish to use to promote and develop learning.

In the future we hope the site may be developed to provide other opportunities to extend the work of this book.

The activities below appeared in *Social Work Practice* and *The New Social Work Practice* and are now freely available for download from our website at: www.shu.ac.uk/chscr/mswp.html

Believe It or Not

Dear Mrs Sunderland, Did You Know?

Endings

Essence of Social Work '98

Ethnic Realities

Fruit Salad

Gulliver's Travels

Headlines

In My View

Ladders and Snakes

Left Hand Column

Mapping the Work

Matter of Fact:
- *Less Transplants for Black People*
- *Emily Asserts her Manhood*

Perfect Timing

Playing Field

Sanction

Signposts

Steps

Sticky Moments

Supervision - reflections

Taboo

Tainted Spectacles

Tree

Topical Islands

Whanau

What is the Problem?

Who Takes the Sugar?

You Are What You Eat

# Part I

Foundations of Practice

# CONTEXT: New opportunities for practice learning

Social work students learn much of their practice in field settings. In the United Kingdom this kind of practice learning has long constituted 50 per cent of the programme; this continues to be the case with the three-year social work undergraduate degree which has become the minimum qualification for social workers across the UK.

During the 1990s the content of practice learning in the UK was closely prescribed by 'six core competences' (CCETSW, 1991a). This approach reflected the view that students should focus on learning competences, which in turn centred on the training function of placements. It emphasized what social workers *do* rather than what social work *is*.

However, during this same period, the notion of the reflective practitioner also gained ground. Here, learning about social work practice was based on principles of adult learning, with an emphasis on the education, rather than the training, of students, and a greater awareness of context and meaning. The tension between these two approaches led many to polarize the debate. Eventually, however, a holistic view of this apparent conflict emerged, which enabled students and practice teachers to find ways to synthesize competence and context (Doel *et al.*, 2002).

Taking the most common structure for the new award in the UK, the move from a two-year period of study (the Diploma in Social Work) to a three-year under-graduate degree is increasing the length of time for students to learn about social work practice by over 50 per cent (on average, from 130 days to 200 days).[1] However, it is not just the amount of time which has increased. A desire to see changes in the *kind* of learning has been reflected in a change of language, such as the development of the notion of a 'practice learning opportunity' rather than a traditional placement. Although the occupational standards for social work practice have to be taught, learnt and demonstrated, like the six core competences before them, there is less prescription about how, when and where (TOPSS, 2002).

---

[1] Although there are significant variations across the countries of the UK.

# Where does social work take place?

This may seem a strange question to ask, but the hegemony of local government social services departments in England and Wales and social work departments in Scotland since the early 1970s has created a very close association between the profession of social work and the way in which social workers have been employed. This has not necessarily been the case in many other countries, where examples can be found of the service user's own place of work acting as the main provider of social work services. Now, the situation is changing in the UK. Increasingly, social workers are being employed outside social services departments, which themselves are finding new names such as 'Social Care and Health' and 'Housing and Social Care'. Yesterday's vision of a unified social work service, epitomized by the social services department, has transformed into a variety of forms, with significant movements into health and education. This trend is likely to be accelerated by developments such as the consolidation of children's services across health, education and social services. It is too early to say whether this will constitute a dilution of social work (as it gets stirred into some kind of multiprofessional soup) or whether this represents an opportunity to extend its influence and impact (spicing the soup with its own distinctive flavour). Whether it is a case of diluting or spicing, social work is no longer consolidated in one primary location.

This diversification opens the way for more flexibility. There are indications that the search for practice learning opportunities is widening. In the state sector, practice learning sites are likely to extend from the traditional base of social work and social care settings into health, education, prisons, police and so on; in the voluntary, independent and private sectors, these opportunities could extend to the wider world of social welfare, including small, community projects and user-led organizations. Social work students will therefore have more opportunities to learn about social work processes in settings which are not primarily social work agencies, even theatre groups (Billington and Roberts, 2002). The practice learning opportunity should therefore do exactly what it says on the tin, and not be seen as 'work experience'.

Students will also need to be broad-minded and creative in their approach, which means not being 'concerned that unless they have a certain type of placement their employment prospects following the course will be hampered' (Billington and Roberts, 2002: 31). Employers, too, will need to be less restrictive in their selection criteria for interviewing newly qualified social workers.

# Teaching and supervising the student's practice learning

There is a difference between being a good practitioner or an experienced service user and being able to help somebody learn about good practice or to benefit from your experience. There are already a number of excellent texts to guide this transformation (Bogo and Vayda, 1987; Brown and Bourne, 1996; Caspi and Reid,

2002; Gardiner, 1989; Hawkins and Shohet, 2000; Shardlow and Doel, (forthcoming) Shulman, 1999). However, despite the growing literature on practice learning, Brodie's (1993) verdict still stands: that we know very little about what actually takes place within the supervision process generally or the practice tutorial (supervision session) specifically. This also seems to be the case in North America: 'much of what occurs in supervision goes on behind closed doors, leaving all involved unsure whether the [student] is receiving quality education' (Caspi and Reid, 2002: 177). By and large, what happens between students and practice teachers remains a very private affair. We hope that using the activities in this book together with other students and their practice teachers will open up these processes. They can, after all, remain *confidential* without being hidden.

The *Code of Practice* for practice teachers published by the National Organisation for Practice Teaching (NOPT, 2000) is a useful checklist of the areas which teachers and work-based supervisors need to consider, listed under these headings:

- Anti-oppressive / anti-discriminatory statement
- Preparation for placement
- Assessment
- Managing marginal or failing students
- Monitoring and evaluation
- Professional development.

In addition to referring to the NOPT code of practice and reading some of the wider literature mentioned earlier, it is important that everyone involved in the student's learning asks themselves 'What will make for a good practice learning experience?'. Those who need to ask this question are not just the student, practice teacher/ assessor, work-based supervisor and college tutor, but also other team members, agency managers and service users and carers involved in helping the student to learn about practice.

Clarke *et al.*'s (2003: 110) findings in respect of the three key factors which help to create a positive placement experience for student nurses are relevant to social work, too:

- the ward was prepared for them and had some structure to support the learning of the students
- staff were interested in them and they felt valued in their role;
- students were able to work with their mentor. (Clarke *et al.*, 2003:110)

It is always important to discover what an individual considers important in the context of *this* particular experience. This is increasingly significant as opportunities for practice learning sites are sought outside traditional 'placements', in sites where experience of social work students (or any from higher education) is limited. There also needs to be agreement about how the aspirations for a good practice learning experience will be transformed into concrete reality.

Some state that there has to be a 'fit' between student and teacher/supervisor. However, 'the establishment of a positive supervisory relationship is not solely based on the "fit" between supervisor and supervisee personalities' (Caspi and Reid, 2002: 124), whatever the term 'fit' might be taken to imply. It is erroneous to assume that people with the same kind of biography (gender, ethnicity, age, and so on) are bound to have a better fit, or that aiming for similarity is automatically beneficial to learning. If a core social work value is concerned with the celebration of diversity, let this be modelled in the student–teacher relationship.

Nor, in the excitement about the possibility of new learning opportunities, must we overlook the potential pitfalls. These are likely to become most transparent when making assessments of the student's performance. Of the common mistakes noted by Kadushin (1992: 365–68), the 'contrast error' may be the most frequent. This is the mistake of comparing the student's performance to other workers or to the supervisor's own standard, rather than to criteria that have been mutually agreed (see the next section, 'The Learning Agreement') and which reflect the fact that this is a *student*, not a practitioner.

In particular, new work-based supervisors and assessors need access to support and consultation from experienced practice teachers, otherwise the following findings are likely to be replicated:

> [I] asked colleagues about their supervisory approaches and received two [kinds of] response. One group said that they drew upon their own experiences as supervisees, attempting to do (or not do) what their supervisors did with them. The second group said that they worked extemporaneously, 'winging it' and learning through trial and error. (Caspi and Reid, 2002: 173)

Current and future students deserve better.

## Benefits of supervising students

There are many benefits to supervising students. A study by Shardlow *et al.* (2002) found that practice teachers regarded supervision as an opportunity to reflect on their own practice, which brought increased confidence and motivation to acquire more knowledge of research and theory. Students were seen as providing a challenge, in the best sense of the word.

Experienced practitioners can drift into automatic decision-making, in which service users 'are assessed as only needing services that the agency currently provides within its mission and area of expertise' (Wayne and Cohen, 2001: 18). Teaching and supervising a student encourages practitioners to slow down, in order to explain the thinking behind their actions. This helps not just the student, but also the practitioner, to consider fresh approaches and new perspectives, and to question any automatic tendencies in their own practice.

What are the economics of a student placement? Busy teams are often reluctant to offer a placement to students because of pressure of work, but the balance of input and output can work in favour of the agency (Shardlow, 1988). The memory of an individual student who has been the centre of concern, and perhaps much angst, sadly lives on well beyond the fonder remembrance of the twenty students who gave the agency a good experience. In reality, the benefits to an agency or project of those twenty students far outweigh the resources allocated to the one failing student.

A mindset change is needed in order to perceive students as a potential resource, able to develop innovative services for the agency. For example, practice teachers at the 2003 annual workshops of the National Organization for Practice Teaching (NOPT)[2] described a number of innovations which included:

- direct work with children which otherwise would not have happened
- a tennis club at a mental health drop-in facility, where the practice teachers were amazed at the take-up, including people who would not have been thought as 'sporty' types
- a reminiscence group in an older people's home – a service that was rarely provided to residents by existing staff members
- in a general practitioner setting, a student who produced an information booklet for survivors of suicide attempts, which was widely distributed locally
- a student who designed a questionnaire about the team's knowledge of the Race Relations Amendment Act 2000 and led team discussion.

Of course, it is important that students do not fill the gaps of staff vacancies, since they are not in the agency as a trainee employee; if a student is being used to reduce a pile of referral forms, this is exploitation. With this caveat, there is no reason why students cannot create or support services which might not otherwise have been available. For example, a team might agree that its work would be improved with more information about the way in which users experience its services, or there might be recognition that a group for certain service users would be a valuable addition to current activity. Indeed, students can be a major and positive force for change, and there is evidence that this kind of proactive practice learning project is welcomed by the students as well as by the users and carers who experience it (Butler, 2004; Dent and Tourville, 2002; Muzumdar and Atthar, 2002; Underhill *et al.*, 2002).

## The Learning Agreement

The key to a successful practice learning opportunity is a clear understanding of expectations. That is not to say that every 't' must be crossed and every 'i' dotted, for there will be plenty of learning which is serendipitous. However, the basic ground rules should be agreed beforehand. These include practical details, such as expected times of attendance and resources available (desk, computer and so on),

---

[2] There are also Scottish and Welsh Organizations for Practice Teaching, ScOPT and WOPT.

and should also cover lines of accountability, expectations of the frequency and kind of supervision and the kind and quantity of work available.

The agreement should outline expectations around assessment, examples of how the student will gather and present their practice, and what will count as evidence of their abilities. There needs to be agreement about how the student's practice will be observed; this will be important not just for their learning and the assessment of their practice, but also to monitor the quality of service to the users.

Most important of all is agreement about what would happen if there are difficulties, with concrete illustrations. Although there is a cultural reluctance to discuss what might go wrong ('tempting fate'), rehearsing potential issues makes them less, not more, likely to happen.

It is illuminating to ask students to reflect on their experience so far, and this is assisted if the student has already undertaken a personal learning audit as preparation for the Learning Agreement (West and Watson, 2002). The following account is taken from a *post*-qualifying portfolio, written by a qualified social worker reflecting back a number of years on the first weeks and months on her social work course:

> When I started my Diploma in Social Work I was very naive and knew very little about social work. As a consequence, to begin with, the course proved to be very difficult. I attended every lecture with enthusiasm, taking in the knowledge provided like a sponge taking in water. The hardest part to understand initially was the legal and theoretical framework. With perseverance and a lot of background reading, alongside support from lecturers and a close friend reinforcing that I could do it, I grasped the fundamental issues in this area and never looked back.

It is important to remember that the student might be in the midst of this stage, 'the course proving to be very difficult', and that your expectations should be of a *student*, not a qualified practitioner. The 'escalator' in Figure I.2 indicates a range of responses from novice (towards the bottom of the escalator) to expert (towards the top). Although progress is not linear, it is expected that the overall direction will be upwards and, indeed, some students may well show natural abilities to operate relatively far up the escalator.

> Of course, assessing professional practice is not such an exact science that we can quantify the precise proportion of examples at each step [of the escalator]. The notion of a dilemma or practice issue is itself equivocal, as is the relative significance of any two such quandaries ... [However], this is a more authentic reflection of the shifting reality of professional practice than the illusion of fixed competencies. (Doel *et al.*, 2002: 148)

Teaching social work practice is more than a technical skill, and the context of supervision has a significant impact. The supervisory process is influenced by your perspectives, as teacher and student, as a man or a woman, by your age, ethnicity, class, sexuality, faith, ability and so on. It is crucial that issues of power are addressed openly in order to achieve practice learning which is anti-oppressive. In some circumstances it is appropriate for students to have access to other resources – for example, it might be worth considering a black mentor for a black student in a

Strategy taught to others
Strategy fully integrated
Strategy repeated, refined
Strategy tried and successful
Strategy tried and failed
A hypothetical response
No developed response
Awareness of dilemma or issue
Unaware of dilemma or issue

**Figure I.2  The learning-practice escalator**

predominantly white agency. It is crucial that these questions are addressed at the time of the learning agreement and not in the heat of any later moments.

The student's experience needs to be integrated not just across class and field, but also between the various practice learning opportunities. Current practice teachers and work-based supervisors need to know about the student's past practice learning and help them to prepare for future learning. The development of new, non-traditional settings suggests that students will need even more assistance in transferring their learning from one situation to another (Cree and Macaulay, 2000).

## Support for practice learning

We have noted that students learn about practice from direct placement for half of their time on the course. In their attempts to integrate the learning in class and the learning in the field they will rightly expect assistance from the practice teacher and college tutor and, indeed, from any other people involved in their learning, such as practice assessors, work-based supervisors, service users and carers. As different kinds of opportunity are found for students, it will be important that the supports for this new practice learning are reviewed, especially for people who are new to the role. Perhaps group provision in the form of college-based seminars and workshops will become more appropriate than the traditional tutor visit. The role of e-support systems is also likely to increase; although most experiments in this area have been with students (Quinny, 2004), it is likely that we will see an extension to practice educators.

The tutor role has been somewhat neglected in the literature (Degenhardt, 2003). Fortune and Abramson's (1993) study concluded that tutors can offer more by helping, advising and consulting with practice teachers and less by monitoring the individual student. In a later study, the experiences of over 300 practice teachers (field instructors) were analysed in relation to two models of liaison between college and field – the 'Intensive Model' and the 'Trouble-Shooting Model' (Fortune *et al.*, 1995). Surprisingly, the evidence suggested that the practice teachers involved preferred neither model over the other, suggesting that the Trouble-Shooting Model might, therefore, be a better use of scarce resources. The practice wisdom that the student's placement should be supported by consistent contact with a tutor perhaps needs to be reconsidered in favour of more systematic methods of supporting practice learning opportunities. Certainly, we need more evidence about what kinds of support for practice learning are most effective.

At a strategic level, the partnerships offering the social work degree in the UK will need to consider how a wide variety of smaller agencies and projects can be best represented on formal bodies such as the partnership committees which advise and support social work programmes.

## The tide

In *The New Social Work Practice* (Doel and Shardlow, 1998), we noted:

> It is possible to discern a number of 'tides' in the way the various aspects of the activity we call supervision has, and continues, to progress. Currently, there is a pull between the educative function, with an emphasis on the student as a learner and the use of a variety of teaching methods; and the assessment function, with an increasing concentration on the student's ability to demonstrate competencies. In this latter case, there is a danger that the processes of teaching and learning become buried beneath the weight of minutely detailed competencies.

We would like to keep the spotlight on the placement as a learning experience, not a work experience. As Thomlison and Collins, (1995: 225) note, 'The primary responsibility of the (practice teacher) is to facilitate the student's ... educational plan through the service delivery system of the agency'. The agency is primarily a service organization, and the education of students for professional practice is not a core concern. In these circumstances, practice teachers and assessors have a crucial role to mediate the needs of the student with the requirements of the agency.

In this respect, the tide flows in the same direction as we noted in 1998. However, the widening of practice learning opportunities and the increase in the amount of time in field settings means that the tide carries a larger and more diverse flotilla, with different support and service needs. It is a great opportunity for social work to widen its experience and also to influence the work of others.

# 1 Knowing the service user and carer

## About Activity 1    *Licensed to learn*

*Licensed to learn* emphasizes the educational function of practice learning by allowing students to focus on the potential learning available from knowing the people who use social work services.

### Purpose

As someone with a responsibility to help a student's learning, *Licensed to learn* helps you to focus on the student as a learner. Students are entitled to wear their 'Learner' plates openly!

The obvious question to ask the student faced with *Licensed to learn* is what would you *do* in these situations or, to use the jargon, what is the *role* of the social worker? However, asking students to consider what they think they can *learn* from these situations puts the focus squarely on learning rather than practice (there will be plenty of time for the latter at a later date).

### Method

- Give the students a copy of the activity perhaps a week before a practice tutorial (supervision session).
- Ask the students to follow the guidance which comes with the activity, answering the questions as and when indicated, and making a written note of their deliberations.

### Variations

Most of the exercises in this book benefit from group activity. However, it is the interplay of individual and group which usually works best. Groups are not always as challenging as we hope or imagine them to be; group consensus can subdue real debate and allow individuals to be intellectually lazy. For this reason, it is often better to have a student complete an activity individually before any group

11

discussion is arranged, so that individuals come to the group with their own views, some of which they should be prepared to change and others to defend.

*Licensed to learn* is better completed singly and discussed with the practitioner. At some later stage, a group of students could meet, to be exposed to the different approaches they have each taken to what is a very open-ended exercise.

## Use by other professions

*Licensed to learn* lends itself to completion by a range of different professions. Students from health visiting, housing work, community psychiatric nursing, environmental health, rehabilitation work, education welfare, community work, town planning, policing, medicine, architecture and others can learn from some or all of these situations. You could consider returning to the exercise later with a multiprofessional group of students to see how they would interpret the notion of interprofessional learning in this neighbourhood. See the Introduction to Part II 'Interprofessional learning and practice' for more on this.

The final question in the activity, 'How do you think people might be helped by social work in these situations?' would need to reflect the professional group in question: for example, 'How do you think people might be helped by policing in these situations?'.

## National Occupational Standards for Social Work

The topics in this chapter relate to the following National Occupational Standards (see the Appendix):

1:   Preparing for social work contact and involvement
14:   Accountability
19:   Professional development
20:   Dilemmas and conflicts.

## *Activity 1*    **Licensed to learn**

### Vignette

**Green Hill flats** were built as public housing in the 1960s to provide decent housing for people then living in slums. However, many of these 'streets in the sky' acquired a bad reputation, partly because of the subsequent housing policies of the local authority, which used to concentrate people with problems in certain blocks. Even so, many of the Green Hill residents are loyal to the estate and have lived there for two and even three generations. It has an active tenants' association. There is a popular pub, the Green Hill Arms, on one of the ground-floor streets. It has a community room. Security doors, CCTV and intercoms have all been put in place, and, for some time, the council has had a policy of mixed habitation, so that families, young couples and older people live side-by-side.

**Derby Street** is one of the ground-floor streets in Green Hill flats. It consists of seven flats.

At Number 1 is **Zoë Benner**, a single parent who was in public care for much of her childhood, but is now reconciled with her mother, who lives on another street in Green Hill flats. Zoë has a fourteen-year-old son (Jackson), a twelve-year-old daughter (Kylie) and a baby daughter (Kara) aged eleven months. Jackson was cautioned for shoplifting earlier in the year, and has just been arrested on a charge of criminal damage. Kylie has not been to school for several weeks. She has few friends and is reluctant to leave the family's flat. She has also been referred for help with her bed-wetting problem. Kara is Zoë's daughter by another man who is attempting to gain custody of her. Kara has asthma and seems to suffer from unspecified allergies. Zoë has another child, Tilly, a seven-year-old girl currently living with foster carers on the other side of the city.

At Number 2 live **Jason Dean** and his partner **Sam Weiner**. Jason, a twenty-eight-year-old, has a previous drug-related charge and has just completed a rehabilitation programme. Jason is unemployed, but volunteers at a local drop-in centre for homeless people. Sam is forty-six years old and is on long-term disability benefit, experiencing occasional periods of depression. He relies on Jason for much of his care. Sam is a leading light in the tenants' association for the block of flats.

**Avis Jenkins** lives at Number 3. She is eighty-four years old, and her only son lives in a distant city. Jason Dean gives her quite a bit of support, calling in and helping her with cups of tea and the like. Mrs Jenkins has home care twice a week. Charging policies for home care services have changed recently, and Mrs Jenkins is finding it difficult to cope financially. Her memory is deteriorating and she is a regular member of a group called Memory Joggers at the local day centre. Avis has lived in the area all her life and worked on the local newspaper until she retired.

Number 4 houses a young couple, **Lorretta and Luke Carter**. They both work in low-paid jobs, but put enough aside to run an old secondhand van. Luke also plays

Reproduced from *Modern Social Work Practice* by Mark Doel and Steven M. Shardlow, Ashgate, Aldershot, 2005

in a band, which sometimes comes to Number 4 to practise. The band play gigs most weeks, and about once a month at the Green Hill Arms pub.

**Jim Rafferty** lives at Number 5. He used to work in the steel industry in quite a well-paid job until he retired. He is now seventy-two years old and was widowed three years ago. Over the last five years he has gradually been losing his sight through macular degeneration. His daughter lives a short bus ride away. Jim has written to the council to complain about the noise from Number 4.

In Number 6 two Kurdish brothers, **Gregor** and **Stefan Kiyani** from Iraq, have recently been housed after successfully seeking asylum. They are both trained as engineers. They are currently unemployed but are actively seeking work and are in regular touch with a local Kurdish support group. Gregor has good English, though Stefan's is more faltering. They get on well with the others on the street and have gone out of their way to say hello and invite people round to their flat. However, they have recently been very distressed by an incident in which dog faeces was posted through their letter box.

**Shama** and **Gary Homes** live at Number 7. Shama works part-time in the kitchens of one of the local schools. Gary is a full-time homemaker. Shama and Gary provide respite care for children with learning disabilities. They have an adult daughter with learning disabilities who now lives independently in a supported scheme on a nearby estate.

Number 8 used to be a small corner shop, but it closed four months ago and is currently boarded up. The nearest shop is a supermarket which opened six months ago, but which lies across a busy highway.

**Derby Street**, and a number of other streets on the north side of Green Hill flats, has a recurring infestation of ants. There are also difficulties with mildew from excessive damp. Green Hill flats was owned by the local council (as public housing) but has recently been transferred for redevelopment by a not-for-profit housing association. Tenants will be involved in decisions about the coming changes, which will result in some tenants moving from the block whilst extensive refurbishments are made.

## The Exercise

1   **What do you think you might learn from working in the situations described above?**
*Avoid stating obvious generalisms, such as 'I would learn how to work with someone losing their sight' and aim for learning which is more specific, such as 'I could learn how an older person copes with the practical difficulties of losing their sight, and how it affects them emotionally'.*

Reproduced from *Modern Social Work Practice* by Mark Doel and Steven M. Shardlow, Ashgate, Aldershot, 2005

2   **Prioritize a list of ten possible learning points and make a written note of these**.

*When you have considered what you might learn from these situations, consider question 3:*

3   **How do you think people might be helped by social work in these situations?** *Again, make a written note of your thoughts.*

Reproduced from *Modern Social Work Practice* by Mark Doel and Steven M. Shardlow, Ashgate, Aldershot, 2005

# Teaching notes: *Knowing the service user and carer*

## Opportunities

One of the major functions of practice learning in an agency setting is the opportunities it provides students to work with the people who use social work services. However, just because these opportunities are readily available does not mean that they will automatically result in a good learning experience for the student. *Licensed to learn* is designed to help both you and the student focus on the learning potential.

In order to make the best use of *Licensed to learn* we suggest that you first complete the activity yourself. Resist answering the questions by reference to what you know of 'the social work role', 'agency procedures', 'eligibility criteria', and the like in your own agency, even though this may be surprisingly difficult to do. Answering the three *Licensed to learn* questions for yourself will help you understand the difference between you and the student.

As the authors, we cannot presume exactly who you, our reader, is. However, if you have responsibility for helping a student learn about social work, it is safe to assume that you are probably an experienced practitioner, manager, user or carer. The location of your work may be a social services department (or its equivalent), a voluntary, not-for-profit organization, a private agency, a user-led agency or, indeed, a location in which social work is not a prime activity. Even so, what is important to remember and too easy to forget is that your task is to help the student learn about social work, *not* to train them to do your job. In other words, the specific work in which you are engaged is but one example of social work in practice.

Helping students to move from the specific of your location to the general of social work practice, and back to different specifics (not just yours), is a demanding skill. You may not be wearing the 'L' plates, but this is going to be a learning experience for you, too, no matter how experienced you are.

The Green Hill situation in *Licensed to learn* is designed to help you to give the student permission to focus first and foremost on their own learning. There will be time enough to learn about your agency's policies and mission statements, the limits to your role, the procedures which govern what can and cannot be undertaken. These policies, procedures and roles may or may not have been formalized with Zoë Benner, Jason Dean, Avis Jenkins and the other residents of Derby Street in mind. The people living in Derby Street do not spend their time reorganizing their problems and aspirations to fit neatly into the mission statements of the agencies which may or may not help them. It is right that the student has the opportunity to consider the whole picture of a community's life before the lines are drawn. After all, it is this whole picture which more accurately reflects the lives of real people.

This holistic approach is not a utopian whim, to be indulged before we turn our attention to the serious business of training the student how to be a child protection officer, a mental health worker or someone in adult services. The whole-person approach is embedded in the new three-year social work qualification in the UK. In the new degree there are no particular areas of practice, no pathways, just a solid commitment to generalist social work practice. Where better to begin, then, than our community in Derby Street in the Green Hill flats?

## Learning notes: *Knowing the service user and carer*

### Who is the 'client'?

One of the learning points to note from *Licensed to learn* is that it is not clear-cut how and with whom you might work. This is a long-standing issue and has been characterized in the social work literature in the question, 'Who is the "client"?' (see, for example, Davies, 1994).

'Client' is an old-fashioned term and, for many good reasons, usage has been changing. For a while there was a flirtation with 'customer', but it was clear, even to the most ardent supporters of market forces, that people who use social work services do not have the economic freedom of choice which the term 'customer' implies. Many do not want to purchase social work services and are forced to receive them as an unwelcome gift. 'Citizen' is a worthy egalitarian word, but with nineteenth-century overtones and, sadly, now excluding some people who clearly are not yet citizens, such as asylum seekers, who should have access to services. 'People' is the most inclusive term, but sometimes we need a term specific to people who are using social work services. The term in current favour in the UK is, therefore, service user. Also, there is increasing recognition of the significant role which carers play and the importance of involving carers and users alike in the work.

We pose the question 'Who is the "client"?' in a very particular way. It was put some time ago by Pincus and Minahan (1973) as part of an attempt to help social workers think more widely about the various systems with which they worked. Rather than seeing the social work 'client' as necessarily an individual person (or even family), Pincus and Minahan's work suggested there were 'client' systems, whose boundaries depended on different circumstances. Doel and Marsh (1992) suggested a conceptualization of the problem as the 'client'. In Green Hill flats, for example, one 'client' could be 'the problem of the damp'. Dent and Tourville (2002: 28) describe how a multi-racial inner-city community became the students' 'client' in an innovative project in which students worked alongside medical students and community development students in partnership with the local community. The students also learned to develop and provide one-on-one services with residents. These social work students were working with physical, economic and social issues simultaneously and their 'client' was much broader than any one individual.

### The individuality of service users and carers

As well as emphasizing your learning, *Licensed to learn* has helped you to understand the way in which people and their difficulties are interconnected. Social policy at central and local level affects individual lives; structural racism and sexism limit individuals' potential and oppress them; neighbours have an impact on each other's lives. The people in Derby Street can be seen as members of larger social groups, women and men, black people, white people, gays, lesbians, straights, children, teenagers, adults, carers and cared-for, older people, blind people, able-bodied and disabled people and so on. People are discriminated against and have dog dirt put through their letter boxes because of these social labels. They also find strength in meeting together as groups, such as the support group which the Kiyani brothers attend, the Green Hill Tenants' Association, and the Memory Joggers group for people with memory problems.

To what extent does it help to know Mr Rafferty as a 'visually impaired person', as opposed to someone who was a steelworker, someone with grey hair and brown eyes or someone with a kind manner and soft speech? You might be able to use your previous knowledge of someone with a visual impairment to begin to understand how 'people' respond to sight loss. However, you must also understand that each person's response is unique. The capacity to move between the general and the particular is an important part of becoming a social worker. This is the ability to comprehend the racism which the Kiyani brothers face at a personal and institutional level, whilst understanding their individual circumstances of loss and likely trauma (JRF, 2005).

## The strengths model

It is often joked that the National Health Service should really be called the National Ill-health Service, since it is only when you are ill, sick or injured that you make use of it. A visit to the doctor usually occurs because something is wrong, although there are increasing numbers of 'well-being clinics' to which healthy people can go for a regular check-up. It is not surprising, then, that the doctor fails to comment on how well your legs are working when you are consulting them about your broken arm. Nevertheless, it was your legs (and various other working parts) that successfully took you to the surgery.

It is understandable if your first knowledge of the service user or carer is in reference to what is wrong, since it is these problems and difficulties which bring you into contact. However, there is a process in which the practitioner can dwell on these deficits to such an extent that the service user is seen only as the sum of their inadequacies. This is sometimes referred to as pathologizing the person. At its very worst, users find themselves in a 'Catch 22' situation, in which their opposition to the attempts to pathologize them is taken as a sign that they are in denial, thus providing further 'evidence' of their neediness.

Knowing the service user means knowing about their abilities and their aptitudes, too – the two 'A's, if you like. This is often referred to in the social work literature as the strengths model. Looking back at your work on the *Licensed to learn* activity, to what extent did you focus on the deficits and to what extent on the strengths. 'What strengths?' you may protest! Well, return to the activity and you will see that there are many indications of strengths, both in the lives of individuals and in the community at large. Moreover, most situations which become defined by the

Reproduced from *Modern Social Work Practice* by Mark Doel and Steven M. Shardlow, Ashgate, Aldershot, 2005

language of deficits (*single parent* Zoë Benner with a son *off the rails*, a daughter who is a *school-refuser* and a *sickly* baby) might be reframed as a *survivor* of public care, keeping a family *together* in dire circumstances. Usually the situation is a complex mix of both possibilities, but it is important not to lose sight of the strengths in people's lives. It is these strengths which will enable you to work together to make improvements. We will consider this in Chapter 5, 'Generating options'.

You will also be developing your understanding of how theories which help you to 'understand human beings' (Trevithick, 2000) can influence your work with service users and carers (see the Introduction to Part IV, 'Evidence-based practice').

## The relationship between social workers, service users and carers

How do changes in the tasks and requirements of social workers affect the relationship with service users and carers? Some current commentators are concerned that a focus on the whole person is increasingly being replaced by a focus on their various needs. Lymbery (2000: 132) argues strongly that 'the core identity of the social worker is affected by this process [of focusing on discrete needs] which is further exacerbated by the fragmented pattern of service delivery that is likely to follow'. In other words, the services are organized around specialized aspects of need (for example, a person's mental health needs) rather than the person as a whole. This reinforces the importance of understanding how people's lives are joined up; individuals' lives are connected to others, and their problems are but one facet of their overall experience.

Lymbery (2000) describes three paradigms for the relationship between social worker and user:

- *The traditional view*: a relationship between a professional and a 'client', in which there are differentials in power and knowledge, and social distance between the two;
- *The market view*: the social worker is a purchaser (occasionally a provider) and the service user is a consumer, with a relationship that is supposedly commercial;
- *The partnership view*: a modified view of professionalism, in which social workers engage service users in an active participation, recognizing the expertise which the service user brings to the relationship.

The current rhetoric emphasizes the last of these, but you should observe which of these paradigms is the most characteristic of the relationships between practitioners and users of services in the agency where you are learning your practice. Sometimes there is a gap between the rhetoric and the reality; indeed, the rhetoric can be a barrier to recognizing and appreciating this gap. The increasing involvement of service users and carers in the education and training of social work students means that you will probably have the opportunity to meet people who use social work services in the class setting as well as the practice learning site. Participation by service users and carers in the full range of social work education – planning, delivery and evaluation – is meant to ensure that the partnership view described above is transparent throughout your experience as a student.

## Service user and carer control

Much of the discussion has moved on from notions of participation to ones of empowerment. In research and policy-making, in particular, social work has been exploring how service users and carers can move from participating to initiating. This is a philosophy that moves beyond the satisfaction survey ('how did you find that service?') to more control over the nature of the service itself. There are some interesting examples of this in practice, including research projects in which service users and carers hold the budget.

We have discussed the importance of knowing the service user or carer, as an individual, as a member of a social group, and understanding the user or carer as a whole person in the context of his or her community. Turning this on its head, how might the service user and carer know you and how, as individuals or in collaboration with others, can they acquire more control over the kinds of service that are available?

## Assessment notes: *Knowing the service user and carer*

It will be important to demonstrate an understanding of 'the whole person' – that is, the service users and carers in their wider context and not just in their relationship to the agency where you are studying. This understanding needs to include an appreciation of people's strengths as well as their problems, and an ability to engage with them, even when their circumstances and their biographies are very different from your own. Your ability to identify and work with people's strengths will be part of your assessment as a social work student.

## Further reading

Beresford, P. and Croft, S. (2001), 'Service Users' Knowledges and the Social Construction of Social Work', *Journal of Social Work*, 1(3): 295–316.
See the regular bulletins of Joseph Rowntree's *Findings* for examples of projects in which messages from service users and carers have been conducted by the people themselves: www.jrf.org.uk

Reproduced from *Modern Social Work Practice* by Mark Doel and Steven M. Shardlow, Ashgate, Aldershot, 2005

# 2 Knowing your self

## About Activity 2    *Viewpoint*

*Viewpoint* takes a look at social work from several different points of view. Brief quotations present examples of different views about social work. Students are invited to consider their responses to the various statements.

The activity is best undertaken by a student and practice teacher jointly; it is even better with a group of three, four or more students.

### Purpose

The reasons why people come into social work are numerous. Some have clear, well-rehearsed positions and others have difficulty identifying their motives and beliefs. Some subscribe to an '-ism' or two, and others have muddled views with no obvious guiding principles. Some may have had personal experiences, such as having used social services or being a carer (Parker and Merrylees, 2002); and there may be differences between the motivation of men and women entering social work (Cree, 1996).

We all have some kind of personal philosophy, ways of looking at the world and explaining it, but how aware of them are we? The purpose of this activity is to help students and practitioners to acquire a better understanding of how the way we view the world influences our work – in other words, how beliefs interact with actions.

### Method

Give a clear explanation of the purpose of the exercise, emphasizing the exploratory aspects and making sure that the students know that there is no pressure to take up any particular position.

- Ask the student to read the various statements in the *Viewpoint* activity and write down responses to each of the statements. Arrange a time when you can exchange comments (probably the next practice tutorial) and suggest that the student makes a few notes ready for this discussion.

- Encourage the student to enter a dialogue about the statements and your mutual preferences. It is important to avoid preaching or trying to enforce a consensus; the discussion is an opportunity to share the ways in which you each view the world, and, if these are not clear, to attempt to articulate previously unspoken world-views.
- Help the student relate world-views to professional practice. What are the implications of each of these statements for practice? How do different beliefs affect the choices social workers make about what they do?

## Variations

You can substitute different statements from a wide variety of perspectives. Alternatively, you can use different viewpoints about particular aspects of practice (for example, childcare, work with older people). In many respects, it is irrelevant which views are discussed with the student; the purpose of the activity is for students to become aware of their own views by looking at the world as others see it.

You can use this activity at an early stage in a student's practice learning. It is also the type of activity that can be revisited later using either the same or different extracts to help students identify how their world-view has, or has not, changed.

## Use by other professions

The extracts in *Viewpoint* put social work behind the prism, but other professions have these kinds of different perspectives, too. Should medicine focus on ill-health or well-being? Just as advances in environmental health (drains and fresh water) had the greatest impact on public health in the nineteenth century, should medicine focus more on health promotion than hi-tech laser surgery? Is occupational therapy a radical, political activity (see Kronenberg *et al.*, 2004) or a skills-based profession which should focus on individual rehabilitation? Clinical teachers can gather examples from the literature or articles in the professional journals, which illustrate a wide range of belief about the mission of their profession.

## National Occupational Standards for Social Work

The topics in this chapter relate to the following National Occupational Standards (see the Appendix):

 1:   Preparing for social work contact and involvement
19:   Professional development.

# *Activity 2*     *Viewpoint*

Consider the following four brief extracts about social work, and ask yourself:

- Which of these extract or extracts do you feel most attracted to? Why?
- What are the ideological beliefs that underpin each of these extracts?

## Extract 1: The social work relationship

In much contemporary social work practice, the chief concern is not with causation, but with the practical consequences of given sets of circumstances. Howe (1996) has defined this as a move away from the 'depth' that characterised much traditional social work literature to a concern with the 'surface', based on eligibility criteria, standard service responses, and a concern with the classification of needs. He states that 'it is the category into which the client's behaviour or condition fits which increasingly determines the response required' (*ibid:* 91). It could be argued that, given this priority, it is unnecessary – even distracting – for a social worker to seek to establish a relationship with the service user. The social worker's purpose is defined more simply, as the need to secure sufficient information on which to make the categorisation, on which a subsequent purchase of services within the market is based.

## Extract 2: The messiness of practice

The emphasis on cognitive-behaviourist approaches and positivist methods of evaluation go hand in hand with a contemporary view of social work as a rational-technical activity, characterised by managerialism, systems of audit, procedures, legalism and a concern with outcomes. These characteristics derive from a view of practice dependent on the application of knowledge emerging from objective, testable, replicable techniques. What becomes lost in all of this is an acknowledgement that social work is also a moral, social and political activity, one in which discretion and judgement cannot be discounted. The blunt instruments which measure changes in client behaviours often cannot capture the dilemmas confronted by practitioners, which lead to uncertainty and confusion, and which are key elements in decisions made in everyday situations affecting their clients' lives. To leave these motives, meanings, doubts and influences – the messiness of practice – unavailable to examination is to have an incomplete and distorted picture of the patterns of action in concrete situations.

## Extract 3: Social workers' constructions of power

A major assumption [in the group of ten social workers] was that the power resided either with the managers, supervisors, recalcitrant colleagues and, in some cases, the community groups with consumer voice. In no instances did workers see themselves as powerful. Either each person had exercised what power they thought they had and it had proved inadequate, or they felt they did not possess enough power to bring about any change. The common themes in the stories we shared showed that we had each constructed ourselves as powerless, denying or minimising the influence of different types of power we might possess. Sometimes we identified as powerless with individual clients for whom we were acting, but in other instances we also invested these people with power we did not have. A major assumption therefore was that *other*

Reproduced from *Modern Social Work Practice* by Mark Doel and Steven M. Shardlow, Ashgate, Aldershot, 2005

*people had the power, workers did not.* There was almost a sense in which workers saw themselves as victims.

## Extract 4: Empirical practice

In general, empirical practice draws, as much as it can, on scientific attitudes, knowledge, and processes. In empirical practice one gives primacy to research-based theories and interventions. Due to the emphasis placed on research, empirical practitioners make an effort to become familiar with studies relating to populations, problems, and interventions they are working with. In treating individual clients, families, or groups, the targets of intervention are specifically stated, and devices such as direct observation and standardised tests are used to collect assessment data. Intervention methods are defined in terms of specific actions by the practitioner, and they are used as systematically as possible ... The practitioner monitors change and evaluates outcomes in relation to the interventions used.

*The sources of these extracts can be found at the end of the chapter. It is strongly suggested that you do not consult this until you have completed the activity and had the opportunity for discussion.*

Reproduced from *Modern Social Work Practice* by Mark Doel and Steven M. Shardlow, Ashgate, Aldershot, 2005

# Teaching notes: *Knowing your self*

## Opportunities

There are as many world-views as there are people to hold them. What we know as 'isms' (socialism, feminism and so on) are world-views that are so cogent that we often refer to them as theories. A theory is a coherent explanation of why the world is as it is. It can provide an analysis of some aspect of the world or it may suggest prescriptions about how to improve matters.

There are, therefore, almost infinite opportunities to help the student develop their self-knowledge. However, if you were to ask students 'cold' about their personal philosophy, you would probably get an equally cold response. Looking at the way in which we view the world and the beliefs we hold is a very personal matter, and, for many reasons, we may have learned to be careful about how and whether to reveal them. It can help to start from a less personal position and to move, at the student's pace, to a more subjective point.

*Viewpoint* helps students open up about professional values and the beliefs they hold in order to explain the world. It is difficult to remain disengaged, and the activity triggers sympathies, antipathies and discussion of general issues, and perhaps sometimes reveals confusion on the student's part. For example, how does the use of language differ from one statement to the next and is this significant? How are meanings construed? What does the student make of the similarities and differences between aspects of the extracts?

It is important to be open about your own beliefs, too. It may be difficult to avoid dispute with an opinionated student, or to avoid providing answers for one who is diffident, but your aim is to open up a genuine dialogue. At this stage you are not making a judgement about the student's own world-view; you are helping them explore how it is likely to influence their work.

## Examples

**Molly** was eager to discuss *Viewpoint*. She had read it carefully beforehand as requested, and had made notations on the extracts. However, she quickly became critical of the crude representation of one of the viewpoints and claimed that the others were an irrelevance in the face of a feminist critique. Molly gave a forthright and articulate account of her views and referred her practice teacher to Langan and Day (1992) and Orme (2002) for some perspectives on different feminist positions. The practice teacher suggested that it might be a good idea for Molly to write a specifically feminist position and commentary to use as part of the exercise, but this was met with short shrift on the grounds that a caricature would debase feminism and that there wasn't 'a feminist world-view', just differing interpretations. The practice teacher's views were, in fact, similar to the student's, but she was unhappy that Molly's manner prevented her (the practice teacher) from sharing her own beliefs.

'How do I feel?' the practice teacher asked herself fifteen minutes into the activity. The answer came: 'like a hurricane is blowing me away'. She decided that it was time to turn the session into a more reflective mode and gently shared her impressions with Molly, who was initially surprised. When Molly began to reflect on her approach to the session, she realized that she had assumed that she would be expected to give a good account of her own views. Although she had denied it to herself, she had been nervous but she was determined 'to get it right – to my own satisfaction'. This explained her earnest single-mindedness. 'I suppose I've played the good little girl to your schoolteacher and I resented it, but I realize that wasn't what you were looking for'.

Molly's approach could easily have been interpreted as rigid and, in part, it did point to a tendency to get hold of the wrong end of the stick. However, Molly's honesty and intelligence proved an asset to her work. She had no doubts about the rightness of her philosophy, but she increasingly understood that what motivated her did not necessarily motivate other people.

**James** was very quiet during the discussion of *Viewpoint*, tending to follow his practice teacher's lead. When he was asked more directly for his views he suddenly became dismissive of issues which he had earlier been nodding at. He felt that people were trying to make social work out to be more than it was and that he 'just gets on with the job, finding people as they are'. He didn't think it mattered with which statements he agreed or disagreed. In his opinion it was much more important to learn about social work skills and to get on with the business of just doing your best for people.

The practitioner should not make assumptions about James' practice from this one reaction, but discover what these views indicate. For reasons which are not yet clear, abstract discussion with James has not been successful. Perhaps it would be helpful to introduce a concrete example from practice familiar to James. If this is constructed in order to illustrate a practical dilemma, the practice teacher can help James to find the principles which lie behind his practice, by teasing out the reasons for the choices he makes in the face of the dilemma. James will need reassuring that he is not being asked to adopt an 'ism', but to look at the approaches which he uses, perhaps instinctively, in his own practice and how these pull together. Revisiting *Viewpoint* later in the placement would show how much James had developed; if he is still unable to conceptualize, this would lead to questions about his competence in this area.

# Learning notes: *Knowing your self*

One aspect of knowing your self is knowing why you wanted to become a social worker and how this motivation can be sustained. One practitioner described her own rather rapid experience in her post-qualifying portfolio:

> I went to a Job Centre where a computer program indicated that I should consider social work. I applied the same day; I was interviewed the following day and was accepted on the course. I started on a full-time [qualifying] course the following week.

Life experience is a significant aspect of motivation to enter social work, though we know very little about these connections and it is currently 'a neglected form of knowledge in social work education and practice' (Christie and Weeks, 1998: 55). How have your life experiences led to your decision to become a social worker and in what ways are they likely to influence your practice? We will be discussing motivation to enter social work in Chapter 17.

## Use of self

When people are canvassed for their views about what makes a good social worker, the responses tend to focus on qualities such as friendliness, warmth, kindness, sincerity, reliability and so on. There are other qualities which may not be named, but which we might also, on reflection, feel are important, such as optimism and a sense of hope (Trotter, 1999: 116). These basic qualities are fundamental to good practice, though there is much debate about whether you just have them, or whether they can be learnt. It is also important to develop competent skills in order to put these good intentions into practice. Training and education help you make conscious decisions about your behaviour; this does not make the behaviour insincere, but it does mean that you are more aware of your self and how you use your self.

There is much talk of the 'conscious use of self' in social work practice (see, in particular, Minuchin and Fishman, 1981). What does this actually mean? Caspi and Reid (2002: 129) claim that 'the "self" consists of all facets of the person ... including feelings, thoughts and ways of behaving as well as fixed attributes such as age, sex and physical characteristics'. The fixed attributes do not change, or only slowly, whilst the other facets might not even be visible to ourselves. If you want to explore different notions of your self, download 'Tree 1' of The Virtual Placement (Doel and Cooner, 2002) and work through each of the Word Photos in the program.

Why might it be particularly important to know your self in social work? Make a list in the box below and share this with your practice teacher.

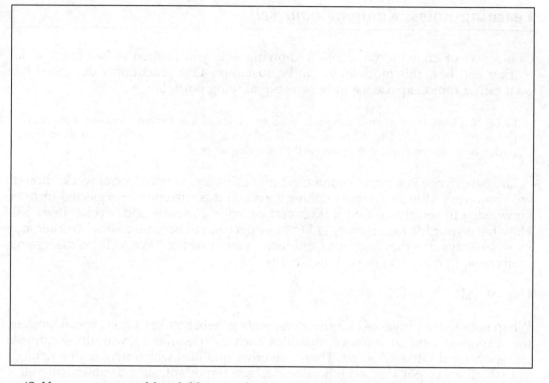

'Self-awareness enables deliberate choices about how to behave' (Caspi and Reid, 2002: 215), whether this is in your professional role as a social worker or, indeed, in your personal life. One significant aspect of self is the way in which you construe the world, as mediated by your beliefs and understandings. In your studies for the social work qualification, you will come across terms such as 'postmodern' and 'constructionist' and these refer to the idea that meanings are not rigid dictionary definitions, but are constructed socially (Parton, 2002). In turn, the term 'reflective practice' is one which builds on this idea that it is important to know your self in order to better understand your professional practice (Lishman, 2002).

## World-views

Everybody has a world-view, even if it is not very clear or consistent. A world-view is just another way of saying how we make sense of the world, including personal theories we use to explain what goes on around us. Problems can arise if we have views which exclude other interpretations to such an extent that we are unaware of other people's world-views, whether they are colleagues or service users. Problems can also occur if we are not aware of the personal beliefs which lead us to act as we do.

Take an example from your current period of practice learning. This may be someone you have been working with, or perhaps one of your colleagues can provide an example. Think of the *case path*[1] for this person and look at it from the different perspectives of the writers of the four extracts in the *Viewpoint* activity.

- How does each viewpoint affect your explanation of the person's situation?
- How does this influence what you do?
- What effect might this have on the case path?

You might want to consider how the beliefs in each of the four extracts might influence your work with the various residents of Derby Street in Activity 1, *Licensed to learn*. It may help if you begin to colour in some additional information, perhaps relating to people's faiths – for example, that the Kiyani brothers are devout Muslims and that Shama and Gary Homes are Adventists.

You have been looking at different world-views, but how about the view which you carry all the time – what does that look like? We get so used to looking at the world through our own particular spectacles that we often forget that we have a distinctive point of view, not necessarily shared by others. The statements below should help to trigger your thoughts about this. Which statements do you feel attracted to or repelled from?

1   Blood is thicker than water.
2   Behind every cloud is a silver lining.
3   Women are unpredictable.
4   Under the skin we're all essentially the same.
5   People don't like being reminded of their responsibilities.
6   In general, people respond to reason.
7   Gay men understand women.
8   There's a lot of untapped goodwill in the community.
9   The more things change, the more they stay the same.
10  Men can't do more than one thing at a time.
11  Childhood – the best years of your life.
12  Never judge a person until you've walked in their moccasins.

Compare your responses to the twelve statements with those of other students. What do the differences and similarities in your responses tell you about yourself?

The way in which we make sense of the world is influenced by the sum of our experiences to date, but our world-view is not static. Indeed, the experience of your professional training is likely to have a major impact on your understanding of your self and your perspective on the world, even if it is not so dramatic as, say, that

---

[1] A case path is a way of describing the person's contact with the organization from start to finish.

Reproduced from *Modern Social Work Practice* by Mark Doel and Steven M. Shardlow, Ashgate, Aldershot, 2005

of Ebeneezer Scrooge[2] in Dickens' *Christmas Carol*. So, remember to make a note of how your experiences both in class and in the practice learning sites have changed your world-view, and how these changes have in turn influenced the way you have worked with someone in a practice setting.

## World-views of service users, carers and other professionals

We have so far been considering your own world-view, but it is important to remember that the people you work with have their own world-views, too. For instance, their belief in the possibility or impossibility of change is a strong factor in the success or failure of your efforts with them.

Do you think it is important to find out about the world-view of the service user? If so, how can you do this? One approach is to review the range of research about users' views of the world (see the regular bulletins from J.F. Rowntree's *Findings* for example). You may discover that users' and carers' world-views are in sharp contrast to yours, perhaps even in strong disagreement, and you need to consider whether you would disclose this. Can you think of occasions when it would be appropriate to challenge these world-views? (There is an example on page 74.)

Differences between your world-view and that of other professionals with whom you are working can sometimes explain the sense of not pulling together. These differences can crystallize into stereotypes, so that we do not see a particular person who is a police officer but our own caricature of a police officer. The solicitor does not see you, but his or her own stereotype of a student social worker. It is users and carers who pay the price of this stereotyping, so it is important to learn how to challenge these assumptions effectively.

## Assessment notes: *Knowing your self*

Although this chapter appears early in this book, we recognize that it is a process which continues throughout your practice learning and beyond. It is the *outcome* of this process which is assessed: in other words, how your growing self-knowledge influences your values and practice. Moreover, in addition to the intellectual self-knowledge which *Viewpoint* helps to put into focus, there are other equally important facets to self-knowledge, such as emotional intelligence, in which emotions and thoughts are harmonized (see Goleman, 1996). This, too, has a strong influence on your developing practice.

---

[2] A fictional character who has a life-changing, overnight conversion from mean businessman to kind-hearted philanthropist.

Reproduced from *Modern Social Work Practice* by Mark Doel and Steven M. Shardlow, Ashgate, Aldershot, 2005

# Further reading

Adams, R., Dominelli, L. and Payne, M. (2002), *Social Work: themes, issues and critical debates*, (2nd edn), Basingstoke: Palgrave.

Payne's chapter in this book considers the relationship between social work theories and reflective practice. There are other individual chapters which consider different theories for practice in social work, such as feminist social work, psychosocial approaches and cognitive behavioural practice.

The extracts in Activity 1, *Viewpoint*, are taken from the following sources:

## Extract 1: The social work relationship

Lymbery, M. (2000), 'The Retreat from Professionalism: from social worker to care manager' in N. Malin, (ed.), *Professionalism, Boundaries and the Workplace*, London: Routledge, pp. 133–34.

## Extract 2: The messiness of practice

Humphries, B. (2003), 'What *Else* Counts as Evidence in Evidence-based Practice?', *Social Work Education*, 22(1): 83.

## Extract 3: Social workers' constructions of power

Fook, J. (2002), *Social Work: critical theory and practice*, London: Sage, p. 109.

## Extract 4: Empirical practice

Reid, W.J. (1992), *Task Strategies: an empirical approach to clinical social work*, New York: Columbia University Press, pp. 7–8.

# 3 Knowing the role

## *About Activity 3*  *Boundaries*

*Boundaries* consists of a number of questions designed to expose practice dilemmas. These dilemmas focus on the distance social workers place between themselves and the people who use their services.

This activity gets best results with four to eight participants, but it can be undertaken by a single teacher and learner.

### Purpose

It can be difficult to know what a professional relationship means in practice and how it differs from a personal relationship. This activity is designed to highlight the differences between *friendships* and what we might call *workships* (professional working relationships between practitioners and other people). It helps students become more skilled at deciding where and how the boundaries between the personal and professional should be drawn. It also encourages students to reflect upon how they might be perceived by others, according to how these boundaries are defined.

### Method

- Arrange a time to meet with the students and outline the purposes of the activity, but not the details, since you want spontaneous responses.
- Give each person a copy of *Boundaries* and take each of the nine sections in turn to trigger discussion. It does not matter if you are unable to finish all the categories in the time available. Kick off the first item yourself with a Never, Always or It depends and invite others to join in with their responses.
- Relate the discussion to actual experiences in order to avoid idealized replies; encourage dissent and try to tease out any general principles which have come out of the discussion.
- Summarize the main areas of consent and dissent and write down any general principles which have come out of the discussion. Ask for feedback from everyone about the usefulness of the exercise.

## Variations

This activity has been used successfully in many different settings, usually in the early stages of the practice learning, and even as part of a meeting before the practice learning begins. It has also been used successfully as part of the selection process for a social work course, as the focus of group discussions between candidates. Alternatively, the exercise could be used at different points during the student's practice learning.

A particularly useful variation is to ask students to complete the activity, then to present the activity to a group of service users and/or carers and ask them how they think social workers ought to behave. Some agencies provide excellent opportunities for this – for example, those already working with users and carers in groups, such as residential centres for children and older people, daycare centres and group projects for young people. The comparison between the views of students, users and carers can prove very interesting and highly informative in helping students to define the boundaries of professional behaviour.

You can use *Boundaries* to highlight a particular dimension of practice. For example, students can be asked to consider how issues of race, gender or age would alter their responses. You could cross-reference to Activity 1, *Licensed to learn*, to ask how students would vary their responses if the service user or carer were Zoë Benner, one of the Kiyani brothers, Shama and Gary Homes and so on.

## Use by other professions

The general principle of *Boundaries* can be readily transferred across professions and countries by modifying the situations in the exercise to ensure that they reflect common dilemmas in the profession in question. It is enlightening for groups of students from differing professions to discuss a *Boundaries* exercise together, exploring similarities and differences in their views. The exercise can also be modified so that it considers the boundaries between different professional and vocational groups in relation to their mutual roles in work with patients, clients and service users. In a hospital it may be the boundaries between the healthcare staff and the social work staff that you wish to highlight. There are also dilemmas in the patient–doctor relationship which you could compare with user/patient–worker activities.

The *Boundaries* exercise is just as provocative when used with experienced workers as with students. Interprofessional teams can use a *Boundaries*-style exercise to consider the ways in which roles overlap and are discrete.

## National Occupational Standards for Social Work

The topics in this chapter relate to the following National Occupational Standards (see the Appendix):

  1:  Preparing for social work contact and involvement
14:  Accountability
19:  Professional development
20:  Dilemmas and conflicts.

# Activity 3    Boundaries

- Where do we draw the boundary between personal and professional relationships?
- How should social workers present themselves to service users and carers?
- Can you answer 'Always' or 'Never' to any of the questions below?
- If your answer to a question is 'It depends', what does it depend on?

## Reciprocation

1 Do service users and carers call you by your first (given) name?
2 Do you call them by their first (given) name?
3 Would you accept a service from a user or carer? For example, would you:
   - let them bake you a cake?
   - knit you a jumper?
   - advise you what is wrong with your car?
   - mend an electrical fault in your home?

## Phones

4 Would you give your mobile phone number to a service user or carer?
5 Would you send a service user or carer a text message?
6 Would you turn your mobile phone off whilst interviewing a service user or carer?

## Self-presentation

7 Would you wear on display:
   - jeans and trainers when you meet with service users and carers?
   - an 'FCUK' shirt? A bare midriff?
   - body piercing and/or visible tattoos when on placement?
   - formal dress for a case presentation?

8 Would you think it OK for someone to wear a badge, when meeting with service users and carers, that stated:
   - 'Stop the war'
   - 'Help the Aged'
   - 'Proud to be gay'
   - 'Black is beautiful'
   - 'UK Independence – down with Brussels'

## Interview culture

9 On a home visit would you accept:
   - a cup of tea or coffee?
   - a snack (such as a biscuit)
   - an alcoholic drink?
   - a meal?

10 In the unit, ward or group room would there be circumstances in which you would:
   - talk about personal matters with other people present?
   - make a cup of tea or coffee for the service user or carer?

## Social contact

11 Would you accept from a service user or carer:
   - a wedding invitation?
   - an invitation to a party?

Reproduced from *Modern Social Work Practice* by Mark Doel and Steven M. Shardlow, Ashgate, Aldershot, 2005

- a request to attend a funeral with them?
- offer a lift in your car?

12  Would you avoid frequenting a place where a service user or carer worked?

13  Would you lend money to a service user and carer?

14  Would you take the children of service users to McDonalds on their own?

## Self-disclosure

15  Do you compare life experiences with service users and carers? For example, do you:
- let them know how you feel about their circumstances?
- let them know what sort of day you've had?
- talk about your work with other service users or carers in similar circumstances?

16  Do you share personal information with your users and carers? For example, do you share:
- good news, such as the fact that your partner has been promoted?
- bad news, like your father suffers from Alzheimer's?
- that you have just booked a holiday?

17  Would you give your home address or a personal phone number?

18  Would you disclose how much you disagree with one of your agency's policies?

## Touch

19  When you meet a service user or carer would you:

- shake hands?
- kiss socially on the cheek?
- embrace?
- make a physical gesture?

20  Would you touch a service user or carer who is upset:
- on the arm?
- round the shoulders?
- on the knee?

21  When with a service user's family, would you:
- play with their children?
- romp with them on the floor?

## Looking the other way

22  Do you ignore the illegal activities of a service user or carer? For example:
- the presence of a cannabis plant in their home?
- claiming benefit when they are working?
- electricity that has been reconnected by the user?
- receiving stolen goods?
- an absconder who is being harboured?
- unlawful sexual activity?

## Sexuality

23  Would you:
- flirt with a service user or carer?
- discuss your HIV status with a service user or carer?
- consider having sexual intercourse with an ex-service user or carer?
- help a severely disabled person find a prostitute?
- disclose that you are gay or lesbian?

Reproduced from *Modern Social Work Practice* by Mark Doel and Steven M. Shardlow, Ashgate, Aldershot, 2005

# Teaching notes: *Knowing the role*

## Opportunities

To talk of opportunities for learning about the role is like looking for opportunities for breathing: every moment of the student's practice learning will relate to the question of role. However, you *will* need to create opportunities to help the student consider role dilemmas. For example, guidance about how to behave with people is often paradoxical:

| | |
|---|---|
| *You must be engaging, personable and able to step into people's shoes.*<br>*Act natural.*<br>*Be warm.* | *You must be purposeful, objective and able to stay outside the situation.*<br>*Be professional.*<br>*Keep your cool.* |

It is not surprising if students feel that making a successful professional relationship is like squaring a circle. Asking somebody to be detached and connected at the same time is confusing. Students need to consider how the way in which they present themselves to people can influence the nature of the professional relationship.

This paradox should be discussed early on with the student. It gives you both a reference point later, when things happen in the student's work which illustrate these dilemmas. It might help to avoid the kind of experience illustrated by the following quote from the portfolio of a qualified social worker:

> One parent where I was involved in assessing the family due to neglectful and poor home conditions misunderstood my role. Although I had carefully explained my role at the beginning of my involvement with the family, my assistance and friendly manner and social work approach with the mother was interpreted by her as friendship. When it came to completing reports for court, my assessment of the situation was interpreted [by the mother] as being negative and 'backstabbing' due to the information she had volunteered to me. She stated that she would never of [*sic*] discussed some issues with me if she knew that I would use that information as part of my assessment.

## Different expectations

Students behave now as they have learned to behave in previous settings, which may have been very different from the current one. A student who has been working in a residential setting with disabled people may be used to a lot of physical contact and informal relationships; this student may not understand the different expectations of a formal office setting.

Students are also at an early stage in their careers and may have a strongly-felt desire to help people, perhaps resulting in close identification with the user and an emphasis on personal friendship. In practice, this could mean an interview in a pub, an intimate talk by a resident's bedside, or activities like motorbiking with groups of young people in the evenings. This may be fine in some circumstances, but not in others; professionals exercise considerable power in their work, and students need to appreciate the dimensions of their power early on (Hugman, 1991).

On questions of professional standards, the difference of opinion about what is acceptable is striking. For example, Jayaratne *et al.* (1997: 187) point out that 'virtually no empirical studies of professional standards exist ... in effect, practitioners and those who judge practitioner behaviour are making decisions with relatively little guidance from the profession'. Their own exploratory study of 826 practitioners in Michigan found that hugging or embracing a client was commonplace, but accepting expensive gifts and lending or borrowing money were rare. There were no clear majorities either way for: commenting on clients' physical attractiveness; cursing or swearing during sessions; discussing one's religious belief; and providing a home telephone number. In other words, social workers said that these behaviours were acceptable and not acceptable in roughly equal numbers.

The General Social Care Council for England has published a *Code of Practice* (GSCC, 2002) which, whilst useful at a general level, does not contain the level of detail which practitioners must deal with on a day-to-day basis. This is why it is useful to consider specific examples.

## Example

The following example shows how students who have been used to keeping service users and carers at arm's length might respond to the prospect of practice learning where the users or carers of the agency are not kept at such distance. We also see how *Boundaries* can be used to judge the suitability of a period of practice learning before it is planned.

> **Yusef**, an Asian student, and **Jim**, a black American student on the same social work programme, were interested in a placement in a user-led neighbourhood family resource centre. So far, they had experienced field social work, which was their intended career, and they wanted the chance to have a placement together to run groups for young people. The tutor thought that the style of the centre would be a contrast with their previous experience and arranged for a meeting for Yusef, James and the two practice teachers from the centre.
>
> The practice teachers, **Carmen** and **Nalini**, began by emphasizing that the people who came to the centre were called users, not clients. They had chosen five specific dilemmas from *Boundaries* which they felt highlighted the centre's work and invited Yusef and James to add any others. The subsequent discussion revealed that the boundaries which the practice teachers drew around their relationships with the users were more permeable than Yusef or Jim had known.
>
> Yusef queried some of the boundaries drawn by the practice teachers, but commented that the centre's relationship with its users would be a new experience for him and that he was interested in the contrast. He had reservations about the effects on his family life, especially the policy of letting users have a personal phone number.
>
> Jim answered all the questions with 'It depends', complaining that the circumstances in each case needed elaborating before he could give an opinion on the basis of the information available. When the practice teachers asked him to explain what he thought *it* depended on, Jim said that he would have to meet each situation as it came: 'It would depend on what felt right at the time'.

After the meeting, the practice teachers and the students reflected separately on what had been said. Rejoining the meeting, Carmen and Nalini said they thought Yusef would have an interesting placement and his past experience would be a stimulating challenge to their own work. They understood the strain that this work places on domestic lives and they would respect whatever decision he and his family came to.

They had concerns about Jim's inability to state his position on any of the dilemmas. They had no problem with 'It depends' as an answer, but they would expect James to be able to say what it depended on. More to the point, the users of the centre would expect that, too; an answer which relied on whatever 'felt right at the time' would not be acceptable to them.

In this situation, the activity gave everybody a chance to find out about expectations at the agency and whether they would be acceptable. For the practice teachers it was also useful for assessing the students' willingness to question their own judgements. For example, giving out your personal phone number is neither professional nor unprofessional, but failing to question the principles behind the decision *is* unprofessional.

## Developing a style

The teaching task is to create a climate that enables students to make conscious choices in terms of style, which might be defined as the unique way in which they define and express the boundaries between themselves and users.

Perhaps an analogy will illustrate this: the Norwegians have a saying that there is no such thing as bad weather, just bad clothing. In other words, what is appropriate in one circumstance is inappropriate in another. It is the same with style and personal presentation. It is not that a particular style is right or wrong in itself, but that certain styles might suit particular occasions (though there are some styles, it is true, which suit no occasion). Students need opportunities to try on different clothing and to experiment to find the style that suits them and is consistent with agency expectations.

Finally, there is another role which students need to begin to understand – your role, whether as practice teacher, practice assessor or work-based supervisor. It is important that both you and the student know what you each expect of supervision, especially since the word 'supervision' has different resonances for different people. Keep the focus on student learning and service user welfare, not on a student's personal problems.

## Learning notes: *Knowing the role*

The key to the profession's identity lies in the recognition that what makes something social work is not what is done but *how* it is done. (Davies, 1994: 155)

*Boundaries* places you in the position of a professional person. It reflects some of the dilemmas you will face when making working relationships with people.

Let's turn this situation on its head and think about times when it is *you* who receives a service. This helps you learn about your image of professional behaviour. Make some notes in relation to each of the following:

- As a patient with toothache,
  what would you describe as professional behaviour by the dentist?

- As a borrower with debts to pay,
  what would you describe as professional behaviour by the bank manager?

- As a householder with three inches of water in your cellar,
  what would you describe as professional behaviour by the plumber?

- As a parent of a child experiencing problems at school,
  what would you describe as professional behaviour by the teacher?

- As a buyer seeking to change a product and being referred to a call centre,
  what would you describe as professional behaviour by the telephonist?

Either on your own or with a small group of other students, think about your positive and negative experiences as a user of services. You can use the examples listed above or choose different ones. Use flipchart paper to make two lists – one for the positive experiences and the other for the negative ones.

From the lists, draw up a number of guidelines for professional practice and prioritize them into four or five main principles. How do you think these principles relate to professional social work practice? How do they compare with the GSCC (2002) *Code of Practice* or other similar codes?

Reproduced from *Modern Social Work Practice* by Mark Doel and Steven M. Shardlow, Ashgate, Aldershot, 2005

## Process and outcome

An important theme in social work practice is the extent to which outcome is important when evaluating this question of professionalism. In other words, does the relief of pain by the dentist indicate professional behaviour or is it possible to think of situations when the pain was relieved but the behaviour was unprofessional; or when the pain was not relieved, but the behaviour was professional? This theme is developed in the Introduction to Part IV, 'Evidence-based practice'.

## Occupational control and status

Who defines the social work role? A number of commentators have reflected that the social work profession is losing control over what social work is and what social workers do; Jordan (2003) claims that the factors which used to give the social work profession a strong identity are now its weaknesses – in particular, its close association in the UK with the public sector and local authorities. The relative lack of occupational control has also sometimes called into question the right of social work to be considered a fully-fledged profession. Occupational control is certainly limited by the location of social work in welfare bureaucracies, with constraints on the use of professional discretion and the requirements for standardized responses to people's needs. Is good practice 'defined as being the ability to follow rules and procedures competently, rather than the ability to make individual professional judgements' (Lymbery, 2000: 131) or is it possible to define it as both?

The fact that the knowledge base of social work is contested (in other words, there is no consensus about this knowledge base) and shared with others (that is, it draws from other disciplines) is often cited as another limitation to its right to be considered a profession, although these factors are by no means limited to social work. Certainly, you should consider how the practices of social work are 'different from those of ordinary social intercourse' (Howe, 1996: 117) as, in many respects, it is these differences which make your work that of a professional rather than of a well-meaning amateur.

Some aspects of the social work role have attracted more status than others. For example, work with children and families has been seen as 'offering most opportunity to engage in high status casework activity', whilst work with adults and older people 'has had a greater focus on indirect tasks concerned with the arrangement of services' (Lymbery, 2000: 124). It is paradoxical, then, that, as work with children and families has become increasingly dominated by procedures, it is arguably in some of the less fashionable areas of practice that 'real' social work is still possible, if 'real' is to be understood as less bureaucracy and more direct contact.

As a student, it is understandable if you narrow your focus on the here and now of the work of the agency. Even so, it is important to find time to understand your role in its wider context. How do social policies have an impact on the day-to-day

Reproduced from *Modern Social Work Practice* by Mark Doel and Steven M. Shardlow, Ashgate, Aldershot, 2005

practice of social workers and the everyday lives of people? How will you retain and make best use of the motivation which brought you into social work, protecting it from the effects of the compromises you will make as a routine part of your learning and work? (Occasional dips into Barry and Hallett's *Social Exclusion and Social Work* (2003) will provide a refresher.)

## Metaphors for the social work role

Before you arrive at your first practice learning site you might like to think about a metaphor which, for you, epitomizes the social work role. Make a note of this metaphor and any others that come to mind during your social work education and training. Return to the metaphor at various points during your learning and see how your view has changed, or not. Is the metaphor you chose at the beginning of your course the same as the one at the end?

As a start, you might consider this metaphor from Howe:

[A social worker is] like the sculptor who frees the sculpted form from the marble: the worker recognises the potential of their client and enables him [*sic*] to realise that potential. (Howe, 2003: 113)

## The student role

So far we have been considering the role of professional social worker. You are also coming to terms with another role, that of student. The *Boundaries* exercise could just as easily be modified to consider appropriate boundaries between student and practice teacher. For example, there is now general agreement that it is important to maintain the boundary between supervision and therapy. Support in supervision is different from helping in therapy, not least because of the power which supervisors have in respect of students' professional lives. Caspi and Reid (2002) suggest that knowing the reasons why this boundary is sometimes crossed is probably the best way of preventing it. They suggest four reasons:

- supervision and therapy processes are quite close, so there are overlaps;
- many supervisors are promoted from clinical positions and may fall back on their clinical expertise when confronted with the experience of new challenges as a supervisor;
- some supervisees may prefer the focus to be on their personal life rather than their work performance, as a way of avoidance, conscious or not;
- supervisees may well be in positions of stress (poverty, etc). (Caspi and Reid, 2002: 105–106)

The crucial question is the extent to which any life stresses impede your ability as a student to learn and practise. There are times when practice teachers must address these issues, but as a supervisor of your learning, not as a personal therapist.

Just as learner drivers in the UK carry 'L' plates on their cars, as a student social worker you are officially licensed to learn, and can wear your metaphorical 'L' plates with pride. In some respects, this allows you more discretion than those who have been expected to discharge their 'L' plates. Despite the rhetoric of lifelong learning, it can be very difficult for qualified workers to be seen, or allow themselves to be seen, as continuing learners. So, although it may feel like a relatively powerless role, there are also aspects of the student social work role that are relatively privileged.

As someone who is licensed to learn, you may be in a better position than the qualified and permanent staff in the agency in terms of experimentation and openness to considering a wider variety of 'hows' of social work practice.

## Assessment notes: *Knowing the role*

Your ability to define professional boundaries is an important part of your assessment. For example, if most of your interviews seem to take place in street settings or if you tell every user to attend the office for appointments, concerns may be expressed about your ability to respond flexibly to people's different needs. A preferred style may have become one which is fixed.

You will need to become aware of any unintended messages conveyed by how you present yourself. For example, warmth and friendliness can be interpreted in the wrong way – perhaps as a willingness to give more than you can or should offer. Sexual attraction does not respect user–worker boundaries. A dress code often carries different messages from one situation to another. Style is one of those personal issues which affects your ability to work as an effective professional. Although these may not be part of your formal assessment, they do show your *suitability* for social work practice.

## Further reading

Lymbery, M. (2000), 'The Retreat from Professionalism: from social worker to care manager', in N. Malin (ed.), *Professionalism, Boundaries and the Workplace*, London: Routledge.
This chapter on the retreat from professionalism is an interesting perspective on the changing role of social work.
Loewenberg, F.M. and Dolgoff, R. (2000), *Ethical Decisions for Social Work Practice* (6th edn), Itasca, ILL: Peacock.

You can find out more by looking at the various codes of practice for social workers. These include the following:
BASW (1975), *A Code of Ethics for Social Work*, Birmingham: British Association of Social Workers. Revised 1986 and 1996.

Reproduced from *Modern Social Work Practice* by Mark Doel and Steven M. Shardlow, Ashgate, Aldershot, 2005

GSCC (2002), *Codes of Practice for Social Care Workers and Employers*, London: General Social Care Council at: www.gscc.org.uk

International Federation of Social Workers (IFSW) (1994), *The Ethics of Social Work: principles and standards* at: www.ifsw.org/Publications/4.4.pub.html

NASW (1996), *Code of Ethics*, Silver Spring, MD: National Association of Social Workers.

For a comparison of codes of practice see:

Banks, S. (1995), *Ethics and Values in Social Work*, Basingstoke: Macmillan.

For comment on the limitations of the standards in NASW's *Code of Ethics*, which contains 'no historical or case references, interpretative guides, or formal or informal opinions', see:

Jayartne, S., Croxton, T. and Mattison, D. (1997), 'Social Work Professional Standards: an exploratory study', *Social Work*, 42(2): 187–98.

# Part II

Direct Practice

# CONTEXT: Interprofessional learning and practice

There is a growing emphasis in modern social work practice on the need to remove the barriers between different professional groups, in order to provide a more coherent service for people. These barriers allow professions to protect their own territory and prevent them from working together with other professions. A series of public inquiries have highlighted professional misconduct as a significant factor in the resulting tragedies, with a failure of communication between agencies and different professionals at the heart of this misconduct (Laming, 2003).

Social work practice is increasingly organized around or within other professional disciplines. Whereas social workers in the last part of the twentieth century were more likely to be employed together in a social work team, at the beginning of the twenty-first century, we see them increasingly employed in multidisciplinary teams. These teams usually have a 'client group' focus (people with learning disabilities, people with mental health problems, young offenders), and the team is designed to bring together people with different skills in order to encourage collaborative working for the benefit of the people who are served by the team.

In addition to these developments in professional practice, there have been parallel moves to enable students of different professions to learn together. These opportunities can be in both classroom settings and agency settings, and they are formalized in the requirements for the social work degree in the UK:

> Providers [of social work education] will have to demonstrate that all students undertake specific learning and assessment in the following areas:
> Partnership working and information sharing across professional disciplines and agencies. (Department of Health, 2002:4)

## Terminology

The terminology to describe these developments varies considerably – multi-professional, interdisciplinary, inter-agency, collaborative working, shared learning, and so on (Barr, 2002; Miller *et al.*, 1999; Weinstein *et al.*, 2003; Whittingon, 2003). In some respects, these terms reflect the continuum of possibilities: from a team in which there are two professions who do very little or no joint working, to a team in which there are many professions who are consistently working together directly with service users and carers. There can be different intensities in the level of inter-agency work, as noted by CCETSW, Northern Ireland:

> Most social care and health professionals will have experience of working with people from a number of agencies and professions, but the distinctions between different types of interaction are frequently blurred. The terms multidisciplinary, multi-agency and inter-agency tend to be used interchangeably to describe a variety of working relationships. A multidisciplinary team, for example, may define itself as such in terms of the various skills required to meet the complex needs of a service user, but the team members and services may be provided by the staff of one agency, such as social services (multidisciplinary) or by staff from several agencies including health, community services and the voluntary sector (multi-agency). Equally, the planning, funding and commissioning of services may be the result of joint initiatives by a number of agencies (inter-agency) with the provision of such services requiring the skills base of a number of disciplines and from a variety of agencies.
>
> In developing a definition of what is meant by multidisciplinary working it may be helpful, therefore, to consider it in terms of levels of modes of *co-operation* between professionals and agencies providing social and healthcare services. (5: 43)

Co-operative working can be identified within five modes of interaction:

- Communication
- Consultation
- Collaboration
- Bilateral working
- Joint working

> *Communication* is defined as co-operation at its most basic level, involving one discipline or agency informing another of its actions or intentions.
>
> *Consultation* involves activities where one discipline or agency approaches others for their opinions, information and advice on a proposed course of action.
>
> *Collaboration* involves a degree of mutual activity between disciplines or agencies with adjustments and agreement on the scope and level of participation in that activity but usually with the expectation that each agency or discipline will operate independently in the provision of services.
>
> *Bilateral working* implies the recognition of an overlap in services provision between disciplines or agencies, which can give rise to both individual and collective operational planning and service delivery.
>
> *Joint working* implies agencies working together to plan and operate a mutual course of action. (CCETSW, 2000: 10)

Whilst recognizing these various intensities, we will use the word 'interprofessional' as a convenient single term to cover all aspects of learning and practice between two or more professional groups.

## Issues concerning interprofessional practice

Social workers are well-placed to promote interprofessional practice because they have been doing it for a long time. It may previously have been called something else ('joint working', 'working in partnership' or 'collaborative practice'), but it is a central aspect of social work practice, sometimes called networking, to be able to bring together a wide range of people who are significant to a particular purpose. Above all, social work is a peripatetic activity, both physically and figuratively. Its practitioners go far beyond a narrow technical skill to an understanding of wider systems including the effects of social policy and agency procedure. In essence, then, much of the practice of social work is already interprofessional, and social workers are well placed to advance this approach.

'The Berlin Wall' has been used as a metaphor largely to describe supposed barriers to working between health and social care; it was used as a powerful image by British politicians to describe what was causing them the greatest problem – namely territorial battles over budgets and beds in the health and social care sector. However, social workers work with a wide variety of other professional and vocational groups beyond the field of health – police, solicitors, probation officers, teachers, education welfare officers, housing workers, income support workers, amongst others. Indeed, the chances of most social workers working with some health workers, such as radiographers, is minimal.

So, interprofessional working is not just about health and social care. It refers to any situation in which two or more professions are collaborating in order to provide a better, more seamless, service. Many, perhaps most, social workers, are likely to have more contact with professionals who are *not* health workers.

Interprofessional working is in danger of becoming entangled with notions of multiskilling and flexible working, all of which are often seen as euphemisms for loss of professional identity and care on the cheap. 'As relationships became more flexible, risk of territorial disputes increased' (Barr, 2002: 11). Although there are specific areas of expertise which the different professions can contribute (see the discussion of the social work role in a multidisciplinary team later in this chapter), we need to be open to the fact that there are areas of overlap, too, and that people benefit if we are able to make best use of these.

For example, if you are having an extension built to your house, you will employ builders, electricians, plumbers, plasterers, joiners and decorators, each with their own area of expertise. You might reasonably expect each to have some knowledge of the others' work, in order to understand how it all fits together. Moreover, the plumber should be able to take up a floorboard and nail it back down without calling for the joiner, and the decorator should be able to smooth a dent in the wall without the plasterer being recalled. Whilst you would probably want to be in control of what the extension will look like (and details of where the sink, electrical sockets and so on will be placed), you will also want advice about what is likely to work best, how long it is likely to take and the relative costs. You might also want to employ a project manager with oversight of the whole job, making sure it is properly coordinated and standards are met. This seems a reasonable analogy for the kind of interprofessional working which users and carers should expect from their human services.

Effective interprofessional working requires each profession to value the contribution of the other. Different professions may not share the same value systems, but they must at least have a mutual respect for each other's differences and an understanding of how they might complement one another. Different value systems have very practical consequences, such as how confidentiality is interpreted, whether record systems will be communal or separate, and the terms used to describe the people with whom the professions work (Øvretveit *et al.*, 1997).

## Power and status differentials

There are considerable differences in power, status, income and working conditions amongst the various professions; indeed, the term 'profession' is in dispute for some groups (such as nurses and social workers) but not for others (such as doctors and solicitors). 'Interprofessional working can only successfully take root when there is mutual respect for the *differences* as well as the similarities between the professions, especially where there are notable power differentials' (Doel, 2002a: 170).

Students need preparation for these complex issues so that they can understand the intricacies of interprofessional working before they are exposed to them. Indeed, there is a need for much more research into interprofessional practice, though what is available is well summarized by Barr (2002). As with other areas of practice which become 'favoured sons', the dash to interprofessional working is in danger of trivializing the complexities and failing to build on existing good practices. Perhaps we could learn more from public inquiries into examples of good practice?

## Interprofessional collusion

In the uncritical rush to break down perceived barriers between the professions, there has been little analysis of a quite different risk to good practice arising from the relationship between different professionals. Research evidence is hard to come by, but anecdotal evidence suggests that professionals' commonly held stereotypes of clients and patients is as great a barrier to good practice as any interprofessional rivalry. In other words, a collusive consensus about individuals or families, reinforced by different professionals, can be discriminatory and excluding. Such a consensus is relatively covert and implicit, but perhaps the problem of interprofessional collusion is the more pervasive. Taking our earlier analogy of the extension to your home, it is as though all those different trades (builders, plumbers and so on) were in absolute agreement that you were a complete and utter troublemaker (they have seen your sort before) and were all unified in their determination to build your extension as *they* saw fit because they know best for you.

In their advocacy role, social workers can find themselves having to counter strongly held assumptions made about service users and carers by all the other professionals in the user's orbit. Challenging this perspective and helping other professionals to consider alternatives is a difficult but essential task. Indeed, Recommendation 37 of the report on the death of Victoria Climbié made it clear that social workers should have the confidence to question other agencies and their involvement or conclusions (Laming, 2003).

Combating interprofessional collusion still requires working together, of course. However, it will often first be interpreted as not working together – as being different. A core value in social work is the celebration of diversity, but this is not necessarily a key value for other professional groups, where consensus may be valued over difference. Social workers need the skills to ensure that offering different perspectives is not seen as a cussed desire to break consensus.

## Issues around interprofessional learning

If people from different professions are to work more closely together, logic suggests that they should begin to learn about each other and from one another during their training. The joint education of students (shared learning) from different professions is an increasing feature of the curriculum.

Learning together in the classroom is an obvious place to start. However, there are a number of challenges to be overcome in making this a reality, not least harmonizing complex timetables. The tendency for professional bodies to prescribe the curriculum and to add new content without extracting the old means that there is little room for maneouvre, though there are undoubted areas of overlap, such as communication skills. In respect of inter-agency working, health and social care professions do not share common standards which practitioners are expected to learn (Shardlow *et al.*, 2004). Therefore, expecting these groups to work easily together is naive. However, there are some examples of courses offering joint awards, including a course for social workers and nurses working with people with learning disabilities, a feasibility study for the joint training of social workers and occupational therapists (Alsop and Vigars, 1998) and a post-qualifying initiative for practice teachers and clinical supervisors in social work, occupational therapy and nursing (Weinstein, 1997).

The quality of learning is an important consideration. In most UK university faculties (schools) where both nursing and social work are taught, the nursing students outnumber the social work students by anything up to ten to one, making balanced small groups of students difficult to achieve. There are risks that professional groups are taught together on the basis of convenience, because they happen to be in the same faculty or school, rather than on the basis of the need to develop joint standards and collaborative practice.

It is important, too, that these experiences of interprofessional learning are properly managed. Throwing students together without group-building and opportunities to practise honest communication can only serve to reinforce negative stereotypes. Tajfel's (1981) contact hypothesis suggests that mere exposure is not enough and students will need to find these encounters rewarding if their perceptions of other professions are to shift. These formative impressions are important ones and need to be carefully considered as opportunities for learning. Coming together for common teaching on a shared topic is one way forward, but this will need to be supplemented by sessions that focus quite specifically on the skills and values of interprofessional learning and practice. The groupwork skills we explore in Chapters 7 and 8 are essential to this process.

## The social work contribution in multidisciplinary teams

Social workers have long been located in multidisciplinary teams, and this is an accelerating trend. Rather than see it as a potential threat to social work's integrity, we should see it as an opportunity to influence others and learn from them, provided that social workers have a strong sense of their own professional identity. Social workers in multidisciplinary teams have a particular opportunity to consider what it is to do social work by considering what it is that is different about their role in these teams. This 'contrast effect' – defining social work by discovering what others perceive as the social work dimension – is an invaluable opportunity for social work students to learn about their profession.

In a small-scale study of a multidisciplinary team working with people with learning disabilities, Herod and Lymbery (2002) found that other professions did have a clear understanding of the social work contribution and that this was valued positively. They cite a non-social work team member's observation of the social work contribution:

> I think what is valuable is you just having a broader, all encompassing view of the community and the people and what's out there. A much wider picture than some of the other disciplines. (Herod and Lymbery, 2002: 21)

The healthcare workers in this team saw social workers as focusing on the importance of social models of disability. They appreciated the values and ethics of social work, the holistic perspective and strategic approach to organizations, the coordinating abilities of social workers and, finally, they perceived a certain quality of relationship with service users which was somehow 'closer'. All in all, non-social workers were able to pinpoint what they would miss if social workers were not members of the team.

These are encouraging findings, and they can probably be generalized to many other multidisciplinary teams which include social workers. They suggest that students could gain an interesting understanding of the social work role by asking people who are not themselves social workers. Replicating the Herod and Lymbery study, or something similar, would be an interesting and valuable project for the student and the team.

In summary, interprofessional learning and practice is essential to good communication between all the people who are working together to provide services. The political drive towards interprofessional working in the UK tends to focus on a negative view of professions as protecting their own corners, and a desire to trivialize some of the very real practical difficulties involved. Social work is a profession long experienced in bringing together people with different perspectives and contributions to make, *including service users and carers*. Other professionals seem to value the holistic perspective of social work, though social workers may find themselves confronting examples of interprofessional collusion when this collusiveness is detrimental. Mere exposure to difference does not guarantee better understanding, especially when there are power and status differentials between different professional groups. More important than gathering people in the same room at the same time is the quality of that experience plus a shared belief that other professions have a distinct and valuable contribution to make.

# 4  Preparation

## About Activity 4    Starting out

Once students have completed *Starting out* with one of the hypothetical situations from *Licensed to learn*, they can follow the same process in order to prepare for contact with an actual user or carer.

### Purpose

Students are expected to become increasingly able to reflect on their practice and learning. This usually occurs either during or after the experience itself. However, *Starting out* helps students reflect *before* they have direct contact with people, so that they are reasonably prepared for the encounter.

### Method

Students should be familiar with Activity 1, *Licensed to learn*, so that they can develop it further in *Starting out*. Ask the student to follow the guidance, which includes writing notes of their responses. These can be used in supervision.

### Variations

Once students have completed *Starting out* with other households from *Licensed to learn*, developing their own additional information, they can follow the same process to prepare for contact with an actual service user or carer. This activity can be used both at the beginning of the period of practice learning and towards the end, to see what changes there are in the quality of the student's responses.

### Use by other professions

*Starting out* can be adapted for use by students from different professional backgrounds, in the same manner as *Licensed to learn*. Students can be asked to consider whether the questions in the *Starting out* activity are generic – that is, whether they translate across professions or whether different kinds of question are relevant for different professional groupings. The commonalities across professional groups can come as a surprise to some students.

## National Occupational Standards for Social Work

The topics in this chapter relate to the following National Occupational Standards (see the Appendix):

  1:   Preparing for social work contact and involvement
14:   Accountability.

## *Activity 4*    *Starting out*

### Part One

Consider how you might prepare for work with Jim Rafferty whom you first met in Activity 1, *Licensed to learn*. Use the six clusters of questions below. Remember that your preparation should be tentative and that you would need to be open to very different possibilities when you actually come into contact with the people.

**Jim Rafferty** lives at 5 Derby Street. We know already that he:

> ...used to work in the steel industry in quite a well-paid job until he retired. He is now seventy-two years old and was widowed three years ago. Over the last five years he has gradually been losing his sight through macular degeneration. His daughter lives a short bus ride away. Jim has written to the council to complain about the noise from Number 4.

You now have this additional information:

> Jim came to work in England from Ireland in the 1950s. Until a year or two ago he used to see two or three of his old friends from his days at the steel mill, but his deteriorating eye condition has made him feel less secure about going out. Age-related macular degeneration affects his central vision, but his specialist says it is unlikely to lead to total blindness. However, he cannot recognize facial features and gets little pleasure watching television. Seeing something directly ahead is a problem. He senses that other people do not know that he has a vision problem. He was very depressed after his wife died and he is still feeling lost without her. His daughter visits as often as she can and he gets a lot of joy from being with his grandchildren.

Clearly, there are potentially many kinds of work to do with Mr Rafferty, some of which might involve people other than a social worker – for example, a rehabilitation worker from the sensory impairment team. For now, however, use the following six clusters of questions to consider his situation, and make a written note of your responses.

1 **'Tuning in'**
  How do you think that the person might feel about their current situation? How do *you* feel about their situation? Do you have any similar or parallel experiences you can relate it to, or is the situation very new to you?
2 **Possible problems**
  What aspects of their current situation might the person like to change? Who is involved in the problem and who would need to be involved to work on the problem to make changes? What aspects do you think are most likely to be amenable to change?

Reproduced from *Modern Social Work Practice* by Mark Doel and Steven M. Shardlow, Ashgate, Aldershot, 2005

3   **Strengths**
     What strengths might there be in the person's situation? Thinking of the two 'A's (see page 19) what potential aptitudes and abilities can you identify?
4   **Aspirations**
     What hopes do you think the person may have for their situation? What changes would be necessary to realize these hopes, and what efforts would be required? Are these likely to be relatively long-term or short-term efforts?
5   **Resources**
     What kinds of resource might be needed to help the person with their situation? Where do you think these resources might be found? What other professionals may need to be involved?
6   **Reviews**
     How would the person know that they had accomplished what they wished to? What would indicate to other people that changes had occurred?

## Part Two

When considering the question of resources in the list above, you were asked to consider what other professionals might need to be involved. In Mr Rafferty's situation we mentioned the sensory impairment team as a possible resource. In Part Two of this activity we suggest that you make contact with other professional groups who would be likely to have involvement in the scenario you have chosen and find out more about how they would see their involvement, and yours, in this kind of situation. Make a note of your contacts to discuss in the next practice tutorial (supervision session).

If you have time, repeat the *Starting out* activity with another situation taken from the *Licensed to learn* activity, developing your own additional information, in the way we did for Jim Rafferty.

# Teaching notes: *Preparation*

## Opportunities

Opportunities for students to learn about preparation and to practise this aspect are likely to be plentiful. However, consideration needs to be given to the particular 'career paths' of the people who use your agency. Are most people coming in a voluntary capacity, or not? Will most people whom the student meets be new to the agency or are they likely to know the agency already? The answers to these kinds of question will have an impact on the kind of preparation which the student will need to undertake.

## Expectations

The first encounter with a potential service user can be like wandering on to a football field with few rules or 'painted lines' for guidance. There are a whole host of expectations which each player brings on to the field. Students need to become acquainted with both the general kinds of expectation which people have of their agency and the particular ones which each new contact brings. They must begin to discover the scope of the agency's field of operation, so that they can make a judgement about whether the agency will be able to respond to the potential user's concerns.

The encounter between the student and the service user or carer does not take place in a vacuum. Continuing the football field analogy, some agencies have very fixed lines which leave little room for manoeuvre. In this case, potential service users may think they are entering an open arena, only to be met with a non-negotiable response from agency staff, and students might discover themselves more restricted than they had anticipated. However, in some other settings they may also be surprised by the size of the grey area in which they can exercise discretion.

The student must learn about the way in which boundary disputes between their own and other agencies are resolved. Do people find themselves being referred back and forth? All agencies must also live with expectations in the wider society, which may be near or far from the reality of the work itself. In short, the student is learning to question whether there is 'a mandate' for work and, if so, where the boundaries of this mandate lie (Marsh and Doel, 2005).

## Existing networks

Prior to making contact with professional services, most people have usually considered other options such as seeking advice from friends and relatives. Unless they already have a history of contact, most people have been referred on to the agency, formally or informally by friends, relatives, neighbours or other professionals. The student, therefore, will rarely be the first person with whom the potential service user has discussed their concerns.

Part of the process of introduction involves tracing the path which has led the person to knock at the agency's door. This may have entailed many 'rehearsals' and it is worth asking the student to consider how many other people the potential user has been obliged to tell their story to. These rehearsals may have changed the person's view of their situation or possibly made it more entrenched. All of this information is pertinent to the student's knowledge of how this person or these people have come into contact with the agency, and how existing networks will help or hinder any future work.

The networks for some users are provided by the agency itself. Long-standing users – those who are very dependent or residents in the care of the agency – are likely to know much more about the agency than the student. Even so, it is important that expectations and 'rules' are checked out, just as they would be if the person were completely new to the agency. The fact that the student brings a new outlook can sometimes help long-standing service users to reappraise the service they are receiving from the agency.

Students need to consider the path which has brought the user into contact with the agency. This may extend backwards for some time, especially for long-standing residents and families with a string of social workers under their belts. Whatever the timescale, an understanding of how the person entered into the agency's orbit will develop the student's ability to focus the subsequent work. This ensures that the user's career with the agency is not aimless and neglected.

## Induction

As well as preparing students for contact with potential or actual service users, it is important to help them settle into the agency. In most cases, this should entail some form of induction programme to help students become familiar with their new environment. Sometimes this can best be done by providing an orientation exercise which guides students to significant parts of the agency (Doel and Shardlow, 1998: 17). Although the induction is usually best organized by one person (the supervisor on site, the practice teacher or assessor), the induction process is an opportunity to steer students towards other colleagues who will have some interest in, or impact on, their learning.

There is no doubt that students appreciate an agency that is well prepared for their arrival: 'one [student] commented that the agency had added her name to the door of a shared office space. She said that this gesture made her feel welcome and that she belonged at the agency' (Caspi and Reid, 2002: 158).

# Learning notes: *Preparation*

## First impressions

It is always difficult to know how reliable our first impressions are, and usually we forget them as we acclimatize to a new setting. Nevertheless, it is interesting to compare first impressions with later ones and to think about the ways in which the early impressions have changed or been confirmed.

Make a note of some of the impressions you have gained from your induction to the practice learning setting. These are your private impressions, so you should decide whether or not you want to share them with your practice teacher or work-based supervisor when you discuss your responses to the activity. You may just want to log them. The following are some suggested headings:

- The ease of travel by public transport to the site
- The use of signage to the site and within it
- The access for disabled people
- The physical appearance of the unit or office
- The reception area and the responsiveness of reception staff
- The feelings that your new colleagues express about their work and about the agency
- The attitudes of your new colleagues towards service users and carers
- The opportunity for privacy or quiet space
- The pace of work (especially compared to what you are used to)
- The 'climate' in the team or agency setting.

Towards the end of the period of practice learning, it will be interesting for you to reflect on these first impressions. How do they look now that you know the setting and your colleagues better? In particular, which impressions have been confirmed by experience and which ones have been changed?

## First contacts

The first contact with a potential user sets the tone for the rest of your work. The initial contact may be a personal encounter or it may be a written introduction, such as a letter or, perhaps more common in the future, an e-mail. Whatever the means, it is important to make careful preparations and to consider the best form of introduction.

### Introduction by letter or e-mail

At some time during your education for social work, it is important to have experience of composing written appointments of introduction, especially if these have not been a central part of your practice learning so far. The ability to convey professional purpose in a friendly manner and to write clearly in a way that invites participation is one worth practising. Letters and e-mails convey a particular style, and your choice of words will reflect this style, on a continuum from familiarity to formality (Doel and Shardlow, 1998: 60). You need to strike a balance between overfamiliarity on the one hand and starchy professionalism on the other. It is helpful to discuss with your practice teacher how the particular context should influence this balance. You will also need to consider whether the person is likely to be a non-reader.

## Introduction by telephone

Let us assume that you have the telephone number for a person who has been referred to the agency. In what circumstances would you consider making a first contact by telephone rather than by correspondence? What do you feel would be the advantages and disadvantages of making a phone call to introduce yourself?

## Introduction in person

There are many settings for practice learning in which introductions are informal and unplanned. You are unlikely to write a letter to a resident for whom you are key worker! However, you should think carefully about the means of the first contact and use whatever seems the most appropriate in terms of allowing both of you to be adequately prepared; remember, it is important to allow the service user or carer the opportunity to be prepared, too. If your first contact is in a group (for example, in the residents' lounge), how might you plan a person-to-person session?

## Attitude

A positive view about the possibility and desirability of change is an important factor in the success of any work, and it is important to think about how this is best conveyed. A naive optimism in the face of unremitting grief is not appropriate, and an overambitious agenda for change in the user's life can lead to disappointment and loss of confidence. However, cynicism about the prospect for change and a belief that changes are imposed from outside are unhelpful too, even if they sometimes reflect the user's own feelings. At some point, a sense of realistic optimism should be conveyed. Should this be conveyed in an introductory letter or e-mail and, if so, what is the best way of doing this?

Reproduced from *Modern Social Work Practice* by Mark Doel and Steven M. Shardlow, Ashgate, Aldershot, 2005

## Taboo topics

A clear, open message about the reason for your contact will tend to reduce any anxieties the user might have. However, there are some issues which it is difficult to be open about. These taboo topics need careful discussion with your practice teacher or assessor. Return to the situations in Activity 1, *Licensed to learn*; what taboo topics might there be in these various situations?

The first contact with people should usually start with the topics on which they are likely to want to focus; these may or may not be the most pressing ones, but they are likely to be the ones which are most acceptable, and they will help build confidence so that any taboo topics can eventually be addressed. On the other hand, there are times when it is obvious that the taboo topic is the one which brings you to the person's doorstep and 'beating about the bush' will seem dishonest or shifty. How might you decide at which moment to point openly to a taboo topic?

## Ad hoc contacts

In some settings, people make ad hoc and one-off contacts. In a citizens' advice bureau, for example, people typically drop in and may not require further involvement beyond a one-off session. In these circumstances it is still important and possible to be prepared, but more for the *kind* of problems that people are likely to bring to the agency, rather than for a particular individual.

## Preparing your learning

So far we have been considering your preparation for practice. It is also important to continue to prepare for your learning, as was emphasized in the Learning notes accompanying Activity 1. How can you be best prepared to take care of your learning? An excellent way of developing your learning is to ensure that you have opportunities for direct feedback. There are four main sources of direct feedback:

1  *You*
    You give yourself continual feedback, but it is important for you to learn how to recognize this and reflect on it. What cues do you respond to? How do you feel you are doing, and what do you do with these feelings? How do you respond to challenges and difficult times?
2  *The service user or carer*
    For much of the time feedback from the user or carer is implicit and inferred from reading their verbal and non-verbal behaviour and from your assumptions made on the basis of these readings. However, it is important to learn how to seek explicit feedback, so that you can question these assumptions.
3  *An observer*
    The third source of feedback is from an observer, preferably one who knows

Reproduced from *Modern Social Work Practice* by Mark Doel and Steven M. Shardlow, Ashgate, Aldershot, 2005

what to look for and how to give feedback constructively. Practice teachers, assessors and work-based supervisors are in a good position to be observers. You should be clear as to whether this is part of any formal requirement to observe your practice or whether this is additional, and you should prepare for any observation by agreeing the ground rules for feedback. In some settings, such as group care and daycare, practitioners are likely to be able to see you in direct work with people as a part of their own daily work. These settings are open, with the work taking place in full view of others. In other settings, opportunities for direct observation must be created.

4   *Audio or video feedback*
    An audio or video recorder is a valuable 'observer' of your work, providing a unique source of direct feedback.

   Note that, when using any form of observation an observer will need to be properly introduced, and the purposes of the observation explained, giving every assurance to users and carers that they can exercise their right not to have an observer present. If it is proposed to use audio or video equipment, signed permissions must be obtained from those involved and people must be given a proper opportunity to decline.

## Making your learning explicit

One aspect of your preparation is deciding how you will keep track of it. These arrangements should be included in your Learning Agreement and they will be separate from the records you keep for the agency in respect of your work with people. One method is to keep a record of one of your first contacts from early in the placement; this will act as a 'baseline' of your early practice. This record might be a letter of introduction or it may be a brief description of a personal encounter in the agency or community. Towards the end of the placement, review this record. If it is a letter, how might you rewrite it now that you have had the experience of writing several letters of appointment? If it is a personal encounter, how would your preparation for the encounter differ now that you are more experienced? This review, taken together with the baseline from the beginning of your placement, will demonstrate the way in which your practice has developed and enable you to make your learning explicit. Making the learning explicit will, in turn, enable you to transfer the learning from this specific experience to others (Cree and Macaulay, 2000).

## Assessment notes: *Preparation and the portfolio*

The *portfolio* is increasingly becoming the favoured method of recording your learning and for reflecting on its impact on your practice. This is true not just of social work, but also of many other professions (Doel *et al.*, 2002; Hull and Redfern,

1996). 'Portfolio' is a term used to cover many different kinds of document, and it is crucial that you prepare your self by becoming familiar with the structure of the portfolio so that you can make best use of it (Doel and Shardlow, 1995). As you make observations about your own learning, it is helpful to organize them using the structure of the portfolio, and you can only do this by becoming familiar with it.

## Further reading

Thompson, N. (2000), *Understanding Social Work: preparing for practice*, London: Macmillan.
Trevithick, P. (2000), *Social Work Skills* (3rd edn), Buckingham: Open University Press.

# 5 Generating options

## About Activity 5     Open ends

*Open ends* presents a brief transcript of a service user speaking. The student is invited to consider a number of options for responding to the person and to discuss the implications of choosing different lines of enquiry.[1]

### Purpose

Helping service users to consider different options is an important element in social work practice. *Open ends* is designed to aid students' understanding of their existing communication patterns, how these influence the way in which options are generated, and to consider possible alternatives.

### Method

- Separately, both you and the student read *Open ends* and make a note of the two questions which most closely fit the line of enquiry you would each wish to take, and the two questions which you feel would be most inappropriate. Each make your own brief notes to explain your choice.
- Compare these notes at the next teaching session, opening up a discussion about different strands of enquiry and the likely consequences of taking different routes.
- Subsequently, the student should use the *Open ends* approach with an audiotape of an interview with a service user or carer. The student should choose one of the person's statements and make a note of three or four possible questions which *could* have been asked at that point. The student should then describe why they took that particular line of enquiry, with any suggestions for changes, having had time to reflect.
- The student should consider what options their line of enquiry opened up for the person, and which ones were closed off.

---

[1] The difference between 'enquiry' and 'inquiry' is subtle, the former suggesting a more informal process than the latter; the meaning we seek in this chapter is somewhere between the two.

## Variations

The *Open ends* example can be adapted to different settings, using case material that is specific to the student's practice learning. On the other hand, we have found that the issues and the learning points transcend any particular example of *Open ends*. Students do not have to be familiar with the specific aspects of Jason's situation in order to use the learning points, though they may need extra encouragement if they are not very confident or imaginative. Indeed, if the territory is too familiar, case material can sometimes be a block to new learning, because of a natural tendency to rely on established patterns of thinking when the circumstances feels cosy. It is important to break free from any 'rut'.

You may also wish to introduce the student to a scenario which involves communicating with children. The manner of enquiry with children needs to reflect language which is approporiate to their age; indeed, students may need to consider different kinds of play as a substuitute for language-based enquiry (Horwath, 2001). Consider developing the situation in the Benner family in Activity 1 (*Licensed to learn*, page 13) to help students practise communication skills with children.

## Use by other professions

*Open ends* refers back to Jason Dean, who we first met in the *Licensed to learn* activity (page 13). There are a number of scenarios in that activity which could be developed into an *Open ends* activity for students from various professions. The opportunity for different students to hear each other's choices and to understand how they relate to their own is beneficial in developing understanding, to the benefit of all the people they work with.

## National Occupational Standards for Social Work

The topics in this chapter relate to the following National Occupational Standards (see the Appendix):

2:   Making informed decisions together
3:   Generating options.

## Activity 5      Open ends

In *Licensed to learn* you met **Jason Dean**, who lives with his partner Sam Weiner. At the moment all you know is the following:

> Jason is a twenty-eight-year-old, with a previous drug-related charge and has just completed a rehabilitation programme. Jason is unemployed, but volunteers at a local drop-in centre for homeless people. Sam is forty-six years old and receives long-term disability benefit, experiencing occasional periods of depression. Sam is a leading light in the tenants' association for the block of flats.

After a bit of preamble, during which you smell alcohol on Jason's breath, this is what he has to say:

> *I just want to talk to someone ... I had my first drink when I was about fourteen and one thing led to another and I was soon into drugs in a big way and it was all out of control. My dad died, I think in an accident, and my mother wasn't taking it too well ... (pause) I was sickly as a boy, no brothers or sisters, and it was all too much. Dad was depressed before he died and I don't think they were happy with each other – Dad and my mother. I've been in trouble with the law, but I didn't get sent away, thank God. I've been out of rehabilitation a while now and it's felt good ... but I've been finding it really hard these last few weeks. Sam and me have been arguing and it makes me feel bad and I know I'd feel better if I ... well, the dealers are back in the area and it'd be so easy, but I've got it under control ... We're getting a lot of abuse from people calling us queers and Sam's going into one of his depressions, not going out so much ... I'm OK, but Sam worries and I just don't know how I'm going to see us both through it.*

What lines of enquiry could you follow? The number of possible lines are infinite, but you are going to limit yourself to ones which begin with 'How', 'What', 'When', 'Where', 'Who' and 'Why'. These are interrogatives which introduce open-ended questions that can't adequately be answered with a 'Yes' or 'No'.

Out of the twenty questions below, choose two which most closely fit the line of enquiry you would wish to follow with Jason after he has spoken, and choose two which you would most wish to avoid. Explain your choices.

1   How old were you when your father died?
2   How do you connect your first drink at fourteen with your drug problem now?
3   How were you sickly as a child?
4   How do you feel about your parents' unhappy marriage?
5   Why did you get into trouble with the law?
6   What kind of help did you receive from the rehabilitation programme?
7   How long did your addiction last?
8   Where are you most likely to come across the dealers?

Reproduced from *Modern Social Work Practice* by Mark Doel and Steven M. Shardlow, Ashgate, Aldershot, 2005

9   Who did you do drugs with?
10   What do you think the future holds if you go back to the drugs?
11   What do you think is making Sam depressed?
12   When do you and Sam find yourself arguing?
13   Why do you feel responsible for Sam?
14   Why don't you go and see a couples' counsellor?
15   What feelings do you have for Sam?
16   How does Sam get to the tenants' association meetings when he's depressed?
17   Who's been calling you queer?
18   What have you done so far about the abuse you are getting as a gay couple?
19   What would you most like to change about your situation?
20   Where do you see things going from here?

---

**The questions I choose are:**

•
•

**My reasons are:**



**The questions I would most avoid are:**

•
•

**My reasons are:**

---

Some of the twenty questions are more open than others. Which are the less open questions?

Reproduced from *Modern Social Work Practice* by Mark Doel and Steven M. Shardlow, Ashgate, Aldershot, 2005

# Teaching notes: *Generating options*

## Opportunities

It will help the student if you begin by considering some examples from your own practice in which you have helped people to consider different options. This should enable you to identify likely areas of work in which the student will be able to practise generating options in partnership with people, and to develop a realistic picture of how the student might prepare for this aspect of their learning.

## Recognizing and interrupting patterns

Gaining an understanding of the way in which we communicate – the patterns of our communication – is the first step to understanding how these limit or expand the options for service users and carers. Recognizing these patterns can be surprisingly difficult, especially when people are unaware that they are indeed locked into a pattern. Moreover, if it is powerful enough, just one incident can determine our behaviour in a subsequent similar situation. This is powerfully illustrated by the following extract from a portfolio written by a qualified social worker reflecting on her formative experiences at secondary school (as usual, names have been changed):

> A friend, Suzy, confided in me that she believed that her father had made her pregnant. He had, and when Social Services became involved, no adults appeared to recognise that she needed her friends more than ever, and she was moved out of school and placed in foster care with no way of us contacting her. When Antony [another friend] came into school after a long period of absence with his hair hacked off with a razor by his mentally ill mother, I supported Antony by keeping it secret and helping him financially and by washing his clothes, etc. This was due to the fear that we all had about informing the teachers following Suzy being taken away by the Social Services. (Social work post-qualifying portfolio)

*Open ends* is designed to help students become aware of the pattern of responses they use when responding to people. The aim is to broaden the repertoire of these responses, so that students are making clear choices rather than relying on habit. In theoretical terms, this is close to a social constructionist approach, in which a critical stance is taken towards the taken-for-granted ways the student uses to understand the world (Burr, 1995).

Even if the student does not espouse a particular theory or approach, their choice of responses to the *Open ends* activity signifies their 'practice theory'; in other words, it helps them begin to understand how the leads which they pick up from people are guided by their own view of what is important. This is true of your choices, too! *Open ends* can, therefore, be a useful way of returning to some of the issues we introduced in Chapter 2 ('Knowing your self'), especially if the student experienced difficulties in understanding or identifying with any particular viewpoint.

The following three steps are designed to help students to consider their present repertoire of responses and how they might expand these and develop their role as navigator for service users and carers.

### Step 1: Awareness

The student's first step comes with an understanding that each intervention (verbal and non-verbal) moves the work in a certain direction. The student needs to be aware of this process. It is not wrong to be directive in terms of taking responsibility for the direction of a session; abdicating this responsibility is a little like sitting in a car with the handbrake off and wondering why and where the car is moving. The student's aim is not to take over in the driving seat (after all, it is the user or carer's car), but to help with the navigation.

Ask the student to reflect how the lines of enquiry beginning with questions 1–4 in the *Open ends* activity might come to different conclusions from enquiries beginning with questions 18–20. The first set of questions point down the road to 'current problems as a consequence of past traumas', whilst the second set of questions point down another route to 'current problems as a basis for here-and-now change'.

### Step 2: Repertoire

Second, students need an understanding of any established patterns of enquiry which they bring to their work. Continuing with the metaphor of riding in a car, it may be that one student has a preference for navigating down main roads, whilst another has a preference for back routes. If this works and successfully helps people to go where they want to, that's fine. If, however, a student seems always to take right-hand forks, or takes the car straight forward even when the road bends, the journey is likely to be unsatisfactory.

Self-aware practice means the student can develop a broader repertoire of enquiry skills and understand how the shape of questions now influences the outcome of work later. Students should be able to inspect their own practice in order to get this particular perspective. Audio- and videotapes are very useful ways for students to hear and see themselves.

### Step 3: Discernment

The third step is to gain a greater feel for when different kinds of response are appropriate to use. 'Appropriate' always seems an unsatisfactory word to use because it is so ill-defined, but there is no neat answer. The student's ability to reflect on successful and unsuccessful responses will help them approach the elusive definition of 'appropriate'.

When Jason finishes his story in the *Open ends* activity, enquiry is only one of a number of different responses which the student could give. There are other kinds of response which would help generate a range of options for people to consider.

- An example of a *supportive* response would have been: '*I want to do all I can to help you because I can see how difficult it is to make this kind of decision alone.*'
- Some students might feel drawn to a prescriptive response such as: '*You ought to see a drugs counsellor and I think you should encourage Sam to make contact with the community psychiatric nurse.*' Prescriptive responses are characterized by 'ought' and 'should'. Enquiry 14 in *Open ends* is a prescriptive response disguised as an enquiry. Although there are occasions when a prescriptive response is appropriate, it often denotes an untutored 'neighbour over the fence' approach.
- Students are less likely to employ a confrontive response, which requires confidence and needs particular care in terms of timing and phrasing. However, confrontive responses can help someone consider an incongruity or a disparity of which they are unaware. For example, '*Jason, you said you have things under control, but I can smell drink on your breath, and I'm wondering what that is about?*'

Students need your help to consider the question, 'Which kind of response would you choose – enquiry, support, prescription, challenge or some other?' Usually the best answer is 'It depends'; good practice is the ability to articulate what it depends on. Students need to discuss the factors which would lead them to choose a particular kind of response and to learn about as wide a range as possible (Trevithick, 2005). Generating options for themselves is an important step towards helping generate options for others.

# Learning notes: *Generating options*

## Spirit of enquiry

As the *Open ends* activity has shown, your choice of enquiry has a profound effect on the direction of the work with people, and even a brief piece of dialogue provides opportunities for enquiry in many different directions. It will, of course, be necessary to develop a repertoire of communication and interviewing skills which build on this spirit of enquiry. These are developed in more detail in Chapter 6.

There are circumstances when it is difficult to continue in a spirit of enquiry – for example, when you disagree strongly with the person's views. Are there times when it is right not to continue the enquiry?

Suppose that you are visiting Avis Jenkins on the Green Hill estate (Activity 1, *Licensed to learn*) In the preliminary 'social chat', Avis suddenly says:

*Two immigrants have moved in at number 6, you know.* [She looks very disapproving] *They come here taking our own people's jobs, sponging off the state and expecting to be handed a living on a plate. I can't be doing with it and it's about time they put a stop to it.*

How would you respond to Mrs Jenkins? Would the purpose of your visit alter the way in which you might respond and, if so, how?

## Positive reframing

So far, we have been considering the effect of your communication patterns on the choices for people. The detail of your discussion with them can have a significant impact on how they see their situation. Initially, it is important for the person to feel confident that you are able to listen to them and to understand what they are experiencing, even if it is outside your own personal experience. It is tempting to offer solutions at this point, such as 'Have you thought about ... ?' or 'Why don't you ...?', or to offer reassurances like 'I'm sure things will get better ... it's quite natural to feel like this ...'. Even if they make you feel better, these kinds of response are not likely to be experienced as helpful and supportive. Take a moment to think why this might be the case.

Attempts to help a person feel better about their situation by offering solutions or normalizing their experience spring from good motives. However, helping someone to begin to reframe their situation is a slow and skilful process. Positive reframing is one of the most powerful skills you can develop as part of your repertoire of communication skills. An example of this is provided by de Bono (2000: 64) in terms of someone losing a tennis game: 'Don't look at it as a defeat. Look at it as a powerful way of finding out the weaknesses and strengths of his tennis game.' This kind of prescriptive reframing is usually less appropriate in social work communication and, of course, it is crucial that you do not use positive reframing as a way of glossing over real difficulties.

Indeed, the best reframing is that done by service users and carers themselves as a result of your enquiry with them. This is likely to take some time. Often, people will have told their story many times and will have become familiar with the well-rehearsed trials and tribulations of their situation. Careful and sensitive enquiry can lead people to discover new aspects to their circumstances, opening up options which they have not so far had the opportunity to explore. Generating options is very much what de Bono has called an opportunity for speculative thinking: 'People are forced to solve problems but no-one is ever forced to look for opportunities. However, everyone is *free* to look for opportunities – if they so wish' (de Bono, 2000: 108).

## Non-verbal and symbolic communication

Only part of our communication is verbal and explicit. The way in which the words are spoken also reflects our meaning: the same phrase can sound sincere or sarcastic depending on the tone, gestures, facial expressions, body posture and context of the spoken words. Sometimes the content of the verbal communication and the message conveyed can be contrary or ambiguous (Trevithick, 2005).

Watching the television with the sound turned down is a good way to develop your recognition of non-verbal communication. It is also worth noting when you find the non-verbal communication unclear (silences are often difficult to interpret) and the way in which cultural norms influence the way we read situations. This is particularly evident when creating a physical distance between ourselves and other people; what is considered an acceptable social distance varies considerably.

You should also be aware of 'symbolic communication' (Lishman, 1994: 18), such as punctuality and attention to detail, which can be symbolic of your concern, or lack of it.

## Action techniques

We have considered the way in which the style and detail of your communication influences the choices open to people. In addition to your verbal and non-verbal communications, you also have a choice of actions which can be used to help people generate options. Social work, and particularly counselling, has been referred to as 'talk therapy', but talk is only one way in which people may communicate. Children, for example, often use play as a means of developing understanding and communication (Horwath, 2001).

As a student in the classroom you will be familiar with the use of flipcharts to generate ideas and discussion. If these methods are effective in generating new pathways of thought and action for you and your fellow students, why deny other people this opportunity? Restricting yourself and the service user to talk is to limit

Reproduced from *Modern Social Work Practice* by Mark Doel and Steven M. Shardlow, Ashgate, Aldershot, 2005

the possibilities, and there are many kinds of action technique which you can use with service users, either individually or in groups (see Doel and Sawdon, 1999: 130–59).

## Assessment notes: *Generating options*

One of the most effective ways of capturing your ability to help people generate options is by making a tape recording. We hear our interactions with other people very differently when they are not immediate, and there is much learning to be gained from listening to yourself as objectively as possible. However, tape recording must be processed very carefully. Of course, permissions are necessary, and you should always consult with your practice teacher about the agency's guidelines.

## Further reading

For a comprehensive account of social work skills see Trevithick (2005).
Lishman's (1994) *Communication in Social Work* (Basingstoke: Macmillan), remains useful.
Horwath (2001) is a helpful text for a wider view of the child's world and different styles of communicating with children.

Reproduced from *Modern Social Work Practice* by Mark Doel and Steven M. Shardlow, Ashgate, Aldershot, 2005

# 6 Making assessments in partnership

## About Activity 6      Hold the front page

*Hold the front page* aims to help students consider making assessments from the point of view of the service user and carer. This may seem an obvious aim, but the proliferation of assessment frameworks can take the focus away from the person and on to the assessment process itself. *Hold the front page* should enable students to keep people's needs, wants and problems at the forefront of their assessments.

### Purpose

Finding out about a person's situation is not unlike investigating a story as a journalist. There may be a number of different, interrelated stories, each with its own headline and more detailed storyline. When listening to people's stories, it is important to listen for quotes from what they have to say; these quotes summarize the story and help to keep it authentic by using the person's own voice. This activity, and the chapter which follows, emphasizes the skills of active listening as core to making assessments in partnership with people.

### Method

- Give the student a copy of *Hold the front page* well in advance of the practice tutorial (supervision session). Ask the student to construct a draft 'front page' consisting of a main headline and four or five other headline stories, with a possible quote for each topic and some text by way of a storyline.
- Discuss with the student why the headline story and the other topics were chosen. Emphasize strongly that this is speculation for the purpose of the learning, and that work with actual people will not be speculative.

### Variations

It is interesting to repeat *Hold the front page* later in the practice learning, in order to reflect work with an actual person. It is especially effective when used with flipchart (butcher's block) paper and can unlock creativity in people's responses to assessment. The *Hold the front page* technique can also be used in direct work with people, as has been done very successfully by a number of students and practitioners.

## Use by other professions

This method of making assessments in partnership is relevant to all professionals who need to find out people's stories. Students from different professions could use the technique together, either speculatively or in practice. It would be interesting to see what differences there might be in the kinds of story they are likely to focus on.

## National Occupational Standards for Social Work

The topics in this chapter relate to the following National Occupational Standards (see the Appendix):

2:   Making informed decisions together
6:   Planning together.

## Activity 6 Hold the front page

In Activity 1, *Licensed to learn*, we met Zoë Benner and her family:

> At Number 1 is **Zoë Benner**, a single parent who was in public care for much of her childhood, but is now reconciled with her mother, who lives on another street in Green Hill flats. Zoë has a fourteen-year-old son (Jackson), a twelve-year-old daughter (Kylie) and a baby daughter (Kara) aged eleven months. Jackson was cautioned for shoplifting earlier in the year, and has just been arrested on a charge of criminal damage. Kylie has not been to school for several weeks. She has few friends and is reluctant to leave the family's flat. She has also been referred for help with her bed-wetting problem. Kara is Zoë's daughter by another man who is attempting to gain custody of her. Kara has asthma and seems to suffer from unspecified allergies. Zoë has another child, Tilly, who is a 7-year-old girl currently living with foster carers on the other side of the city.

If there was a newspaper devoted only to Zoë and her family, what might the front page look like? (You will need to elaborate on Zoë and her family's situation.)

Construct a front page for Zoë Benner (see the outline on the next page). What might the main headline be? Fill in the storyline and a likely quote from Zoë to illustrate the story. As well as the problems and difficulties, what might she say that she *wants*? What other headlines and stories might there be? Construct the rest of the front page by adding four or five other headlines. Add the more detailed stories, and likely quotes, to summarize them in a nutshell. Include what Zoë or other family members might want to happen in relation to each particular storyline. Add your own 'editorial' about how you see her situation.

Reproduced from *Modern Social Work Practice* by Mark Doel and Steven M. Shardlow, Ashgate, Aldershot, 2005

# The FRONT PAGE

**Headline:**

**The story:**

**The story continued:**

**Zoë Benner says:**

**Another headline and story:**

**Also:**

**More news:**

**And finally:**

Reproduced from *Modern Social Work Practice* by Mark Doel and Steven M. Shardlow, Ashgate, Aldershot, 2005

# Teaching notes: *Making assessments in partnership*

## Opportunities

Assessment has been defined as:

> ... the process of objectively defining needs and determining eligibility for assistance against stated policy criteria. It is a participative process involving the applicant, their carers and other relevant agencies. (Department of Health, 1990, Appendix B/1)

When preparing opportunities for the student to learn about the assessment of people, you will need to decide how much autonomy the student should have in this process. This, in turn, will depend on the risk factors associated with the assessments and the circumstances of the particular student – for example, does the current period of practice learning come early or late in their programme of study? A helpful model is for the student to shadow others making assessments before taking supervised responsibility themselves.

### Your role in teaching about assessment

In the Introduction to Part I we touched on the difference between good practice and good practice teaching. The distinction is especially strong in this area of 'assessment'. The student is indeed *a student* and not a trainee, and it is important that the learning goes above and beyond the specific assessment frameworks used in your own particular agency or area of practice. Students are not learning to 'do assessments' as a worker in your agency, they are 'learning about assessment'. However, doing assessments will be a tool for them to learn about assessment. So, they will learn how to do an assessment within a particular framework (depending on the opportunity in any particular setting), but also learn to generalize from this particular experience to learn about the notion of assessment.

During a period of practice learning, students should be enabled to understand:

- the philosophical principles that underpin the idea of assessment
- the practice skills necessary to make a good assessment when working with service users, carers and other colleagues in an interprofessional context
- one or more assessment protocols, by being able to use these in practice – that is, one of the standardized approaches to assessment, such as the English Assessment Framework for Children (Department of Health, Department for Education and Employment, and Home Office, 2000).

As part of understanding the idea of assessment, students should be encouraged to recognize what is *general* to all assessments, what is *specific* to an assessment protocol and what is *particular* to the context in which the assessment is made (the agency context). It might be a good idea to encourage students to keep a CV (resumé) of their practice, perhaps by keeping a list of the number of assessments they have made using a particular assessment protocol, rather in the way that those in the medical profession keep a record of the number of assessments made using a particular protocol. (See below for a discussion of protocols.)

The vagueness of the term 'assessment' presents one of the greatest challenges to your practice teaching, not least because of the potential confusion caused by the fact that the same term describes the process to which students are submitted in relation to their practice abilities. Experience in doing assessments does not necessarily mean that you will feel confident of your ability to teach about assessment, so you might want to familiarize yourself with Milner and O'Byrne (2002) and Parker and Bradley (2003), the suggested texts in the Further reading section at the end of this chapter. We discuss some of the issues around assessment in more detail later.

## Assessment and intervention

There has been a tendency for assessment to be seen as a separate activity from intervention, and this has been underlined by successive legislation in the UK. However, the student is learning both about social work practice and agency practice; social work practice emphasizes the close connection between assessment and intervention. Indeed, assessment in the sense of 'finding out and making judgements together' continues throughout the intervention period.

By asking the student to include statements about what Zoë Benner and her family might *want*, you have also been encouraging them to consider what kinds of intervention the assessment might lead to. This is crucial to social work practice, since we doubt whether an assessment without an intervention is, in fact, social work. The assessment should be theoretically grounded and based on available evidence (see the Introduction to Part IV on 'Evidence-based practice').

# Learning notes: *Making assessments in partnership*

## Assessment: a note of caution

The term 'assessment' is deeply embedded in the social work vocabulary at professional, organizational and governmental levels. We need to be honest about the reservations we have about the term. Nevertheless, it is here to stay; hence our willingness to follow the lead of the National Occupational Standards and include it in a chapter title. Even so, there are two good reasons to sound a note of caution.

First, it is a confusing term. Is it a process, a skill, an outcome, or all three? In addition to its principal use in this chapter in connection with judgements made in respect of service users and carers, you will find it used to describe the process and outcome of your own competence to practise social work. Indeed, the Department of Health uses the word twice in one sentence, with both meanings (our italics):

> ... providers [of social work education] will have to demonstrate that all students undertake specific learning and *assessment* in the following key areas:
> - *assessment*, planning, intervention and review. (Department of Health, 2002: 3)

Second, and more seriously, the term 'assessment' has connotations that are contrary to the spirit of partnership. The preposition which most commonly follows 'assessment' is 'on' rather than 'with' – for example, 'Have you completed your assessment *on* Mrs Smith?', rather than 'Have you completed your assessment *with* Mrs Smith?' This is not a mere semantic point; it lies at the heart of a fundamental dilemma – namely, that assessments usually comprise professional judgements about people, their state of mind, their risks and their eligibility for resources.

Clearly, there are times when it is necessary to use professional judgement about a situation, in which case it would be more honest to use the term 'judgement'. Judgement is more candid than assessment because it recognizes the element of discretion (and room for mistake), whereas assessment makes a claim to objectivity which is not necessarily justified. Assessment is about making judgements based on information (Middleton, 1997). A professional judgement should, of course, take full account of the views of a range of stakeholders about needs and wants.

## Feedback from *Hold the front page*

If we think of assessments as an 'exploratory study' (Coulshed and Orme, 1998: 21), it is possible to see links with a journalist's skill. The aim is to find out what is happening, who it involves, what people think about what is going on, what they have tried to do about it, and what their aspirations are. The journalist does this to sell newspapers, and the social worker does it to see what kind of help might be appropriate. Journalists often have their own agenda of what spin can be put on the story to sensationalize it (to sell *more* papers); all too often social workers have their

Reproduced from *Modern Social Work Practice* by Mark Doel and Steven M. Shardlow, Ashgate, Aldershot, 2005

own agenda, too – for example, what parts of the person's story fit into the proforma, the assessment criteria and so on. Unfortunately, this processing by the social worker for a 'fit' can lead to an inability to hear the full story.

Of course, resources are limited and they must be fairly allocated (Department of Health, 2001b), so at some point there has to be a process of assessing a person's *need* and not just their *wants*. However, in closing off discussion so that it only fits the agency's agenda, we are acting contrary to the spirit of partnership and, indeed, to the principles of good social work practice. The *Hold the front page* activity lays the foundations for 'open-book' listening, unguided by assessment structures, so that you learn what an open assessment can, at least, look like.

## A wide range of assessments

Social workers are involved in a very wide range of assessments, including:

- assessment of children in need and their families (Department of Health, Department for Education and Employment, Home Office 2000)
- assessment in childcare, with three domains: the child's developmental needs; parenting capacity; family and environmental factors (Department of Health, 2003)
- community care assessments (National Health Service and Community Care Act 1990, section 47)
- mental health assessments for admission to hospital or guardianship (Mental Health Act 1983, sections 2, 3, 4, 7)
- single assessment process (SAP) – NHS Plan (Department of Health, 2000) and the National Service Framework for Older People (Department of Health, 2001a)
- specific assessments for carers (Carers [Recognition and Services] Act 1995).

## Assessment and government guidance

Many assessments carry the authority of statute in the UK, so they are exceptionally powerful, as is the whole notion of assessment. Although the format may be prescribed and limiting, McDonald (1999) acknowledges that assessments do carry statutory authority and legitimation. Revisions in UK government guidance have had an impact on assessment practices, particularly in increasing the 'emphasis on ensuring that assessments are evidence-based [and] consider risk more comprehensively in all its contexts, and accountability' (Milner and O'Byrne, 2002: 1).

We noted earlier that social workers are involved in a very wide range of assessments, which can be thought of as a series of separate *protocols* governing how an assessement might be undertaken in a particular context. Some of these are mandatory and some are advisory: you need to be very clear which is which!

Reproduced from *Modern Social Work Practice* by Mark Doel and Steven M. Shardlow, Ashgate, Aldershot, 2005

Although you will learn about a wide range of assessments, it will not be possible or necessary to practise all of them to understand what assessment is about. As we have already emphasized, it is important that you learn how to help somebody to tell their story before you then learn how to squeeze it into an assessment framework.

## Working in partnership with people

An assessment can be transformed from a formalized checklist to a genuine partnership of enquiry by good communication skills, especially those of listening and interviewing (Trevithick, 2005). This ability is especially important since, in reviewing the literature, Milner and O'Byrne (2002: 3) were struck that there was 'little evidence of the existence of well-developed skills in involving service users in the assessment process'. The following quote from a social worker's portfolio reflects some of the confusion over the nature of assessment:

> Following a visit, my initial assessment was that she had let the tasks of the household get on top of her and she also appeared to be isolated. (Social work post-qualifying portfolio)

This statement indicates that the everyday interpretation of the term 'assessment' is that it is a judgement made by a relative expert about another's situation. Was it the service user's assessment that she had let the tasks get on top of her and that she was isolated? We think not. Service users do not 'make assessments'.

Of course, practitioners and agencies have to make judgements about people's circumstances and these will sometimes be quite different from those made by the people themselves. In that case, let us be honest and call them judgements, rather than hide behind the white-coat term 'assessment'.

We have to exercise caution, too, in our use of the word 'partnership'. It is an 'apple pie' term and can be 'used to describe anything from token consultation to a total devolution of power and control' (Braye and Preston-Shoot, 1995: 102). Genuine partnerships are not easily established, and the differences in power within the relationship between social workers and users and carers will always place a limit on the scope of the partnership.

Partnership involves an approach which is centred on the person rather than on the proforma. For example, Kitwood and Bredin (1992) developed person-centred approaches in relation to work with people with dementia, looking at the care process and its effect on well-being. These highlight the service user's point of view and remind us of the importance of considering strengths as well as problems.

## Holistic assessments

We have mentioned several conceptual and practical problems with 'assessments'. A further difficulty with highly structured assessment procedures is their tendency to blinker the person who is assessing, so that they only assess for narrow aspects of

Reproduced from *Modern Social Work Practice* by Mark Doel and Steven M. Shardlow, Ashgate, Aldershot, 2005

a person's life rather than allowing a fuller picture to emerge. The following quote from a social work post-qualifying portfolio illustrates this:

> One of the difficulties of the assessment that Sure Start[1] completed was that it was about Ms X and the assessment was not a child-centred assessment. The difficulty was that Ms X was very needy herself and it is my belief that the Sure Start staff lost sight that the assessment was meant to be child-centred. (Social work post-qualifying portfolio)

We cannot be confident that the social worker would have approached this from a holistic (all-encompassing) perspective either. Two assessments would emerge – the one parent-centred and the other child-centred. Which, if either, tells us the full story?

It is important not to confuse a holistic assessment – one which takes account of different dimensions in people's lives, including their strengths and not just their problems – with a single assessment, which is carried out by one professional, rather than many. A single assessment is designed to prevent people having to endure multiple assessments from a number of different professionals, but it does not guarantee that the assessment process itself will take account of the service user as a person rather than as a 'pain sufferer' or 'an applicant for daycare services'.

## Assessments and interventions

Finding out is just one aspect of an assessment. Unlike journalists who do nothing more with their story than print it, social workers must use an assessment as a basis for further action or recommendation. Social work practice goes beyond assessments to interventions; indeed, assessment is one aspect of the social work intervention, though it may mark a definite stage (via a report, for example) before further work is, or is not, indicated.

What follows an assessment will vary from one agency to another, but in social work practice there are a number of models to guide the whole of your intervention, the best known of which is probably task-centred practice (Marsh and Doel, 2005). In this method of practice, the assessment stage is called 'problem exploration'. Task-centred work emphasizes people's strengths as well as their problems. It models making assessment in partnership, precisely because the social worker's expertise does not lie in making judgements about the person's situation, but in engaging them in a new experience which builds confidence to solve or lessen problems, and to achieve goals.

Interventions range along a continuum from 'short and fat' to 'long and thin' (Doel and Marsh, 1992: 90); in other words, your work may be characterized by relatively frequent contact over a short period of time, or extended over a longer period with fewer contacts. It is important that your learning about assessments is

---

[1] Sure Start is an organization working with families.

Reproduced from *Modern Social Work Practice* by Mark Doel and Steven M. Shardlow, Ashgate, Aldershot, 2005

linked to your wider learning of planning, completing and evaluating interventions, and that all of these processes are tied to an understanding of what partnership with people means in practice.

## Assessment notes: *Making assessments in partnership*

It is important not to lose sight of the 'in partnership' in the title of this chapter. The temptation is to focus on the skills of making assessments for the agency in which you are placed, rather than focusing on learning about the assessment process as a whole and how it links to other aspects of your intervention with people. By all means use a particular assessment framework as an example, but keep in mind that it is just that: an example. The assessment of your abilities as a student in this area should focus on your capacity to enquire, and to plan, complete and evaluate your work together with all the people who have been involved.

## Further reading

Crisp, B.R., Anderson, M.R., Orme, J. and Green Lister, P. (2003), *Learning and Teaching in Social Work Education: Assessment*, London: Social Care Institute for Excellence (SCIE)/Policy Press.

Department of Health, Department for Education and Employment, and Home Office (2000), *The Framework for the Assessment of Children in Need and their Families*. London: HMSO.

Milner, J. and O'Byrne, P. (2002), *Assessment in Social Work*, [2nd edn], Basingstoke: Macmillan.

Parker, J. and Bradley, J. (2003), *Assessment, Planning, Intervention and Review*, Exeter: Learning Matters Ltd.

Reproduced from *Modern Social Work Practice* by Mark Doel and Steven M. Shardlow, Ashgate, Aldershot, 2005

# 7 Working in and with groups

## About Activity 7    No-one is an island

*No-one is an island* is designed to help students think about the kind of learning that can be achieved from involvement with groups. This activity builds on familiarity with the residents of Derby Street (Activity 1, page 13).

### Purpose

Social workers are not independent clinicians. They must work closely with other people, both in formal teams and informal groupings. Service users and carers often live and work in groups; if they live alone they may miss the company of others, too. This chapter helps to develop awareness of groups and the potential of groupwork, especially as a means for people to achieve collective control over their lives and a way of sharing power between workers, users and carers. The chapter also makes links between groups and teams, and between sessions and meetings.

### Method

- Both you and the students will need a copy of *Licensed to learn* (page 13) to accompany *No-one is an island*. Once the student has decided which of the four group scenarios to work with, you might wish to provide further reading for the student to pursue.
- Give the students time to prepare Parts One and Two before you discuss the activity with them – perhaps the period between one practice supervision and the next.

### Variations

You can add to the four group scenarios in the activity to reflect the kind of group which is, or could be, characteristic of the agency setting. However, it can be more instructive to use situations which are less, rather than more, familiar.

## Use by other professions

Groups, teams and networks lend themselves to multiprofessional involvement. Co-work with another professional in a group can help students to learn about both groupwork and interprofessional work. Three of the proposed groups in *No-one is an island* involve a group leadership which is bi-professional, and it is illuminating to use the exercise with students from different professions if you have the opportunity.

## National Occupational Standards for Social Work

The topics in this chapter relate to the following National Occupational Standards (see the Appendix):

  8:   Working with groups
11:   Meetings and other decision-making forums.

## *Activity 7*     *No-one is an island*

You will need a copy of Activity 1, *Licensed to learn*, to hand. We know from the information in Activity 1 that Avis Jenkins already attends a group called Memory Joggers to help her manage her failing memory, and the Kiyani brothers are members of a Kurdish support group. However, you are now aware that there are four other groups being planned in the district, which might be of interest to some of the people living in Derby Street. The groups are briefly described below.

### A parenting skills group

This is a group proposed by a social worker and a health visitor to help parents who are experiencing difficulties with their children's behaviour. The group will meet once a week for a time-limited period; the co-leaders are planning 8–12 sessions of an hour and a half, with about eight group members. The group will use cognitive behavioural methods to help parents understand their children's behaviour and also to rehearse different ways of responding.

*You consider Zoë Benner to be a potential group member.*

### A school refusal group

This group will be led by an education social worker and a teacher based at the school into which Kylie Benner's school feeds. At the moment they are thinking to recruit children aged between eleven and fourteen years old whose problems are leading them to withdraw from school. This would be a voluntary group, with no legal requirement, and parental permission will be needed for children to attend. It is proposed that the group will meet weekly for an hour to an hour and a half. It will be an ongoing group, with new members joining and existing members leaving as their attendance improves. The group will use activities, as well as discussion.

*You consider Kylie Benner to be a potential group member.*

### A volunteers' group

A local drop-in centre, The Hearth, opens its doors to homeless people and people with mental health and drug problems. The Hearth is helped out by a good number of volunteers, some quite regularly and others on an occasional basis. A project worker at The Hearth is planning a group for local volunteers, not just for those based at the centre. The main purpose will be to develop volunteers' skills and to share problems and experiences.

*You consider Jason Dean to be a potential group member.*

Reproduced from *Modern Social Work Practice* by Mark Doel and Steven M. Shardlow, Ashgate, Aldershot, 2005

## A support group

A community psychiatric nurse and a social worker are publicizing a new group which they want to start for people with depression. It will be community-based, and their intention is to withdraw when the group can become self-help. They see the group as an opportunity for people to talk about their experiences and to offer mutual support, meeting once a week, but perhaps fortnightly when it has become established.

*You consider Sam Weiner to be a potential group member.*

Choose *one* of the groups above and consider the questions below.

## Part One: Offering the group to a potential member

- What further details would you like to know from the group proposers before you discuss the group with the potential member?
- How might the potential group member benefit from this group?
- What reservations might the potential group member have about the group?

## Part Two: Participating in the group as a co-worker

If you were invited to be a co-facilitator in this group:

- What would you bring to the group leadership?
- What changes might you wish to suggest to the purpose, methods or shape of the group as currently proposed, and why?
- How would you find out whether the group had been successful?
- What would you hope to learn from involvement in the group?

## Further suggestions

If you have time, choose another of the groups and repeat this process with the new group and potential group member.

Later in your period of practice learning, return to the notes you kept from this activity and review them. What changes would you make in the light of your subsequent learning?

Reproduced from *Modern Social Work Practice* by Mark Doel and Steven M. Shardlow, Ashgate, Aldershot, 2005

# Teaching notes: *Working in and with groups*

## Opportunities

It is not the purpose of these notes to detail groupwork processes and purposes. These can be found elsewhere (for example, Doel, 2005; Doel and Sawdon, 1999; Wayne and Cohen, 2001). Our focus is the way in which students can learn about working in, and with, groups during their practice learning. To begin with, it is important to establish what knowledge of groups and groupwork the student brings. There is very little research in this area, but an American study has suggested that groupwork is poorly integrated into the social work curriculum in the US (Birnbaum and Wayne, 2000). The situation is likely to be similar in the UK, though the inclusion of groupwork in the National Occupational Standards may begin to reverse this decline.

Whether there are plenty of opportunities to 'do groupwork' or none at all, group processes are impossible to avoid. Your role as a practice teacher or work-based supervisor is to help students recognize these processes and to make best use of them.

Even if there are no existing groups with service users or carers in your agency, it is worth considering whether there are unmet needs which a group could satisfy. This brings us to a fundamental issue; the purposes of the practice learning. On the one hand is the imperative to train the student to learn how to do various specified tasks; on the other is the student as an adult learner developing increasingly independent thinking and practice. This tension is reflected in the balance between the student observing and emulating 'the expert practitioner' and the student creating and developing a new service.

Groups offer a real opportunity both for students to express their creative potential and for the agency to develop a service. However, this needs very careful consideration, because the student will need a great deal of support (Cohen, 1995). In some circumstances, it may be necessary for both you and the student to consider strategies to influence agency policy. Again, this will be valuable learning for the student.

## Balancing various needs

Clearly, a group cannot be created just for the sake of the student's experience or practice. There has to be an established need for a group, and decisions will need to be taken about what impact the involvement of a student will have. Will the group be single leadership, dual leadership, observer, user-led, or what? Dilemmas in balancing student, user and carer needs are not unique to group encounters, but they are more public in these settings, and the dynamics are more complex. Groupwork offers great potential for providing a vehicle for user participation (Ward, 2000). Expressing this potential in ways that fit with current concerns about social exclusion may be significant in attracting the necessary funding to support a new groupwork initiative.

If you and the student are co-working a group, power issues in co-leadership are heightened, and you both need to consider how these will be addressed. Co-work in a group provides good opportunities both for direct observation of the student's practice and for coaching. However, the student's need to develop more autonomous group leadership styles should be taken into consideration.

## Fears about groupwork

It is important to acknowledge that groupwork is an area of practice learning which can generate much anxiety for students (Knight, 1997). Fears are often related to the semi-public nature of a group. Making mistakes or an inability to cope is more exposing in a group. Other apprehensions may arise from a worry that people will not attend, that there may be hostility, silence or other difficult behaviours, or from being intimidated by the number and potential power of people in a group. Indeed, some of these fears might also be your own. It is important, therefore, to reflect on how *you* feel about supervising groupwork and whether you need support in this area. What is your own experience of groups, and what have been the positive and negative aspects of this experience?

Discuss possible fears about groupwork openly with the student as early as possible and clarify the expectations of the course in this area. The extent of the student's knowledge and experience will determine whether it is appropriate for them to be a sole groupworker.

## Other opportunities

There are other ways in which students can learn about group processes. One of these is through participation in group supervision. In a study of the effects of reflective team supervision, Thomlison and Collins (1995: 234) found that students felt that they received more feedback than in one-to-one supervision; team and group supervision gave them information about how other students experienced them and how they came across to others. There were some concerns, too, about the need to adapt to different supervisors' styles and the anxiety of being observed. Used with care, group supervision can provide a more rounded experience for students and staff, and help bring different perspectives and a potential power shift into the supervision.

Bourne's study in Brown and Bourne (1996) perhaps explains why group supervision is not prevalent in social work. The group supervision in four out of the five teams which he studied folded shortly after the spotlight of his research terminated. He points to the public nature of group supervision (it takes a confident team leader to 'perform' in front of the full team) and the difficulties arising from the different supervisory needs of the group members as key reasons for the relative absence of groupwork approaches to supervision. In addition, it is important for teams to be clear about the place of the group supervision sessions in relation to their other meetings; group supervision has to be qualitatively different from other forums, otherwise it becomes yet another time-consuming meeting.

Conversely, group practice teaching might have more success because of the relatively common purposes and standing of students on placement. In many respects, the learning and support gained by students from one another balances the additional workload involved in supervising more than one student. Alternatively, if there are other students in your agency or vicinity – not necessarily social work students – you may wish to consider involving them in group supervision sessions, though you will need to make sure that lines of communication are well established with their individual supervisors.

If you intend to make use of the group of students *as a group* (that is, consider the group dynamics of the student group), this must be made explicit from the start, with ground rules agreed so that the experience is guided and constructive. However, you should exercise caution in using group supervision in an experiential way, especially if you have the power to assess the students' practice.

Students might also be learning from one another in the performance of group tasks or working on group assignments as part of their practice learning (Underhill *et al.*, 2002). They need to have the chance to learn from this group experience, especially since an awareness of group processes is likely to improve their ability to work together and therefore to complete the task.

## Teamwork

The creation of a new group with service users, or joining an existing group of service users, is not the only learning opportunity in this area. A much neglected group is the team. Students can learn much about groupwork from their experience of group dynamics in teams. You need to give some thought to how you will help the student understand the dynamics in the team or teams with which they will be involved, and how they can begin to relate this to groupwork principles.

The following questions can be used as an observation checklist for the student to complete over time in preparation for discussion with you. However, given that you are probably also a member, or possible leader, of the team, it is crucial to agree how the student's observations may be used.

- What do you see as the team's purposes?
- How and why is the team structured as it is? Is it clear who is and who is not a team member?
- What kinds of role do you see individuals playing in the team?
- Who holds what kind of power in the team?
- What rewards and sanctions are there in the team?
- What are the team's values? Are these widely shared in the team, or are there many differences? How are values demonstrated in practice?
- What happens to conflicts in the team?
- How are team processes recorded and reflected on?
- How does the team monitor its work?
- How do people outside the team view the team?

## Learning notes: *Working in and with groups*

### Social action

There are many models of groupwork, and those which are implied by the four proposed groups in *No-one is an island* are worker-initiated. In contrast, the social action model of groupwork hands over the agenda for action to the people themselves (Mullender and Ward, 1991). The four groups proposed in Activity 7 would imply different levels of partnership with the group members, different kinds of dialogue between group members and different degrees of democracy and equality (Douglas, 1993). How might the proposals for each group be reframed in such a way that issues of social inclusion, rather than social functioning, are brought to the fore? How might group members be empowered to take collective control of these groups?

### Links between groups and teams

A careers choice survey[1] found quite a contrast between the views of students and those of employers in respect of the place of teamwork abilities. The survey of more than 1000 students found only 25 per cent of respondents thought it important to develop teamworking skills. In contrast, employers rated teamwork as their number one priority. It is perhaps understandable that students are focusing on developing their own individual competence, but in the world of practice it will be crucial that you have good abilities in both teams and groups.

Teams vary considerably. Some consist of people doing much the same kind of work, in face-to-face contact (such as a team of workers in a residential unit) or independently (a team of field social workers). Others are composed of people with different but complementary skills, such as multidisciplinary mental health teams. Some teams are formalized as 'Team X', with a life that transcends the membership of individuals, whereas others are time-limited, formed around a particular task or person.

Groups, too, cover quite a range. Some are long-standing and open-ended, with a life that is independent of the individual membership; others are created for a specific purpose, with a definite beginning and ending. There are, therefore, a number of characteristics which link groups and teams, so that your learning from the one can be transferred to the other.

#### Groups and Teams:

need to be fit for purpose (in terms of size, resources)
need clarity about roles, responsibilities and expectations
should consider process as well as outcome

---

[1] The survey was conducted by the Careers Research Advisory Committee and reported in *The Times Higher Education Supplement*, 13 June 2003.

are characterized by a range of leadership styles
are influenced by their context
members need to share a common sense of purpose
members need both affirmation and challenge

What are some of the differences between groups and teams?

## Meetings and sessions

The focal point for teams and groups is the meeting or session, which can be actual or virtual. Although the work of teams and groups goes on outside meetings and sessions, it is at these times that they consolidate, refocus, consider progress, work on problems, negotiate present and future plans, review, reflect on past successes and failures, and celebrate individual and collective achievements.

The business of a meeting is often formalized around an agenda, whilst the degree of structure in individual sessions of groups varies considerably. In a meeting, leadership is usually formalized around the chairperson, whereas the styles of leadership in group sessions are, again, very varied indeed. Teams usually have just one chair, whilst groups commonly, though by no means always, have co-leaders (Doel, 2005). The degree of democracy and partnership differs from group to group and team to team, though teams are more often characterized by a formal hierarchy, whereas the very reason for many groups is to empower the membership through collective action and experience. Individual meetings and group sessions are usually part of a larger pattern of meetings and sessions, though single sessions can also be appropriate (Ebenstein, 1999).

## Learning from groups and teams

You will need to ask about the opportunities for working with and in groups in the preparation meeting prior to the beginning of your time in the agency. A realistic timescale will need to be agreed if you are to be involved in establishing a group, and, in most cases, you are more likely to be joining an existing group or taking part in plans that are already underway.

As well as these practical details, you need to be open about your feelings about groups. Do you feel comfortable in groups or are there issues which concern you? Groups can be powerful, and this power can be used to various effects. There are some well-known experiments which have demonstrated this power, such as the Asch experiments (1952), which showed how people were influenced to agree with judgements they considered to be obviously wrong (the respective lengths of two lines, for example) because the 'plants' in the room all subscribed to them. Group pressure can work for good and ill.

## Making the work more visible

The relative invisibility of the work done by social workers fails to promote social work in the wider community. Indeed, much of social work practice is invisible even to social work managers (Pithouse, 1998). Groupwork is one way in which social work processes can be made more public, especially if the group's purposes are outward-directed, such as campaigning groups. Doel *et al.* (2002) have described how portfolios of groupwork practice at a post-qualifying level have helped document the impact of social work with groups, making these accounts accessible to the agency and to other workers.

## Assessment notes: *Working in and with groups*

It is important to know what agency expectations there are for recording groupwork practice. With appropriate anonymity it may be possible to make use of these records for your learning and assessment purposes. If you are co-working in a group, your co-workers may be able to play a role in giving evidence of your practice, and group members themselves also have valuable perspectives on your work. As with any aspect of your assessment, it is crucial that everyone involved is clear about the expectations and that any potential conflicts in role are discussed. Group members need to be aware of how any feedback they give about your work will be used and be reassured that it will have no consequence on their position in the group.

## Further reading

Doel, M. and Sawdon, C. (1999), *The Essential Groupworker: teaching and learning creative groupwork*, London: Jessica Kingsley.
Douglas, T. (1993), *A Theory of Groupwork Practice*, Basingstoke: Macmillan.
Ward, D. (2000) 'Totem Not Token: groupwork as a vehicle for user participation', in H. Kemshall and R. Littlechild (eds), *User Involvement and Participation in Social Care*, London: Jessica Kingsley.

Reproduced from *Modern Social Work Practice* by Mark Doel and Steven M. Shardlow, Ashgate, Aldershot, 2005

# 8 Working in difficult situations

## About Activity 8      *Difficult behaviour in groups*

*Difficult behaviour in groups* is an article reproduced from *Groupwork*, Vol. 14.1.[1] This activity marks a different style from others in the book, since virtually all of the chapter consists of the article. As will become apparent, this activity will serve two different, but equally important, functions.

### Purpose

Social workers are expected to be able to work with behaviour which is sometimes difficult and challenging. Who defines behaviour as difficult or challenging is not straightforward, and the contextual factors are invariably very significant; nevertheless, social workers work with difficult situations and it is important that students are adequately prepared for these circumstances. *Difficult behaviour in groups* explores the group context for challenging behaviour; the conclusions are readily transferable to individual situations.

As a separate consideration, students need to develop a critical understanding of research findings in social work. Promoting best practice means keeping abreast of latest evidence and integrating the social work literature into everyday practice, in a discerning way. The *Difficult behaviour in groups* activity is, therefore, also an opportunity for the practice teacher to enable the student to consider what this means in practice, and how to consider the literature critically.

### Method

- First, familiarize yourself with *Difficult behaviour in groups*.
- Give the student a copy of the article to read well in advance of the practice tutorial (supervision session). The activity consists of both the article itself and the brief accompanying notes. The student should read the notes first and follow their guidance.

---

[1] We are most grateful to Whiting and Birch for kindly allowing this article to be reproduced in full.

## Variations

- Other articles can be substituted for the one reproduced here. It is important that the topic of the article reflects some of the dilemmas and conflicts which the student is likely to encounter. It is usually better if the scope of the research on which the article is based is relatively small, so that 'research' is not seen as something that always has a capital 'R' requiring an enormous budget and a large research team.

## Use by other professions

- As we saw in Activity 7, *No-one is an island,* many other professions are likely to be involved in groupwork and therefore encounter the kinds of difficult situation that are explored in *Difficult behaviour in groups*. Other professions must similarly learn how to critically appraise reports, articles and research digests and to integrate the findings from this kind of evidence into their regular practice. Articles from interprofessional journals such *Learning in Health and Social Care* (Blackwell) can provide useful exemplars for interdisciplinary groups to learn from each other about critical appraisal of the formal professional literature.

## National Occupational Standards for Social Work

- The topics in this chapter relate to the following National Occupational Standards (see the Appendix):

- 4:  Respond to crisis situations
- 5:  Achieve change
- 8:  Work with groups
- 9:  Address behaviour which presents a risk
- 20:  Manage complex ethical issues, dilemmas and conflicts
- 21:  Promote best social work practice.

# Activity 8    *Difficult behaviour in groups*

## Guidance notes

Read the article which follows. It first appeared in *Groupwork* journal and is an account of a training programme for groupworkers in a children's services agency in the English Midlands. The abstract which introduces the article provides an overview.

While you are reading the article, keep the following questions in mind and make some brief notes in response to them. The first questions are related to the issue of working with difficult or challenging behaviour and the second set of questions are concerned with your critical appraisal of the article.

### 1   *Working with difficult behaviour*

- Once you have read the six Examples (A–F) on pages 107–110, add your own example (G), using the same five trigger questions. (This may be in a group, a team meeting, or a one-to-one situation.)
- The nine elements of practice guidance on pages 111–115 are not prioritized. How would you prioritize them? Explain why you have made these priorities.
- What particular learning from this article can you transfer to situations where the difficult behaviour is one-to-one, rather than in a group?

### 2   *Critical appraisal of a published article*

- What do you think are the strengths of this article?
- What do you think are the weaknesses of this article and how would you have improved it?
- What relevance do the findings reported in the article have to your learning and practice?

Reproduced from *Modern Social Work Practice* by Mark Doel and Steven M. Shardlow, Ashgate, Aldershot, 2005

The article

# Difficult behaviour in groups

**Abstract:** *This article is based on work with 24 groupworkers in a Children's Services agency in the English Midlands. Focus groups to consider the training priorities for groupworkers revealed one of the most pressing issues was difficult behaviours in groups. (This was initially referred to as challenging behaviour, but it was recognised that the word is ambiguous, so it was replaced by 'difficult'.) The groupworkers were asked to present an example of difficult behaviour, some of which are reproduced here, as part of a process to understand the meaning of difficult behaviour and to add context. Nine themes arose from the work with the Children's Services groupworkers, and the article explores each theme and its implications for groupwork practice. The article relates the topic of difficult behaviour to the wider literature and suggests that the key to understanding and working with these behaviours in groups is the ability of the groupworker to unlock the meaning of the behaviour, and to find a way to articulate this alongside group members. Groupworkers' honesty with themselves about the feelings aroused by difficult behaviours emerges as a significant factor.*

**Keywords:** *groupwork education; difficult behaviour; group behaviour; co-working; children's services; focus groups.*

## Introduction

The enthusiasm to lead and facilitate groups is often tempered by the concerns which potential groupworkers have about their confidence and skills in this role. In order to support a major groupwork initiative by a Children's Services Department in the English Midlands, the author was asked to work with 24 workers in three teams in the agency. The teams were Community Support (to prevent accommodation of children and assist rehabilitation), Family Solutions (also to prevent accommodation, using solution-focused approaches) and 16+ (after-care for young people leaving care). The teams were experiencing a reorganisation but wished to maintain a groupwork service. Most of the workers had facilitated at least one group, but their groupwork had largely been learned through experience and they had received little to no formal training in groupwork. The group of workers was ethnically diverse, and all but four were female.

## Focus groups to identify priority areas for groupwork training

An initial half-day with 22 groupworkers was an opportunity for introductions and for focus groups to consider what aspects of groupwork were considered most important to

Reproduced from *Modern Social Work Practice* by Mark Doel and Steven M. Shardlow, Ashgate, Aldershot, 2005

cover in the available two days of training. 'Focus groups are a data collection method in which people reflect together on selected themes or questions' (Home, 1997, p. 128). Unlike Delphi and Nominal group approaches, focus groups harness rather than control the group process, and are especially apt when the participants are knowledgeable about the topic and interested in it, as was the case with the Children's Services groupworkers.

As a warm-up, a 'name game' was used in which each person makes an introduction by reflecting on their name, what it means to them, how their name was chosen, how it might have been personalised and adapted (for example shortened). This is an effective way to help people to begin to think beyond the surface, to disclose a little, and to ease into reflective ways of thinking, which may require a different pattern to the regular working day. Reflecting on what your name might signify and listening to others working through this process anticipates the search for meaning that will underpin later work. It is also usually fun.

In three focus groups, the groupworkers were asked to work on this question: *What aspects of groupworking would you like the training to focus on?* They were reminded that there were just two one-day events, so it would be important to prioritise the topics. Each group did this by asterisking the points which gained deepest and broadest support. Feedback from each group was both verbal and written (on flipcharts) and shared across all groups so that we could establish collective priorities.

The responses were relatively sophisticated and a number of agreed priority areas emerged during the plenary group discussion. The flipcharts and record of the discussion enabled further work to determine topics, six in all, each of which formed the basis of a session in the subsequent two days with the groupworkers.

These topics were, in no priority:

## 1    Planning groups and underpinning theory

Choosing an appropriate model of groupwork, linked to purpose. Practicalities such as attendance, and getting group members there; contingency plans; timing of the group. Crisis intervention theory and groupwork.

## 2    Co-working groups

Co-workers' different 'thresholds' with regard to group members' behaviour; professional boundaries; confidentiality; self-disclosure; establishing groundrules; diversity and difference in the leadership and the group.

Reproduced from *Modern Social Work Practice* by Mark Doel and Steven M. Shardlow, Ashgate, Aldershot, 2005

## 3   Groupwork techniques

How to use and choose from a variety of techniques to achieve the group's purpose; techniques to work with quiet members and contain dominant ones; effective icebreakers; confidence to broaden methods, e.g. drama and activities.

## 4   Difficult behaviours in groups

What to do when you experience behaviour which you find challenging; understanding group dynamics; challenging prejudice; handling a clash of value systems; working with uncertainty; motivating groups.

## 5   Subgroups

Understanding and working with subgroups; groups within groups; understanding and working with youth subculture.

## 6   Evaluating groups

How to bring sessions to a successful close; how do we know whether the group has been successful, in what ways? Involving service users in 'measurable' outcomes; sessional closure; getting the best from group endings.

The findings from a single project of this nature cannot be generalised, but they do help to illuminate the kinds of priorities made by workers in human services (or certainly children's services), in terms of preparation for groupwork. We should remember, too, that there is a culture of groupwork in the teams involved in this project and that these participants probably have more active experience of groupwork than is typical.

The topic of 'difficult behaviours in groups' emerged as one of the most urgent concerns for the groupworkers and it is this aspect of groupwork which this article considers in detail.

### What is 'difficult' behaviour?

How might we understand this notion of difficult behaviour? (First named as 'challenging' by the participants, but this was found to be ambiguous, so re-named 'difficult'.) Behaviours in groups have often been conceptualised in terms of role theory. However, the groupwork literature has tended to anthropomorphise roles by describing individuals as if they *were* the role itself: the scapegoat and the deviant member; gatekeepers, clowns and monopolisers (Northen and Kurland, 2001; Shulman, 1999); visitors, complainants and customers (Sharry, 2001); even Sherman tanks, snipers, exploders and clams (Bramson, 1981). An understanding that these behaviours are

Reproduced from *Modern Social Work Practice* by Mark Doel and Steven M. Shardlow, Ashgate, Aldershot, 2005

much more fluid and volatile reflects the reality in groups more accurately (Szymkiewicz-Kowalska, 1999). Understanding scapegoating behaviours in a group, rather than identifying the scapegoat, helps groupworkers focus on the meaning for the whole group in the context of the wider world, and not just on the individual (Doel and Sawdon, 1999).

Even with this transformation from the person to the behaviour, it remains unclear whether there are any advantages to being able to name and categorise behaviours in this way. We have no evidence that labelling some behaviour in a group as 'defensive' makes the groupworker any more capable of working with it.

Although difficult behaviour is not necessarily conflictual, an understanding of conflict in groups and how to work 'with it rather than against it' is likely to be helpful (Lordan, 1996, p. 74). Tuckman's (1965) classic 'storming' stage does, after all, envisage difficult behaviour as part and parcel of a group's development. The literature on the notion of 'practice dilemma' is also relevant (Maram and Rice, 2002; Preston-Shoot, 1992), though the idea of 'a difficult behaviour' is more specific. Authors who give honest accounts of making mistakes in groupwork also contribute to our understanding of difficult behaviour (Malekoff, 1999; Manor, 1996), even if the mistakes are not necessarily technical errors, but missed opportunities (Manor, 1999).

It seems reasonable to suppose that definitions of 'difficult' will be subjective and that different kinds of behaviour will challenge different groupworkers in different ways. Indeed, to elicit more information about what 'difficult' meant, each groupworker in the project was asked to consider a recent example from their groupwork practice. This began the session on *Working with Difficult Behaviour in Groups,* which took place during the first of the two training days. Each person wrote a response to the following five prompts on an index card:

Briefly describe:
1   What the **behaviour** was
2   What **led up** to the behaviour
3   How it made you **feel**
4   What you **did**
5   What you would **have liked** to have done.

This format evolved from Doel and Sawdon's (1995, p. 199) 'Sticky Moments' concept and has links with the classic ABC (Antecedent, Behaviour, Consequence) approach (Skinner, 1969).

The group's agreement was sought to have the examples typed up (anonymously), and distributed for our collective learning. It might not be easy to dissent to this request in the full group, so the groupworkers were asked to leave their index cards alongside their feedback forms on the 'evaluation chair', if they wished. This was done at the end

Reproduced from *Modern Social Work Practice* by Mark Doel and Steven M. Shardlow, Ashgate, Aldershot, 2005

of the day, with no scrutiny as to who was leaving what. Interestingly, though 19 evaluation forms were placed on the chair, there were only 14 index cards. Indeed, one participant tore hers up, saying that she was 'destroying the evidence!' She was smiling, but it is likely that a number of these incidents brought back uncomfortable feelings.

Immediately after completing the five questions, the groupworkers were asked to rate their perception of the degree of physical risk in the situation, using a scale of 1–10 (lowest to highest risk), and note this on their card. The reason for this was a concern that the volunteered examples in the full group might well be dominated by the dramatic, high risk situations – in effect, *dangerous* behaviour. Situations in the higher risk category are likely to be less ambiguous and it is just this kind of ambiguity which can promote the best learning, an assumption based admittedly more on practice theory than empirical evidence. In addition, examples of dangerous behaviour are likely to demand greater time and support for the individual involved which, though necessary, can be frustrating for the learning needs of the group as a whole. By asking each individual to rate their example high or low risk, the nature of the volunteered examples could be controlled, by asking for examples in one or other category.

When the 14 examples were examined later, nine were rated low risk (1–5) and only five were high (6–10). It is reasonable to suppose, then, that most of the group would wish to focus on the less traumatic examples of difficult behaviour, and this was substantiated in two comments written on the evaluation feedback forms (see later). It was clear that the notion of difficult behaviours differed from that of conflict, though conflict resolution approaches could have useful application in some of the situations (Fatout, 1989). However, amongst the 14 examples of difficult behaviour, none were of the more subtle kind, such as denial (Getzel and Mahoney, 1989), or reluctance (Behroozi, 1992), and none related to responding to racist or sexist comments.

The raw data of the 14 examples of difficult behaviour is illuminating. Most concerned the behaviour of an individual in the group, but some related to the group's behaviour as a whole, and others to subgroups. Some focused on the impact of the behaviour on the group leader or co-leader, others concerned behaviours between group members. Perhaps these differences also reflect the range of groupwork, from working with groups as groups to working with individuals in groups (Kurland and Salmon, 1993; Ward, 2002). By way of illustration, six of the 14 examples are presented below:

## Examples of behaviour in a group that was experienced as difficult by the groupworker

### Example A
*Whole group behaviour towards the groupworker (rated low physical risk).*

Reproduced from *Modern Social Work Practice* by Mark Doel and Steven M. Shardlow, Ashgate, Aldershot, 2005

1    What the behaviour was
     My role as the group leader was questioned by the fact that I had been appointed to a management post, and whether the group would function better without me.
2    What led up to the behaviour
     An ongoing difficulty in establishing a working relationship with the group members.
3    How it made you feel
     Defensive; criticised; upset; uncertain; angry.
4    What you did
     I mumbled something about this was the way the group was set up and looked generally uncomfortable and upset.
5    What you would have liked to have done
     Not to have had such an emotional reaction and been more assertive and confident.

## Example B
*Behaviour of an individual group member towards groupworker (rated low physical risk).*

1    What the behaviour was
     Disclosure of sexual abuse by an individual in the group.
2    What led up to the behaviour
     Discussions in the group about personal experiences, parenthood and childhood.
3    How it made you feel
     Awkward for the rest of the group; slightly out of control as the facilitator; concerned for the person and wanting to support her.
4    What you did
     Listened and acknowledged the difficulty in sharing the experiences, made space for person at end of session, and tried to get back to the group tasks whilst realising dynamics had changed.
5    What you would have liked to have done
     Stopped the discussion earlier as members of the group knew the family in question (that is, prevented it in the first place); taken more control.

## Example C
*Behaviour of the whole group towards a co-groupworker (rated low physical risk).*

1    What the behaviour was
     Whilst facilitating the group, the young people became loud and were talking amongst each other and ignoring my co-facilitator.
2    What led up to the behaviour
     There had been a change of facilitator and a change of focus. It was towards the end of the session and the young people were becoming bored.

Reproduced from *Modern Social Work Practice* by Mark Doel and Steven M. Shardlow, Ashgate, Aldershot, 2005

3 How it made you feel
Annoyed and uncomfortable for my colleague.
4 What you did
I spoke to the group about what was happening, using a firm tone, and about showing respect. I asked them to show the same courtesy they would expect.
5 What you would have liked to have done
*(Not completed)*

## Example D
*Behaviour of an individual towards the rest of the group (rated low physical risk).*

1 What the behaviour was
A young woman (teenager) in a predominantly male group was being loud, disruptive and challenging during a group session.
2 What led up to the behaviour
She had spent some time texting on her mobile phone [cell phone] prior to the group session beginning and during the initial part of the session and presented as not interested.
3 How it made you feel
I felt as though I had no control as the leader/faciliator; some of the young people who were present were interested in the topic but were unable to focus due to the behaviour of the young woman.
4 What you did
I asked the young woman if there was anything she wanted to share with the group, effectively 'putting her on the spot' as she appeared to want to dominate the contributions being made.
5 What you would have liked to have done
Upon reflection, I felt as though I hadn't spent any time with her prior to the group beginning – I also failed to fully appreciate her potentially isolated position in the group. I felt 'putting her on the spot' isolated her further.

## Example E
*Behaviour of a subgroup within the group (rated low physical risk).*

1 What the behaviour was
Disruptive, by [a group of young people within the group] not partaking in the group and actively disturbing others with private conversations, giggling, whispering.
2 What led up to the behaviour
Nothing particularly – the behaviour was exhibited from the start of the group session.

Reproduced from *Modern Social Work Practice* by Mark Doel and Steven M. Shardlow, Ashgate, Aldershot, 2005

3   How it made you feel
Increasingly frustrated. I wanted to stop it as it was affecting other group members who were wanting to participate. What was the point?
4   What you did
Initially I asked them to settle down and explained it was affecting others. I reinforced the groundrules. Finally, I was becoming stronger in my 'requests' to stop, stating the group would either have a shorter break or finish later to cover the items on the agenda.
5   What you would have liked to have done
Maybe taken them [the subgroup] out and spoken in private, but this may have made it worse if they felt singled out.

*Example F*
*Behaviour of one individual towards another individual in the group (rated high physical risk).*

1   What the behaviour was
One young person started to push another young person and was swearing. This became a fight.
2   What led up to the behaviour
The group were working in pairs about body language when angry, and the young person said the other one was 'copying' him.
3   How it made you feel
Frustrated, angry (with co-groupworker as well).
4   What you did
Made light of it initially but had to remove the young person from the group and told him off.
5   What you would have liked to have done
I would have liked to have made links between his [the young person's] reaction and the content of the session.

Four examples were volunteered in the plenary group, two from the low risk and two from the high risk range. This was an opportunity to model a systematic approach to enquiry, already begun in the clear instructions given by the five questions on the index card. The incident and the difficult behaviour were considered in careful detail, borrowing techniques from the problem exploration stage of task-centred practice (Reid, 1992) and from critical incident analysis (Fatout, 1998; Henchman and Walton, 1993). This forensic process of detailed and careful examination is important before moving on to any problem solving or speculation about alternative approaches. Once this forensic method had been demonstrated and repeated in the plenary, the participants moved into small groups to use the method to work on the examples which they had generated.

Whilst the groupworkers were discussing further examples in the small groups, the author collected the learning from the plenary discussion to present at the conclusion of the session. An invitation to include any further points arising from the small groups did not produce any additional themes.

## Practice guidance

The following nine themes emerged from the detailed process of considering specific examples of difficult behaviour in groups. They have been shaped and refined to provide practical guidance for groupworkers to respond to difficult behaviour in groups.

### 1   Importance of prior and contextual knowledge

Although difficult behaviours could be experienced at any stage in the group's progress (and not just in 'storming' stages), it became apparent that preparation and awareness of the wider context was a key factor to anticipating possible difficulties, even though the good groupworker should always 'expect the unexpected' (O'Connor, 1992, p. 84).

One groupworker described how she was troubled by the silent, withholding behaviour of a group member, and only later discovered that the silence was explained by her being bullied outside the group by a number of the other group members. One way to increase the likelihood that such knowledge becomes available is to ensure that each potential member of a group is offered the groupwork service individually (Doel and Sawdon, 1999; Manor, 1988). The groupworker in Example D noted that 'upon reflection, I felt as though I hadn't spent any time with her prior to the group beginning'. Developing a knowledge of an individual outside the group is possibly even more important in work with young people where there is a need to understand the youth subculture, which has a particularly strong impact within the group itself. The experiences of group members and group leaders *outside* the group are significant in understanding their responses *within* it.

### 2   Sampling the behaviour

Although some difficult situations arise suddenly, like the disclosure of sexual abuse in Example B, in most cases there is a build up and the point at which the behaviour becomes defined as 'difficult' is not clear cut. There is often a need to sample behaviour, sometimes even over a few sessions, to identify it and to understand it. Example A describes 'an ongoing difficulty in establishing a working relationship with the group members' as leading up to the difficulty. In Example C we learn that 'the young people

Reproduced from *Modern Social Work Practice* by Mark Doel and Steven M. Shardlow, Ashgate, Aldershot, 2005

*became* loud' (my italics), indicating that this was a process not an event. In some cases the 'outside' is brought into the 'inside' of the group from the very beginning of the session, as in Example E: 'Nothing particularly [led up to the behaviour] – the behaviour was exhibited from the start of the group session'.

Reflecting later on the cues which indicated difficult behaviour, and the point at which the groupworker defined the behaviour as 'difficult' helps future learning and recognition of cues.

### 3   Groundrules

Establishing a reference point to guide the behaviour of the individuals and the group is especially important in groups with young people, where issues of control are likely to predominate. Negotiating what is acceptable and what is not and recording this in a way that it can be displayed (for example flipchart / butcher's block) makes it possible to call on the group's sanction, avoiding a sense that it is the groupworker's whim. Of course, groundrules cannot detail every possible circumstance, but their principles can be called on in most cases. All six examples above would benefit from recourse to groundrules; for example, groundrules about disclosure in the group would have guided the facilitators in Example B. However, Example E ('I reinforced the groundrules') shows that agreeing groundrules does not guarantee that they will be respected.

We should also allow for groundrules which 'accept resistance as legitimate' (Sharry, 1999: 85). In other words, groundrules should not just concern themselves with control and containment, but should also acknowledge that there will be resistance and that the group can accept this.

### 4   Exploring the meaning of the behaviour

The concept of *difficult* behaviour can imply that it needs to be managed and controlled, even eradicated. True, in groups with children and young people, issues of control are keener than in groups of adults. However, there is a balance between working with the behaviour and controlling it. Unless there are evident physical and emotional risks, it is usually important to explore the meaning of the behaviour rather than containing it. As Trevithick notes (1995, pp. 11–13), establishing meaning for and with the group is essential for the group's success, and it is always important not to pathologise difficult behaviour (Sharry, 2001).

What often seems to prevent this exploration is the strength of the groupworker's feelings, which is why the third statement on the index card, *how it made you feel* is so important. The range of feelings expressed in the 14 examples of difficult behaviour included:

Reproduced from *Modern Social Work Practice* by Mark Doel and Steven M. Shardlow, Ashgate, Aldershot, 2005

defensive; criticised; upset; uncertain; out of control; frustrated; angry; uneasy; unsure; afraid; anxious; annoyed; embarrassed; vulnerable; undignified; childish; wary.

Frustrated, angry and annoyed were particularly common feelings. Discussion of anger goes back some way in the groupwork literature (see Redl, 1966), and more recently Malekoff considered whether it is a help or a hindrance to express anger in groupwork with adolescents. He felt that his mistake in expressing anger was 'not in the doing but in the understanding ... it felt to me as if I was on a runaway train or, perhaps, left behind' (Malekoff, 1999: 74).

When strong emotions are experienced, we focus on our own needs rather than those of others, which closes off new avenues of thought and action, just when we need to open them up. 'I mumbled something about this was the way the group was set up and looked generally uncomfortable and upset' (Example A). In response to 'what you did', one groupworker wrote 'panicked'. Unless acknowledged, these feelings can make it difficult to explore the meaning of the difficult behaviour and to move on to 'find the positives in the challenge' (Sharry, 1999, p. 84). Groupworkers can find themselves scolding the group or individual members (Sharry, 2001).

If groupworkers have the opportunity to prepare for these kinds of situation there is more likelihood that they will be able to manage their own feelings so that they are able to focus on the needs of the group. Difficult behaviour can be useful behaviour, in the sense that it is an opportunity for the groupworker to help the group to practise how it collectively responds to the challenge. Sometimes the behaviour reflects little more than an individual's state of mind, but most times it is an important piece of communication about where the group is, and controlling or removing the behaviour is a missed opportunity for learning. In Example F, there was an exact match between the topic of the session (body language and anger) and the angry behaviour of one of the individuals. As the groupworker notes, 'I would have liked to have made links between his [the young person's] reaction and the content of the session'. This could have entailed introducing an activity that drew attention to group processes (Craig, 1988).

## 5   Self, the individual, the group

Even if we are able to focus beyond our own feelings in these difficult situations, it is not uncommon to find oneself centring entirely on the individual whose behaviour is experienced as difficult. Sometimes this is unavoidable, especially if there are physical risks, but groupworkers need to find a balance between their own feelings, the demands of the individual concerned and the needs of the group. This is the challenge. Actually, *this* is the difficult behaviour, in the sense that it is difficult to achieve!

Although we need more empirical evidence in this area, it seems reasonable to suggest that if groupworkers can articulate feelings and meaning in all three arenas – that is, in respect of themselves, the individual(s) concerned and the group as a whole – this is the

Reproduced from *Modern Social Work Practice* by Mark Doel and Steven M. Shardlow, Ashgate, Aldershot, 2005

significant step to achieving learning from the behaviour. 'Articulating' will usually suggest an actual verbal dialogue with the group, but might sometimes be an inner dialogue as part of the careful balance in groupwork between suppression and expression of feelings (Turkie, 1995).

The groupworker in Example B shows an awareness of these three elements (in this order: group, self, individual) in response to the statement *how it made you feel:* 'Awkward for the rest of the group; slightly out of control as the facilitator; concerned for the person and wanting to support her'.

The groupworker in Example D attempts to make a link between the individual and the group, but is aware even at the time that this is not successful:

> I asked the young woman if there was anything she wanted to share with the group, effectively 'putting her on the spot' as she appeared to want to dominate the contributions being made ... Upon reflection ... I failed to fully appreciate her potentially isolated position in the group. I felt 'putting her on the spot' isolated her further.

To Schwartz's (1976) classic notion of the 'two clients' (the individual and the group) we should perhaps therefore add a third 'client', the self.

## 6    First stage and second stage strategies

Most of these groupworkers faced decisions about whether and when to move from a first stage position of working with the behaviour *in* the group to a second stage position of calling time-out to work with the behaviour *outside* the group. The dilemma about whether to move to the second stage is succinctly described in Example E, in response to the statement about *what you would have liked to have done:*

> Maybe taken them [the subgroup] out and spoken in private, but this may have made it worse if they felt singled out.

Working with the behaviour inside the group is an opportunity to enable the whole group to take some responsibility and to learn from the way in which difficult behaviours are processed. Second stage responses may be needed if the first stage is proving ineffective or the behaviour is sufficiently severe or disruptive.

We should also be alert to those times when group members themselves can work with the dificult behaviour without the groupworkers taking over. 'Over time, the workers learned to hold back when the children showed that they could challenge or support one another which will, of course, always be more effective' (Mullender, 1995, p. 90).

Reproduced from *Modern Social Work Practice* by Mark Doel and Steven M. Shardlow, Ashgate, Aldershot, 2005

## 7   Co-working agreements

Co-workers need to know each others' threshholds, and to have a sense of what each might define as 'difficult' behaviour. Consensus about the definition is not essential (indeed, diversity can be less oppressive), but agreement about how they will work together is. Lebacq and Shah (1989, pp. 130–1) describe how 'one worker was often used to control behaviour whilst the other worker led the exercise' in a group for sexually abused children. Co-workers need to develop mutual awareness (non-verbal signals, and so on) and rehearse strategies to work with a range of likely behaviours in the group.

The examples earlier make two explicit references to co-workers, one in which the groupworker felt angry *for* the co-worker, (Example C) and another where the groupworker felt angry *with* the co-worker (Example F). A preparatory questionnaire is one way of helping co-workers to work though potential difficulties by anticipating them (see Doel and Sawdon, 1999, pp. 214–16 for two examples).

## 8   Policy issues

A group does not take place in isolation, and it is important that there are supports available to groupworkers from their agencies and communities. Especially where risks of physical confrontation are not unusual (and this would include Children's Services), it is important that there are well-developed policies to which groupworkers can refer as non-negotiable elements in the group's groundrules. It might be appropriate to display public notices in group rooms which lay out clearly rules and expectations around personal conduct; discussion would revolve not around whether but around *how* the statements were to be enforced.

Support for all workers (in groupwork or not) should be available if difficult behaviour has been experienced. This may take the form of peer and supervision support; if the experience has been more traumatic, other forms of help need to be on hand. Groupworkers should feel confident that they will receive the support of their managers when dealing with difficult behaviour.

## 9   Dangerous and violent behaviour

Finally, it is important to make a clear statement that dangerous and violent behaviour is never acceptable. There is, therefore, 'a bottom line' and groupworkers should not consider that they can or should be able to handle all challenging behaviour. If personal safety is at issue, for groupworkers or members, external help must be sought.

Reproduced from *Modern Social Work Practice* by Mark Doel and Steven M. Shardlow, Ashgate, Aldershot, 2005

## Conclusion

The examples of working with difficulty in this article are, naturally, coloured by the fact that the groups are based in a Children's Services agency. However, the range of groups involves not just young people but their carers, too. It would be an excellent resource to build a data set of examples from across a whole range of practice settings, across professional disciplines, agencies and communities. Examples of difficult behaviour could be supplemented with growing experience about successful interventions, similar to the encyclopaedia of task strategies arising from research into task-centred practice (Reid, 2000). Accepting that novice groupworkers in particular are reluctant to confront in groups (Reid, 1988, p. 132), these examples could provide knowledge and encouragement and prevent missed opportunities for group learning.

The focus groups proved very effective in ensuring a programme which was in tune with the groupworkers' needs, and mirrored the good practice of the 'offer of groupwork' to potential members. The careful analysis of examples of difficult behaviour proved effective in helping to understand the wider meaning of the behaviour, and revealed the pivotal place of the groupworkers' feelings. However, having devised a scheme to regulate the flow of examples to the plenary group, I failed to use it properly and asked for two high risk examples as well as the two low risk ones; I think the urgency with which these examples were volunteered reflected the strength of residual feelings about traumatic episodes in groups, and a co-facilitator would no doubt have helped to keep this better balanced. Participants would have benefited from more time to consider their own examples in the small groups, and I should have placed more trust in their readiness to take the forensic method forward for themselves.

A ready-made example of a nuanced behaviour (around silence, denial or reluctance, for instance) might have encouraged more case studies of that nature, though it is clear that this group of workers, largely female groupworkers working with mainly adolescent male group members, felt the issue of raw control quite keenly, and the session responded to that. One person reflected the concerns described above: 'an area that needed more time was further discussion to include issues of oppressive language, undermining behaviour and unwilling participants'; and the ambiguity of the term 'challenging' was illustrated by one participant writing, 'perhaps more discussion on how to divert and change this behaviour rather than "challenge"'.

Overall, the groupworkers' evaluations were very positive. We all learned much about difficult behaviour and we felt it was important to share this learning with a wider audience. I hope that aim has been successful.

Reproduced from *Modern Social Work Practice* by Mark Doel and Steven M. Shardlow, Ashgate, Aldershot, 2005

Complete the questions on page 101 ready for your next practice tutorial.

## Further reading

Doel, M. (2005), *The Groupwork Book*, London: Routledge Community Care.
Malekoff, A. (1999), 'Expressing our Anger: hindrance or help in groupwork with adolescents?', *Groupwork*, 11(1): 71–82.
Manor, O. (1996), 'Storming as Transformation: a case study of group relationships', *Groupwork*, 9(3): 128–38.
Sharry, J. (2001), *Solution-Focused Groupwork*, London: Sage.

Reproduced from *Modern Social Work Practice* by Mark Doel and Steven M. Shardlow, Ashgate, Aldershot, 2005

# Part III

## Agency Practice

# CONTEXT: Creative practice and procedural requirements

> Everybody at the Conference was asked to stand in a line. The line represented a continuum of how creative people felt they were able to be within their working lives. Sadly, the end of the continuum which marked 'not creative at all' was very much the most crowded place on the continuum. (Doel, 2002b: 3)

One of the tensions in professional work is that between individual practice and organizational performance. In this contextual chapter we consider how discretion and creativity can be balanced with regulation and standardization.

## Principles underpinning procedures

Few people would disagree with the need to have procedures in place to ensure the quality and consistency of services available to the public. When it is a question of making resources available, it is important that there are agreed procedures to help regulate and distribute these resources, and these should be fair and transparent. Similarly, procedures are needed which help to ensure not only standards of service, but also accountability to the community at large for the costs of these services. It is important that people in one part of the country can expect as good a quality of service as those in another, hence the introduction of the Fair Access to Care Services procedures.[1]

A procedure should build on what we already know to be good practice, so that it can act as guidance for practitioners, helping to embed this experience in future practice. All of this is right and proper; indeed, much of it is enshrined in law, statutory guidance and notions of 'best practice' (see Chapter 15).

Students must learn about procedures for a number of reasons. They need to learn how to translate general notions of fairness and efficiency into actual practice, using the procedures which the agency has made available. This may be general guidance or, more commonly, a particular proforma or set of proformas designed to chart the practitioner's work with people. Students should also be helped to consider procedures critically. This does not mean moaning about them as a chore, but a genuine analysis of their usefulness in achieving the principles of fairness,

---

[1] Located at www.doh.gov.uk/scg/facs.

transparency and good standards. The practice teacher and work-based supervisor should prepare examples of the use of procedures, illustrating aspects which are successful and others which are less successful in applying these principles. In this way, the student can begin to learn not just how to use a procedure, but also how to think about it critically.

## Problems with procedures

Procedures carry dangers, too. A procedure can too easily become a tool to aid the smooth running or self-protection of the agency rather than a means of promoting the benefit of the users. Procedures that are hastily designed in reaction to a single high-profile event can have unintended negative consequences on many more low-profile events. There is a tendency to follow any shock to the system with a set of procedures designed to prevent a recurrence of this shock but, unfortunately, the trauma from the shock means that a cool analysis of the potential secondary effects of the new procedure is neglected. Consequently, although the procedure may be successful in preventing the highly unusual events which led to the initial shock, it may have unfortunate consequences on all the rest of the agency's less dramatic work. For example, is it likely that there will be an evaluation of the possible negative effects of the twenty-six recommendations referred to in the newspaper report which follows?

> Social services and health managers in Cityville were this week criticised after two-year-old Andrew Coldwell died after drinking his drug addict mother's methadone ... They were 'too tolerant' of Rebecca Hodgkins' drug habit and had not made a proper assessment of her parenting skills, an independent report said ... A total of 26 recommendations were made on how procedures should be tightened to avoid tragedies. (*Names have been changed*)

In this case, the two-year-old toddler had drunk from a bottle of methadone, left with the top unscrewed. The same report went on to record that 'there is no guarantee that a perfectly working childcare protection system could have prevented his death'. Would there have been the same reaction if a child had died because a parent left a bottle of bleach, rather than 'a drug', with the top unscrewed? Would there be a reference to the 'bleach-using parent' in the way that Rebecca is called a 'drug addict mother'? The report continued, 'each year more than 500 children in Cityville [pop. 500 000] are taken to hospital because they have taken substances (medicines and alcohol) meant for their parents. Between 130 and 140 have to be admitted.'

Procedures are an expression of power. Those who design a procedure have considerable power to shape future practice, yet they are often not the people who will have to implement the procedure directly. This can lead to procedures which are unwieldy and impractical, and this, in turn, can generate opposition, merely because those who must use the procedures do not feel any ownership of them. In these circumstances, the people who designed a procedure can view critical feedback from the people who are obliged to use it as obstructive rather than insightful. When procedures are developed and evaluated in your work setting, what opportunities exist for consultation or participation in these processes by practitioners and service users, and how can the student be involved in this?

Procedures can lead to lazy practices if they become a substitute for critical thinking and action, and a reliance on procedures can slip into routinized practice. Of course, routines are essential to manage a heavy workload and are appreciated by users if they guarantee a punctual and reliable service. However, if the routine fails to acknowledge important differences between one situation and another, it becomes dangerous practice, with automatic decision-making replacing individual plans and interventions (Thompson, 2000b; Wayne and Cohen, 2001). Procedures can lead an agency to feel it has done all that is necessary, and, because it can become difficult to change a procedure once it is in place, the procedure may come to reflect a past reality rather than the current one. What opportunities for reviewing and changing procedures can the student learn about in your agency or work setting?

As a standardized process, a procedure does not lend itself easily either to the highly individual nature of much professional practice or the complex circumstances of the people with whom these professionals work. Procedures might be bypassed or sabotaged, with the result that they become discredited. If the lines of communication in the agency are open, this will lead to a revision of the procedure but, where communication is poor, a gap will grow between what an agency thinks is practised and the practice itself. The need for discretion should be openly discussed, so that there can be healthy debate about the limits of discretion and the kinds of circumstance where it can be applied. To close off this dialogue is to drive discretionary behaviour underground and, therefore, to encourage dangerous practices.

One set of procedures can contradict another. In a residential home for older people, procedures based on personalized care had allowed care staff to make individually tailored breakfasts for each resident, many of whom enjoyed the opportunity of a soft-boiled egg. When a new principal was appointed, she was horrified that 'procedures were not being followed'. The procedures she invoked were health and safety which, she said, required only catering staff to make breakfast (of whom there were insufficient to make individualized breakfasts) and did not allow the cooking of soft-boiled eggs for residents 'because of the risk of salmonella'. Whose procedures should be followed? Did anyone ask the residents?

Perhaps the greatest challenge is how to achieve a balance between the need for procedures which can ensure quality, fairness and accountability and, at the same time, allow for professional discretion to deliver an individualized and personal service. In short, students need to learn how to use procedures in ways that are not proceduralized, and to develop routines that are not routinized. How can the student learn about the use of professional discretion in your agency and are there open forums where these kinds of issues are discussed?

## The retreat from professionalism?

The size of welfare bureaucracies, the perception that they are insensitive and inefficient and driven by the needs of those employed by them rather than those using them all combined in the closing years of the twentieth century to undercut the confidence of the professions. Tightening control of resources, coupled with central government's suspicion of local government, led to the introduction of private-sector managerial techniques such as performance indicators. This has all led to what has been termed a retreat from professionalism, with the implementation of community care heralding increased managerial control over practice (Lymbery, 2000).

Procedures are not value-free, and Sheppard (1995) has argued that importing case management procedures from the US to a different UK environment was an ideological, rather than an evidence-based, decision. This ideology has a language as arcane as any Marxist, Freudian or postmodernist, what Humphrys (2003) calls 'the hen-house language of "delivering objectives" by "thinking outside the box" or "stretching the envelope" by "building on best practice"'; to which we might add 'creative synergy' and a myriad other buzzing clichés.

The terms of debate in the social work profession are seen, therefore, as increasingly determined by the managers of social work services rather than the practitioners or the users. In respect of community care, Lymbery (2000: 129) notes that the central problem 'has therefore been re-ordered – it is not the attempt to meet the needs of individuals and communities but is, rather, the management of budgets and resources'.

This analysis concludes that one of the many consequences of the retreat from professionalism has been the increase in proceduralized practice, as evidenced in assessment procedures such as eligibility criteria to ration services and the reduction of the social work role to a 'technical operative' (Lymbery, 1998), with decreasing opportunities for practitioners to work in direct practice with service users (Jones, 2001; Reed, 2002).

Much of this analysis seems so far away from creative practice that the reader may wonder how we are able to include it in the title. Is there any way forward?

## Creative practice

It is no surprise that the social work literature is sharper in its analysis of the problem than it is in its presentation of examples of solutions. There is much analysis of the pathology of current practice, but what is urgently needed are specific examples of creative practice and practice learning. In line with the moves towards positive psychology, social work needs to focus less on what does not work and more on what does.

One of the difficulties possibly lies in recognizing what creative practice might be. Those conference participants who gathered around the 'not creative at all' pole of the continuum (see the quote opening this chapter) might need some prompting to recognize some of their current practices as being creative. For example, one practitioner did some innovative work with a family, using flipchart sheets to help them represent their situation in graphic form and working in a way that was quite different and challenging for her; yet she did not see this as being creative, despite the novelty and the excellent evaluation from the users. Some people do not see themselves as creative, perhaps isolating the idea of creative as something for the arts rather than a possibility for applied social science. 'Creatives' are cast as artists, advertising executives, actors and so on, with social work airbrushed out.

Is there an *art* of social work (England, 1986)? What does creative practice look like? For some it has to be something new and original, an innovative way of using existing resources, a special ability to be imaginative. In fact, creative practice is a way of looking at one's own practice rather than something that can be objectively defined. Let us remember that creativity is no less objectively defined in the world of art: is an unmade bed a work of creation? Tracey Emin certainly believes so. A social worker who sees their work as creative would recognize that every time they meet with a service user they create an atmosphere which they hope is conducive to the work, they create space for the user to express themselves, they create opportunities for the user to seek solutions, agree plans and involve other people, and so on. And, paradoxically, this social worker might experience all of this creativity quite routinely.

As an aside, we should also acknowledge the pejorative use of the word 'creative', meaning intentionally deceptive, as in 'creative with the truth'. We might worry if a colleague crowed about their 'creative record-keeping'!

There are many reasons why you should aim both to recast your existing work as creative and to seek new opportunities for creativity in your practice. Foremost is the question of job satisfaction. We are familiar with the impact of stress and burnout on social workers, but we know much less about those social workers who continue to enjoy their work. We have little evidence one way or the other, but it seems unlikely that the satisfied group are any less busy or committed than the former burnt-out group, so what is it that makes the difference? Once again, we need to change the focus, in order to learn from those who are using successful strategies, rather than learn even more about those who do not. Job satisfaction is crucial if the students we are educating today will continue to be practitioners the day after tomorrow.

As well as a responsibility to yourself, you also have a responsibility to the people you work with. Creative practice is likely to be more engaging for service users, more stimulating for the team and other professionals whom you involve, and is also likely to lead to innovations in the ways in which services are given. If one of a social worker's talents is to see situations from different perspectives, this is surely a key aspect of creative practice – reframing a situation so that it can be seen in a different light, triggering a fresh approach and offering a new range of potential solutions or courses of action.

Some agencies may be suspicious of creative practice because it is likely to call into question existing practices. However, the 'change agenda', as the jargon has it, has too long been driven by government and senior management. The battery of changes imposed from outside the profession as part of the modernization ideology has tended to make people averse to the notion of change itself. This is understandable, but mistaken. How much more powerful it would be if the direction and drive for change came directly from practitioners and service users. Creative practice would provide the evidence and the energy to promote changes (as opposed to 'change') from the bottom up, rather than from the top down.

## Procedural *and* creative practice

We have a great need, then, to consider how we can add the 'c' of creativity to the other common 'c's of criteria, compliance and competence (Phillipson, 2002).

Let us return to the idea of procedures. First, they are with us, like it or not. Second, the underpinning principles which we spelled out early in this chapter are important and necessary ones. Fairness, transparency and good standards must be incorporated into all professional practice, and the development of procedures is an important mechanism to promote these principles.

The dictionary has a definition of procedure as 'established method: an established method or correct way of doing something'. However, a second definition states, 'any method: any means of doing or accomplishing something, [as in] an extremely unorthodox procedure' (Encarta, 1999).

This is a very helpful insight. Yes, its first meaning suggests that there is only one correct way of doing things, but the second reminds us that procedures are just ways of doing something, and that these can be unorthodox as well as established. Basically, a procedure can be followed in a routinized way or in a creative way; it can be highly formalized or it can be any method used to accomplish something.

If we consider a method of working such as task-centred practice, we see that there are certain procedures associated with this method (Marsh and Doel, 2005). The various stages of the method have recognized procedures which help to guide the practitioner and the user. These procedures can be administered in a tick-box fashion, with outcomes implying that users seem to need or to want only the services which the agency can afford to provide, or they can be used to develop a spirit of partnership with service users, in which the users are, as far as possible, in the driving seat. Though some procedures are undeniably more helpful than others, it is not the procedures themselves which determine the nature of the experience for the service user, it is the way in which they are used, creatively or not, by the practitioner and the agency.

# 9 Making priorities

## About Activity 9    Home truths

The activity *Home truths* takes us back to the residents of Derby Street on the Green Hill estate (See *Activity 1, Licensed to learn*, page 13). Priority rehousing is possible for just one household, and the student is asked to consider the statements by each household before putting the applications into a rank order of priority. The learning from the activity comes from a consideration of the values that have underpinned the student's choices.

This activity can be undertaken by two people (you and the student) or by a small group of practice teachers and students. A group of students in different settings can often provide contrasting perspectives.

### Purpose

The purpose of this activity is to encourage students to think about how they make decisions when there are conflicting priorities. Too often, these kinds of decision are made without an awareness of the knowledge, values and beliefs which underpin them. This activity makes these factors explicit and teaches students a framework, which will help them continue to review the way in which they make decisions.

### Method

- Ask the students to study *Home truths* before the practice tutorial, making a brief note of their response to each household's statement, and to bring a list of their priorities (from the household they think should have first priority to the one they think should have least).
- Discuss the student's reasoning in the practice tutorial (supervision session) and develop an 'objective' list of criteria.
- Together with the student, apply the 'objective' list of criteria to see what differences (if any) this would make to the student's original order of priorities.

## Variations

In 'real life' there would be formal criteria and a set of procedures to decide how a resource such as new housing would be allocated (as well as the practical issue of a match between the size of the new accommodation and the applicants' needs). However, the ability to suspend these practical factors can lead students to recognize greater home truths about the way in which priorities are too often made – on the basis of 'the deserving' and so on.

Once the *Home truths* activity has been completed, you may like to draw up a set of competing priorities, which are more specifically tailored to the kind of situations found in your work setting. However, before setting the student down to the application of existing agency procedures, the *Home truths* activity enables students to think critically about how criteria should be developed and to understand the link between procedures and the values which those procedures seek to enforce.

## Use by other professions

Whatever the professional group, some form of prioritization is needed to manage the gap between demand and resources. The *Home truths* activity is applicable across a range of professions (indeed, social worker students have been using the activity to do what some would say is a housing worker's task). You may wish to revisit the exercise by tailoring it to the particular situations in your setting, pointing the student to literature in your professional area. There are many examples of prioritization of services and treatment in healthcare professions; Harries and Harries (2001) explored how four occupational therapists managed and prioritized community mental health referrals using a form of 'social judgement theory', for instance. Where students work in a multiprofessional environment, they can be encouraged to explore the forms of prioritization used by other professionals.

## National Occupational Standards for Social Work

The topics in this chapter relate to the following National Occupational Standards:

  6:   Planning together
 15:   Managing resources and services.

## *Activity 9*      *Home truths*

For this activity, you should also refer to Activity 1, *Licensed to learn*, for more background detail on each household.

Read the statements for rehousing made by the various applicants. Make a brief note of your response to each household's statement and bring a list of your priorities – from the household you think should have first priority to the one you think should have the least. Revisit these notes and make a list of the criteria that you have used to help you make your priorities.

Assume that the new accommodation is the appropriate size for each of the applicants (even though this could not be the case in reality).

### Applicants' statements

*Zoë Benner*

> As a single parent with two teenagers and a baby daughter, I think I have a strong case for moving off this estate. Jackson, my fourteen-year-old, has been getting in with a bad crowd and we need a fresh start and our Kylie needs the opportunity of a fresh start at a new school. I would like to live nearer my daughter Tilly who is currently living with foster parents and this new accommodation would give me the opportunity of seeing much more of her. The chance of having our own garden at the new accommodation would improve our quality of life as a family, especially since my baby suffers a lot from asthma.

*Jason Dean and Sam Weiner*

> We are very excited at the prospect which this new accommodation would give for us to move to more suitable accommodation. Although we are on the ground-floor currently, the flat is very unsuitable for Sam's disability; the prognosis suggests that Sam will need wheelchair access in one or two years, and this would make it impossible for him to use the bathroom in our current accommodation. Attached is a letter of support from our GP and the Occupational Therapist.

Reproduced from *Modern Social Work Practice* by Mark Doel and Steven M. Shardlow, Ashgate, Aldershot, 2005

## Avis Jenkins

I am writing this statement on behalf of my mother, who currently lives at 3, Derby St. I have recently divorced and I am planning on moving back to Cityville to be near my mother. However, because of the schooling situation for my son, for whom I have custody, I will be living across the city from Mrs Jenkins' current address. The possibilty of this new accommodation for my mother is ideal since it would be close to my new home and I could give her the kind of support she clearly needs. I fear that without this support she will not be able to maintain her independent living and that she is at risk of needing residential care. Also, she tells me that she is much disturbed by her current neighbours and is unhappy about the general quality of the area and the type of people who are moving in.

## Lorretta and Luke Carter

We see this as a great opportunity to better ourselves. It is very important for us, as we start to think about a family, to have a home with a garden where the children will be able to play. My husband's band is getting very successful, which means he needs to practise more frequently, and we are getting complaints from neighbours. He tells me that the new accommodation is close to some sound studios which it would be possible to hire, so our new neighbours wouldn't be disturbed.

## Jim Rafferty

I like this neighbourhood, but I have to be honest with myself that, as a partially sighted person, I'm finding it increasingly difficult to find my way around and I now hardly go out. The local shop has closed and I can't use the supermarket which is across a very busy road with no nearby crossing, so I'm dependent on the kindness of others. Through the local residents' association, we have tried very hard to lobby for improved street markings, but with no success. My sister took me to the new accommodation and the surrounding area is very well-marked for blind and partially sighted people – my independence and quality of life would be transformed, as well as escaping from the noise next door! I'm afraid that the prognosis for my sight is not good and I enclose a letter of support from my Rehabilitation Worker and from the RNIB.

Reproduced from *Modern Social Work Practice* by Mark Doel and Steven M. Shardlow, Ashgate, Aldershot, 2005

## Gregor and Stefan Kiyani

*We hope to have successful application in account of very bad treatment we receive in our current home. People on our street are friendly, but there is gang which continually threatens us from near here, and police seem not able to help us with this problem. We have many contributions to make to our new country but are frightened by possible violence where we live now. Also, the rooms are not good, with some wet on the walls, which has been told to Mr James, but nothing is happening. We hope respectfully to have opportunity for better life which can be safe for us.*

## Shama and Gary Homes

This application is based on our role as carers and the possibility which the new accommodation (with more rooms) would give us to increase this role. We successfully care for a number of children with learning disabilities, giving them, and their own carers, a valuable break. We enjoy our work, and treasure the many letters of thanks and appreciation we have received over the years. The new accommodation would enable us to expand our capacity and to give much-needed respite to even more children. Our own adult daughter has learning difficulties but is well-established in an independent living foundation and we now feel able to take on more responsibilities.

# Teaching notes: *Making priorities*

The value of *Home truths* is that it gives students permission to reflect carefully on the reasons behind the decisions they make. In the safe environment of simulated practice, students can begin to question the reasons for their choices, because there is time to reflect on them. This helps students to make better decisions at times of great pressure, and gives a framework to evaluate the way in which they have made their priorities.

Good social work practice is self-aware and accountable. Students learn how to *give an account* of what they are doing and why they are doing it. Those students who can answer the question 'What am I doing and why am I doing it?' make their practice accessible, with every prospect of becoming accountable, too. Students often learn to describe what they did and why they did it *after* the event, which only improves their skills in post hoc rationalization. As practice teacher, you hope to improve the students' abilities to give an honest account of the choices that are available to them and to become aware of the criteria used to make these choices. This kind of activity can accelerate students' understanding (see Doel, 1988).

Below are a dozen criteria to tease out during the discussion with the student. The situations in *Home truths* are not especially urgent, so you may wish to inject some urgency into some of the situations to see how this might alter the student's rankings.

- How does the student think these criteria are ranked in practice?
- How does the student think these criteria *should* be ranked?

## Ranking criteria

1 *Consequences of delay and risk*
   In these situations, the individual's life is at risk. What are the consequences of delay? How urgent is the immediate risk?
2 *Legal obligation*
   What is the legal framework for the powers and responsibilities that govern this situation? What are the legal requirements on social work and other professionals in these situations?
3 *Agency expectations*
   Does the agency have any policies that determine the priorities, and are these clear and accessible?
4 *Social pressures*
   What are the broad influences on the worker's decisions? Is there such a thing as society's priorities and expectations? How do we determine what these are and who defines them?
5 *Available resources*
   To what extent do we make priorities in order to fit the available resources, so that resources define needs?

6   *Others' responsibilities and skills*
    What other people could and should be helping? When would you expect other
    people, in your agency or other agencies, to be involved?
7   *Previous knowledge*
    To what extent do previous assessments influence present attitudes?
8   *Degree of need and disadvantage*
    Can one person be said to be more needy than another and how can this need
    be measured? Are specific service user and carer groups particularly
    disadvantaged and how should this influence the way we treat particular
    individuals?
9   *Likelihood of success*
    Is it important to put energies into effective work, providing help to those who
    can use it? How is the possibility of a successful outcome to be judged and what
    do we do about those situations where failure is almost inevitable?
10  *Personal preferences*
    How far does the acknowledgement of personal preferences for particular
    kinds of work – for example, a preference for working with women – clear or
    cloud the judgement? Is this an honest self-assessment of personal skills and
    limitations, or a rationalization of prejudice?
11  *Problem sensitization*
    Are we more likely to respond quickly and favourably to problems which we
    can relate to in connection with our own personal lives?

## Opportunities

If there are clear agency policies which define priorities, it is important to let the
student know that you will be discussing these. However, agency priorities are not
necessarily synonymous with professional ones and, to begin with, you want
students to express their own priorities. Make sure that students do not try to avoid
the issues by claiming they would never have to deal with all these things alone and
that others would be involved. Of course, others would be involved, and students
would not have to determine the priorities independently, but the point of the
activity is to look at reasons for making choices and deciding priorities, not at ways
of avoiding them.

You can ask students to reconsider their priorities from somebody else's point of
view, such as the director of the agency, the local newspaper or 'the man or woman
in the street'. You are not looking for a rapid response. Encourage students to think
about how they manage to deal with competing demands and set priorities, both in
terms of making effective decisions as well as managing any stress they may
experience.

Finally, encourage students to consider how they might manage the priorities of
their own day-to-day practice as well as the broader considerations about how the
agency, in which they are currently working, approaches the problems associated
with making priorities.

# Learning notes: *Making priorities*

Decisions about priorities are variously set at governmental, regional, local and individual level. Within any complex organization, all staff, whatever their position and role, will make decisions about priorities. Some will make decisions that affect many; some will have scope only to prioritize their own work practices. In a complex society, levels of expectations among the public about the availability of health and social goods is almost infinitely elastic. This means that decisions have to be made about not only those programmes to be funded, but also which service users and carers, at the individual level within a programme, will receive priority over others and how much support they will receive. Making decisions about priorities may be assumed to be a responsibility of the politician and the civil servant at national level. However, in Oregon, an experimental approach has been developed by politicians to involve the public in setting priorities. This state has pioneered in setting health and social care priorities by asking the electorate directly what level of taxation they are willing to accept for a given level of services (Bodenheimer, 1997).

Deciding on priorities is not just a matter a matter of money; there are some hard moral choices to be made – sometimes as fundamental as whether to live and let live.

## Live and let live

Consider the following vignettes:

---

**Vignette One: Better use of resources**

Jaymee Bowen (Child B), then aged six, was diagnosed in 1990 as having non-Hodgkin's lymphoma for which she was treated at Addenbrooke's Hospital in Cambridge. In 1993, Jaymee was diagnosed as having a second cancer, acute myeloid leukaemia. She was treated at the Royal Marsden Hospital in London with chemotherapy and a bone marrow transplant. When she suffered a relapse and the cancer reoccurred in 1995, she was denied the opportunity of a second transplant by Cambridge Health Authority on the grounds that this would be an 'experimental treatment' that would cause considerable suffering and would have only a limited chance of success. The authority recommended palliative care only. At the Court of Appeal the judgment concluded in favour of the health authority on the grounds that its resources could be better spent on other cases where treatment was likely to be more effective (that is, more deserving).

---

Reproduced from *Modern Social Work Practice* by Mark Doel and Steven M. Shardlow, Ashgate, Aldershot, 2005

### Vignette Two: Disability matters

According to Hinsliff, the parents of 'Nadia', a severely disabled eleven-year-old girl suffering from a chest infection, were told by doctors at the Royal London Hospital that 'it was not worth putting the child on a ventilator and that she should be allowed to die' (Hinsliff, 2004: 12).

David Glass, aged twelve, born profoundly disabled, suffered complications following an operation. Both treatment and feeding were stopped; he was given diamorphine and was to be allowed to die peacefully.

In both cases, the parents have challenged the medical decision.

### Vignette Three: Don't be old – the case of Alice C

The case of Alice C, who at the age of eighty-eight was believed to be dead and was resuscitated, is described by Levinsky (1998: 1849):

> ... 3 min after she reached the emergency room, Alice C (name changed for confidentiality) stopped breathing. The 88-year-old woman had been talking to the doctor – word by laboured word, separated by gasps for breath. She had told him that she had been well until the previous evening, when she had begun to feel short of breath. By morning, her breathlessness had become so severe that she had overcome her repugnance for medical care and allowed her granddaughter to drive her to the hospital.
>
> The physician in the emergency room had never seen Alice before. Her granddaughter did not know whether she wanted to be resuscitated. In the absence of any advance directives, the doctor – although he believed the elderly woman was 'as good as dead' – opted for vigorous treatment. Within minutes, a tube had been positioned in Alice's airway and attached to a ventilator. She was transferred to the medical intensive-care unit for further treatment.
>
> The next morning I was making rounds with the residents assigned to the intensive-care unit. 'Do you think', one resident asked me, 'that it is appropriate to give such expensive treatment to an 88-year-old woman who is probably going to die anyway?'
>
> Three unstated ideas underlie the resident's question. First, that so much of our national wealth is consumed by the cost of healthcare that it is appropriate to withhold potentially beneficial care to save money. Second, that such rationing should be based on age. Third, that much of the expenditure on medical care of elderly people is wasted on aggressive care of old people who are dying. [ ... ] Alice was found to have pneumonia and was treated with an antibiotic. Within 3 days, she was taken off the ventilator. Within 10 days, she went home and resumed her independent lifestyle, living near but not with her children and grandchildren. When I lost track of her 3 years later, she was still alert and enjoying life at age 91.
>
> When we obtained her old hospital record, we learned that 5 years earlier, when Alice was 83, she had been fitted with a cardiac pacemaker. The use of this device and her stay in our intensive-care unit 5 years later are prime examples of the application of expensive technology 'at the end of her natural lifespan'. Except that, as it really happened, her lifespan was extended by at least 8 more years by the use of aggressive treatment with a pacemaker and later in an intensive-care unit.

Reproduced from *Modern Social Work Practice* by Mark Doel and Steven M. Shardlow, Ashgate, Aldershot, 2005

Now that you have read the three vignettes, consider the following questions:

1   Do you agree with the treatment decisions made in these cases?
2   What priority would you give to treating the people in the vignettes?
3   Is there any further information you would like to gather before taking action?
4   What criteria have you used to help you decide your position?
5   Can you envisage other situations that would have greater priority?

## Rationing

Rationing has been more explicit in healthcare than in social care for some time. There is much to learn by exploring issues in healthcare, not least because social workers are increasingly likely to be involved in situations where there is:

1   *Rationing of resources on the grounds of quality of life*
    Individuals may be denied access to resources because these would not sufficiently improve their quality of life, or because their current quality of life does not justify the allocation of further scarce resources.
2   *Rationing of resources on the grounds of age*
    Priorities may be set on the grounds of age. In respect of healthcare there is a well-established debate concerning the virtue of this form of rationing. In a debate format, Williams (1997) supports rationing healthcare on the grounds of age, advancing the argument that there is 'no compelling argument to justify the view that the young should sacrifice large benefits so that the old can enjoy small ones': that is, younger people's quality of life is to be preferred over that of older people. Those who are older have had life opportunities and similar opportunities should not be denied to those who are younger; (to pursue a cricketing analogy), 'they've had a good innings'. Evans (1997) argues against age as a grounds for rationing healthcare because it is fundamentally unacceptable on ethical grounds to discriminate on the grounds of age.

Rationing on the grounds of quality of life or by age are by no means the only grounds upon which health priorities operate, either explicitly or as a consequence of the operation of particular systems. Rationing also occurs *on the grounds of choice of lifestyle* – for example, when smokers are denied treatment for smoking-related illness unless they stop smoking. In such cases they are treated as having made a lifestyle choice to smoke, rather than being treated as 'nicotine addicts'. There have also been reports of *rationing of resources on the grounds of moral worth*, such as the denial of treatment to vagrants for renal dialysis, when such treatment is being offered to others in similar need but with different lifestyles. You might like to consider these examples of rationing and consider whether you agree with any of them and, if so, why. Are there similar examples, known to you, in social work, where the setting of priorities is managed through moral-worth rationing

Reproduced from *Modern Social Work Practice* by Mark Doel and Steven M. Shardlow, Ashgate, Aldershot, 2005

mechanisms, whether deliberately adopted or as the accidental consequence of policy decisions? If so, what are the rationing mechanisms?

During the First World War, the medical services were faced with the kinds of priorities we hope we will never have to make. With scant resources, they had to make decisions, which were, literally, life and death. They divided the casualties into three categories:

- those whose injuries were such that they were likely to recover, even without treatment
- those whose injuries were such that, without treatment, they were likely to die, but with treatment they were likely to survive
- those whose injuries were such that they were likely to die, even with treatment.

The medical services put all their energies into the middle category, leaving the first group to recover unaided and leaving the last group to die. This method of making priorities was called triage. Fortunately, the choices in social work are not so stark, but they are difficult nonetheless. The principle of putting your efforts where they are most likely to be effective is one you need to consider.

> Effectiveness is an important ethical consideration not only for individual workers but for the agencies in which they work. There is a disproportionate unconcern within agencies with self-evaluation. (Hudson and Macdonald, 1986: 11)

The latter part of this assertion, concerning agencies, may or may not remain the case, but if you had used the criterion of likely effectiveness as the main guideline for your work on a placement, would there have been a difference in the kinds of priorities you made?

What do you think are the benefits and the limitations of using the effectiveness criterion in social work?

## Extent of rationing

The extent of rationing is a measure of the degree to which available resources are in balance with perceptions of need, whether professionally defined or service-user and carer defined. As Bergmark (1996) notes, it is financial constraint due to cuts in public spending that has increased the interest of Swedish municipalities in considering the way in which priorities are implemented. There is some evidence that decentralized decision-making processes lead to people in similar sets of circumstance being treated differently in different geographical areas. From an examination of the provision of mental health services for older people, Murphy (2000) suggests that the planning and purchasing mechanisms for health and social care services in the UK actually increase the inequalities in services for older people.

The real world of social work practice is being radically and speedily reconstructed as organizations merge, shift and change, as the boundaries between healthcare and social care become more permeable and fluid. Setting priorities for services is no longer a matter for one organization but has to be undertaken in partnership, especially at local and regional levels. Glendinning, Coleman and Rummery suggest three current policy initiatives: 'an emphasis on partnership; active demonstration of improved performance; and increasing involvement of frontline health professionals in decisions of services development' (2002: 185). These factors shape the form, nature and priority of services for older people, amongst other groups.

## Assessment notes: *Making priorities*

Making decisions between competing priorities is not necessarily a particularly difficult task. We all have to make choices about all aspects of our lives – whether to have tea or coffee in the morning for breakfast, which job to apply for, with whom to develop relationships and so on. What distinguishes each of these decisions is the extent and permanence of their impact on our lives, from the banal to the life-defining. Some may matter a little; others may matter a lot. What is truly important about making decisions is that you understand the reasoning lying behind the decision; this is the case whether the decision concerns making a cup of tea or how to allocate resources between the competing needs of different service users and carers. It is this reasoning – the grounds upon which you make decisions about priorities – that will be used to assess your abilities to make priorities.

## Further reading

Coulshed, V. and Mullender, A. (2001), *Management in Social Work* (2nd edn), Basingstoke: Palgrave.
Orme, J. (2002), 'Managing the Workload', in R. Adams, L. Dominelli and M. Payne (eds), *Critical Practice in Social Work*, Basingstoke: Palgrave, pp. 236–43.

# 10 Managing resources

## *About Activity 10    Travel agent*

*Travel agent* invites students to consider buying one of a number of different holidays, the purchase of a holiday providing an analogy for the purchase of social services (care management). The student is asked to consider factors such as high, medium or low season, the price of the holiday, and the remaining monies available for spending and so on.

   *Travel agent* is best undertaken by a group of three or four students. It can also be undertaken by two people, such as the practice teacher and student.

### Purpose

*Travel agent* is designed to encourage students to consider some of the factors involved in making choices about services – in this case, a service they might wish to obtain for themselves. Thinking about the factors that are important in making decisions about a holiday helps us to a better understanding of the type of decisions that must be made in the provision and management of social services. However, although it is possible to survive without a holiday, it may not be possible to continue living in the community without adequate social services.

### Method

- Ask students to read *Travel agent* and, independently, consider the options for holidays. Ask them to decide on their first choice of holiday. In making this selection, students may want to find out if others in the group are considering the same package. If two or more students take the same holiday package, they are entitled to a 20 per cent discount on the price, thus increasing their available spending money.
- Once students have decided on their holiday package, ask them to review the reasons for their selection, including the following factors:
  - type of holiday
  - overall cost
  - balance of costs (meals/accommodation and so on)

139

  – time of year
  – location and facilities offered
  – whether the holiday is 'protected' and facilities inspected
  – available spending money
  – other factors.

The students should compare the relative importance of different factors in deciding on their preferences.

• In the practice tutorial (supervision session), students should be encouraged to consider the differences and similarities between the purchase of a holiday and the purchase of services to help a person remain in the community.

## Variations

This simulation can be modified in a variety of ways to affect the issues considered by students. For example:

• Different factors can be introduced into the holiday, such as the safety or reliability of the travel agency. (Dice could help here to make some holidays riskier than others – students could lose part or all of the holiday for which they have booked.)

• Service users and carers often have little real or effective choice, and students can experience this by having another student choose the holiday they think is best for them for, without consultation.

• The student can be placed in a position, similar to that of a manager, with responsibility for purchasing 'block services', such that the student is given the responsibility, as a travel manager, for buying holidays in bulk to then sell on to others.

## Use by other professions

Effective management of resources is central to all health and social care professions, so this activity can easily be used by other professions that allocate resources. It is often assumed that early intervention and delivery of services will produce significant benefits. Does early intervention lead to significant change or resources being taken from other parts of an overstretched system? Pelosi and Birchwood (2003) attempted to answer this question in respect of early intervention for psychosis by reviewing the arguments about whether early treatment of psychotic symptoms results in a higher success rate in symptom management and control and whether early intervention can minimize the psychosocial effects of a psychosis. They concluded that the rationale for early intervention is overwhelming. Therefore, by analogy, is it better to buy your holiday early and, if so, is it guaranteed that you would find the holiday of choice? Conversely, if you buy the holiday later do you get a bargain because the travel agent has reduced prices in order to sell the holidays that are still left?

# National Occupational Standards for Social Work

The topics in this chapter relate to the following National Occupational Standards (see the Appendix):

4: Respond to crisis situations
15: Managing resources and services.

## Activity 10    *Travel agent*

Read the following extracts from holiday brochures and decide which holiday you would like to purchase, taking account of your income. Your choice will be influenced by a number of factors, such as the proportion of your budget you wish to spend on the holiday and the proportion this leaves you for spending money.

**DISCOUNTS**

Holidays are cheaper if you can share with another; if you want to negotiate with a fellow holiday-maker to share a holiday, you will both benefit from a 20% reduction (i.e. there will be a commensurate increase in your spending money – indicated in italics).

Note that Holiday G is a half-chance lottery – a 50% chance of your name coming up.

(A) Access for disabled people

(G) Guaranteed by the International League of Travel Agents

### Holiday A

Two weeks in a self-catering cottage near Snowdonia in the heart of North Wales at the height of the summer season. You travel in your own car.

| | |
|---|---|
| Travel: | €100 |
| Accommodation: | €500 |
| Meals: | €300 |
| Spending money: | €300 |
| *Spending money with discount:* | *€450* |

(A)

### Holiday B

Ten days' cycling in Brittany, Northern France. Accommodation is provided in farmhouses and small family-run *chambres d'hôte*. You buy your own lunches. Travel to France is by train and a six-hour ferry.

| | |
|---|---|
| Travel: | €250 |
| Accommodation: | €550 |
| Meals: | €200 |
| Spending money: | €200 |
| *Spending money with discount:* | *€370* |

### Holiday C

Two weeks on a caravan site in April on the coast of Northumberland. Travel to the campsite by own car. The campsite includes leisure complex with indoor heated pool, bars and theatre. A full programme of entertainment is provided.

| | |
|---|---|
| Travel: | €100 |
| Accommodation: | €200 |
| Meals: | €300 |
| Spending money: | €600 |
| *Spending money with discount:* | *€690* |

(A)

### Holiday D

Three weeks' camping in the South of France during August. The campsite is located by the beach and also has its own outdoor swimming pool, tennis courts, crazy golf, etc. Travel by your own car and through the Channel Tunnel.

| | |
|---|---|
| Travel: | €350 |
| Accommodation: | €200 |
| Meals: | €350 |
| Spending money: | €350 |
| *Spending money with discount:* | *€490* |

(G)

### Holiday E

A fly-drive one-week holiday at Disney World in Florida. Accommodation is in one of several different themed hotels with meals included. This holiday can be taken at any time of the year.

| | |
|---|---|
| Travel: | €900 |
| Accommodation: | included |
| Meals: | included |
| Spending money: | €200 |
| *Spending money with discount:* | *€370* |

(A)

(G)

### Holiday F

A two-week cruise on the Nile, visiting all the most famous monuments such as the Pyramids. All meals are included and travel is by charter flight.

| | |
|---|---|
| Travel: | €1000 |
| Accommodation: | included |
| Meals: | included |
| Spending money: | €100 |
| *Spending money with discount:* | *€290* |

(G)

### Holiday G

A 50:50 chance of a once-in-a-lifetime trip to Australia for three weeks, which includes stopovers in Sydney, Adelaide and Canberra, as well as a chance to explore the bush with Australia's Aboriginal peoples. You pay the all-inclusive price and have *a one-in-two chance* of being selected from the draw.

| | |
|---|---|
| Travel: | €850 |
| Accommodation: | included |
| Meals: | included |
| Spending money: | €250 |
| *Spending money with discount:* | *€410* |

### Holiday H

A ten-day Easter-break holiday in the Greek islands, staying in small hotels. Cost includes all flights, but meals are paid for separately.

| | |
|---|---|
| Travel: | €650 |
| Accommodation: | included |
| Meals: | €200 |
| Spending money: | €300 |
| *Spending money with discount:* | *€450* |

Reproduced from *Modern Social Work Practice* by Mark Doel and Steven M. Shardlow, Ashgate, Aldershot, 2005

# Teaching notes: *Managing resources*

## Opportunities

Complaints about the shortage of resources are commonly heard in social work agencies – indeed, across the public sector generally. Students should be encouraged to hear these voices, whether they originate with other professionals, service users or politicians. Although these complaints are frequently made, it is important for students to evaluate their validity. Are resources really insufficient? Could they be put to better use? In all agencies, the day-to-day business of providing social work will highlight many examples that illustrate how resources are prioritized. These can all be used to provide good opportunities for reflection and learning.

*Travel agent* is an activity that simulates some aspects of choosing a holiday. At first sight, this seems far removed from social work practice; however, the factors that influence the selection of a holiday are similar to some aspects of the available choice about services for those living in the community.

## Key influences on holiday choice

No matter which route we take to choose a holiday, certain factors are likely to influence our final decision. The importance of each of these factors will vary from individual to individual and family to family. A disabled person might look first at accessibility, and then have to take their budget into consideration. A well-to-do family might look at available entertainment for the children, with less concern for price. Below are some of the factors that may apply when choosing a holiday; these should be discussed with the student during the practice tutorial.

- Access
- Climate
- Entertainment
- Location
- Time of year
- Availability
- Convenience
- Facilities
- Price
- Budget
- Diet
- Lifestyle
- Quality of service

Encourage students to think about the relative importance of these factors in making their decision about their chosen holiday. Broaden the discussion so that students consider the importance of holidays relative to a service that a person may depend on for their day-to-day well-being, such as home care, meals delivered to their home, washing and bathing, respite or permanent residential care.

Students should also consider the possible kinds of information they would expect to have available to guide their choice:

- choice of travel agents for independent advice
- information direct from holiday companies (the providers of holidays)

- online information services to provide updated information about availability and price
- ability to negotiate directly with the holiday company
- information available at no charge
- availability of detailed brochures about a variety of holidays worldwide
- availability of many different types of holiday
- varying levels and packages of insurance (concerning cancellation, theft, loss and medical costs; and the company's liability and so on)
- procedures for complaints.

Students can think about the similarities and differences inherent in the process of selecting a holiday and 'choosing' a care package. People choosing a holiday are able to decide independently, to book directly with a holiday company and to purchase the service they require; they are not obliged to consult a travel agent. Compare this with the process of gaining access to social services when the person has to consult an 'agent' (a social worker or care manager)

*How far are similar facilities and options open to the person who is making choices about care in the community?*

Oliver, recasting Titmus's ideas, has argued that it should be possible in principle to go for a social services system to provide choice for people:

> It should be possible to allow for choice and control in service provision within a universal infrastructure if consumers have social rights to these services and if there are mechanisms whereby the needs of groups and communities, whether local or interest communities, can be articulated by them, themselves. (Oliver, 1990: 99)

Similar themes are expressed in the 1975 UN Declaration of Rights for Disabled People, which emphasizes the importance of being self-reliant, to have choice over how to live, and to be able to participate in the social, recreational and creative opportunities of communities. However, the real question is not one of principle about desirability, but how to achieve the UN Declaration of Rights' or Oliver's prescriptions in practice, within existing political and social structures.

> A package of care is not like a basket of goods and services; it is a fluid set of human relationships and arrangements. The care manager's main tasks will be to make the efforts of the people involved coherent; to ensure that the care of a dependent person is not dropped like the baton of a badly co-ordinated relay team. (Smale *et al.*, 1994: 4)

# Learning notes: *Managing resources*

## Care management

The dominant approach to managing resources found within the UK in social work is 'care management'. According to the Social Services Inspectorate (1991a, 1991b), care management can be understood as a number of processes:

*Stage 1*

Prospective users and carers receive information about the needs for which care agencies accept responsibility to offer assistance and the range of services currently available.

*Stage 2*

If an enquirer requests more than information or advice, basic information is taken about the need in question, sufficient to determine the type of assessment required.

*Stage 3*

A practitioner is allocated to assess the needs of the individual and of any carers, in a way that also recognizes their strengths and aspirations. In order to take account of all relevant needs, assessment may bring together contributions from a number of other specialists or agencies. The purpose of the assessment is to define the individual's need in the context of local policies and priorities and agree on the desired outcome of any involvement.[1]

*Stage 4*

The next step is to consider the resources available from statutory, voluntary, private or community sources that best meet the individual's requirements. The role of the practitioner is to assist the user in making choices from these resources, and to construct an individual care plan.

*Stage 5*

The implementation of that plan means securing the necessary finance or other identified resources. It may involve negotiation with a variety of service providers, specifying the type and quality of service required, and ensuring that services are

---

[1] See the reservations we have expressed about this view of assessment in Chapter 6.

Reproduced from *Modern Social Work Practice* by Mark Doel and Steven M. Shardlow, Ashgate, Aldershot, 2005

coordinated with one another. The responsibility of practitioners at this stage will vary according to the level of their delegated budgetary authority.

*Stage 6*

Because circumstances change, the implementation of the care plan has to be continuously monitored, making adjustments as necessary to the services provided, and supporting the users, carers and service providers in achieving the desired outcomes.

*Stage 7*

At specified intervals, the progress of the care plan has to be formally reviewed with the user, carers and service providers: first to ensure that services remain relevant to needs and, second, to evaluate services as part of the continuing quest for improvement.

Within this process there are many necessary social work skills, some of which are detailed in other chapters of this book (see especially Chapters 4–8). The essence of the process of care management, as stated by the Social Services Inspectorate, is located in the assessment of people's needs, the construction and purchase of a care plan to meet those needs, and the review of the effectiveness of this plan. Hence the so-called 'purchaser–provider' split in agencies has developed, where some staff will be entirely concerned with assessing people's need for services, purchasing those from within a limited budget, while others may be concerned with the provision of services.

Care in the community provides considerable opportunities for the involvement of service users and carers. The question is, how to achieve involvement in the process of care management? Breeforth (1993: 23) characterizes traditional professional attitudes to the involvement of service users and carers, in relation to an example drawn from the provision of mental health service, as follows:

> *The officials' view.*
> we're the providers of mental health services
> we know what is best
> we have to organise services
> we must have user participation
> let's set up a users' group
> do we know any users we can ask?

Breeforth suggests instead that social workers must adjust the way that they think about the involvement of users as follows:

> *How to involve service users (and carers)*

Reproduced from *Modern Social Work Practice* by Mark Doel and Steven M. Shardlow, Ashgate, Aldershot, 2005

get users together
leave us alone to talk
invite us onto your committees
listen to what we say
give us information
pay our expenses

Involving service users in the process of community care is not a simple process. Lindow and Morris (1995), reviewing then published research, found evidence of several barriers to their involvement:

- the division of people into service user groups (for example, older people, people with sensory impairment)
- consulting with carers rather than service users
- exclusion of service users' views because of perceptions about the incapacity of the user to understand or communicate (for example, due to dementia)
- differences of culture and language
- the marginalization of some groups (for example, older people)
- the difficulties of being clear as to who is representative of whom and to whom people are accountable.

These barriers can be overcome. In advancing the involvement of service users, equal attention should be paid to carers. For example, there is a legal requirement to assess their needs under the terms of The Carers (Recognition and Services) Act (1995).

## Resources and change

WE TRAINED VERY HARD, BUT IT SEEMED THAT EVERY TIME WE WERE BEGINNING TO FORM INTO TEAMS WE WOULD BE REORGANIZED. I WAS TO LEARN LATER IN LIFE THAT WE TRIED TO MEET ANY NEW SITUATION BY REORGANIZING, AND A WONDERFUL METHOD IT WAS FOR CREATING THE ILLUSION OF PROGRESS WHILST PRODUCING CONFUSION, INEFFICIENCY AND DEMORALIZATION.

(Petronius, AD 166)

The ground is continually shifting. Just when it seems as though we might have grasped the processes for managing resources, we find ourselves in a changed world. Moreover, the process of change is itself changing. It is accelerating. In the social care sector, multiple changes in policy and practice are occurring simultaneously. Bruggen (1997) found that 75 per cent of middle and senior social work managers reported that their organizations were undertaking two or more change initiatives at any one time. Such a rate of change places considerable demands on those who manage resources. The effect, apart from possible 'change fatigue', is that it is increasingly difficult to separate out the various consequences of

Reproduced from *Modern Social Work Practice* by Mark Doel and Steven M. Shardlow, Ashgate, Aldershot, 2005

different changes, to coolly weigh up which changes lead to a particular improvement in a service or, indeed, to a deterioration (Lindow and Morris, 1995).

## Managing your time

Your own time is one of the most important resources at your disposal. Yet the skills of managing time are not intuitive; they can be learned. A placement can start to go wrong when practice teachers make incorrect assumptions about students' basic abilities to organize their own time. This is the first step to managing the workload. It can seem pedantic to investigate how you remember the tasks you have set yourself, or how you collect and store information for regular use. Perhaps this is one reason why these core abilities are often assumed to be present; they are the day-to-day backdrop to the 'real work'.

Two students, Cathy and Henry, were on placement in a small social work team. They met to discuss how they had arrived at their decisions about managing their own time. These principles came out of their discussion with the practice teacher:

1   *Be clear about the status of each diary entry – is it tentative or definite?*
    'Can you tell at a glance what you're doing on Thursday at 2.30?' Henry confessed to making frequent scribbles and deletions; Cathy suggested using pencil until it was confirmed. 'Some feasts are movable and some aren't'.
2   *Prioritize diary entries according to urgency and others' expectations.*
    'Are you aware of the criteria you used to plan your diary time?' Cathy and Henry had both used urgency as their main priority. Whose circumstances warranted contact early in the week and what promises, if any, had been made about contacting people? They had made very similar decisions about this and expressed pleasure at their like minds.
3   *Pace appointments economically.*
    'What about the space you've allowed between diary entries?' Cathy and Henry were conscious of working in a neighbourhood and were committed to the localization of services. They were careful to group their destinations to avoid either zipping back and forth across the map or twiddling their thumbs between appointments. They had taken account of their method of transport – car in Cathy's case, foot and bus in Henry's.
4   *Consider what times will accommodate other people involved in the work.*
    'Have you considered the use of other people's time?' Cathy and Henry had thought about the circumstances of individuals and their families when planning appointments. Nine o'clock in the morning might be a convenient time to visit eighty-three-year-old Mr Cook, but was not a time that Mr Cook would welcome. Planning a first visit to a family around school collection time or meal times was not wise either. Cathy liked Henry's suggestion of an evening appointment to include a working parent, and both students had scheduled their diary to accommodate part-time and job-share staff.

Reproduced from *Modern Social Work Practice* by Mark Doel and Steven M. Shardlow, Ashgate, Aldershot, 2005

5 *Anticipate the unanticipated by building dual-purpose times into the diary.*
'How do you cope with unexpected work which disrupts your programme?' Cathy and Henry developed a metaphor that they had found useful in planning their diary time. A diary can be made of cast iron, netting or elastic. A cast-iron diary is unlikely to be able to respond to new demands; on the other hand, the holes in a diary made of netting are liable to see appointments falling through. Ideally, the elastic diary has a mix of firm appointments and dual-purpose times, which are scheduled for one purpose (for example, reading a policy paper or making non-priority phone calls) but can stretch or contract for other purposes if necessary.

6 *Anticipate the 'imprint effect'.*
'What effect is the experience of one event likely to have on the next?' After the first few weeks of the placement, events in the working week are more familiar, so students can anticipate their after-taste. For example, Cathy and Henry could say whether the working party was likely to leave them feeling stimulated/ bored, appreciated/isolated, calm/angry. It is often possible to anticipate how you will feel after visiting service users or carers groups that you already know. Using this information, it is possible to obtain the most 'helpful mix' of diary entries – in theory!

7 *Appointments with myself.*
'What helps you to keep your batteries topped up?' The most difficult aspect of the diary for Cathy and Henry was planning a regular hour's break each day and setting aside time for professional development, when they could pursue their own research interests and keep abreast of developments in social work. These tended to be given the lowest priority and were readily swallowed up. Yet things like a midday swim and time for professional development were crucial to survival and avoiding burn-out. They both agreed to pen, not pencil, appointments with themselves.

If you use these principles clearly, coherently and consistently, you can feel confident that you are gaining command of your workload and helping to reduce the stresses of the job. It is crucial to *work smart, not hard.*

## Assessment notes: *Managing resources*

The student needs to be clear where the limits of their responsibility for managing resources lie and to reflect this in any assessment task for their portfolio. Clearly, for most students, managing resources such as their own time is likely to be more of a priority than the management of high-profile agency resources. It is likely that you will have some responsibility for the management of some resources, such as your own time, from your earliest practice learning opportunity. You will be expected to demonstrate your competence in using time constructively throughout the practice learning. In addition, you will be expected to demonstrate that you understand the

Reproduced from *Modern Social Work Practice* by Mark Doel and Steven M. Shardlow, Ashgate, Aldershot, 2005

difficulties of managing resources from the managers' perspectives and, most importantly, how the constraints that managers face construct the nature of choice for service users and carers. Acknowledging the organization's world-view is not necessarily to accept it and certainly should not obscure the service users' views of the way in which resources are managed. You will, therefore, be expected to demonstrate that you understand the implications of resource management from a variety of perspectives.

## Further reading

Bamford, T. (2001), *Commissioning and Purchasing*. London: Routledge/Community Care.

Payne, M. (1995), *Social Work and Community Care*, Basingstoke: Macmillan.

Sharkey, P. (2000), *The Essentials of Community Care: a guide for practitioners*, Basingstoke: Macmillan.

# 11 Accountability

## About Activity 11     Held to account

There are different mechanisms by which social workers can be held accountable to service users and carers, colleagues and the wider society for their actions. This activity focuses on exploring those mechanisms through which accountability can be made effective.

   *Held to account* can be completed by a practice teacher and student jointly, or by a group of practice teachers and students. A group of students who are placed in different kinds of setting produces a variety of perspectives.

### Purpose

This activity helps the student to think critically about the extent to which professionals can be held to account for their actions by their managers, service users and carers. In addition, students are encouraged to explore the mechanisms that are used to hold professionals to account, and also how the ideal differs from the reality.

### Method

- Each person needs a copy of *Held to account*. The activity can be used without prior preparation or students can be given a copy of the activity in advance of the practice tutorial (supervision session).
- The student (or students) should complete the activity prior to discussion in a practice tutorial.
- During the practice tutorial explore the reasons for any difference of view: it is important for students to consider carefully which principles and values underpin the views that they hold. Encourage a careful consideration of the difference between the ideal and the reality.

## Variations

*Held to account* presents students with a series of examples where service users and carers might wish to find ways to hold social workers to account. Different scenarios can be developed and used in place of those suggested – for example, to explore the particular accountability issues in any given learning environment. You can also ask students to consider how other professionals are held to account, such as Dr Thomas in one of the activity scenarios.

## Use by other professions

Increasing demands for greater professional accountability are not restricted to professionals working in the field of social work. For example, professional practitioners in education and healthcare have experienced similar pressures to be more accountable for their actions.

We should also be concerned about the accountability of policy-makers. In a recent study, Campbell *et al.* (2003) sought to investigate 'public accountability' indirectly by measuring the impact of the myriad government initiatives seeking to improve the quality of healthcare. They compared clinical practice in 2001 with similar practice in 1998 across some twenty-three general practices in England. The study explored key indicators such as the quality of chronic disease management, elderly and mental healthcare, access to care, continuity of care, costs and so on. Campbell and colleagues found some improvements in the quality of care – suggesting that the initiatives had some impact. This is a different level of accountability; it concerns the accountability of public bodies for the way in which they spend public money to achieve specific objectives. (In this example it also concerns the accountability of GPs for the way in which they operationalized the scheme.)

## National Occupational Standards for Social Work

The topics in this chapter relate to the following National Occupational Standards (see the Appendix):

14:   Accountability
16:   Managing information.

## *Activity 11*      *Held to account*

This activity draws on Activity 1, *Licensed to learn*. Three of the people that you met in the first chapter are service users in your practice learning site, and the following issues present you with concerns that relate to accountability and access to information.

1   *Carefully consider the following additional information about three of the Green Hill flats residents.*

---

**Zoë Benner**, then aged 18, returns to her children's home two years after leaving and asks to see her records – having expressed some concerns about her treatment while living at the home. During the placement, you have read some past files, and these confirm your view that they contain very subjective, often destructive, opinions. Some of these workers are still employed in the home, but others have left. You are not sure about the department's policy on past files. At the staff meeting, Zoë's request is discussed. What is your view?

---

**Sam Weiner** is a regular visitor to the mental health day centre where you are on placement. One morning he arrives very angry because he has caught sight of his notes at the local general hospital (he opened the blue envelope carrying information about him from one department to another). He is being treated for a viral infection, and the notes from the consultant to the laboratory describe him as 'a homosexual and a drug addict'. Sam is openly gay, but does not see this as relevant and, although he took an overdose in the past, he has not been dependent on drugs. Sam wants to know what he can do about this and what you can do to help.

---

Dr Thomas, a psychiatrist at the local hospital that serves Green Hill flats, writes a report to you about **Avis Jenkins**, who is about to be discharged following her admission four weeks ago, suffering from delusions which may or may not be a symptom of her physical health. Dr Thomas states at the bottom of his letter that he does not wish Mrs Jenkins to see the report because it might provoke a reoccurrence of her delusional state. What do you do?

---

Reproduced from *Modern Social Work Practice* by Mark Doel and Steven M. Shardlow, Ashgate, Aldershot, 2005

2　*Using the left-hand column of the attached sheet, prioritize these requests. In which order would you respond to these situations?*
Remember that you will be held to account for your decisions, both by your managers and by service users and carers. You must be able to justify your decision, remembering that a personal preference for work with one kind of situation is not a justification (see Chapter 10 – there is a considerable overlap between accountability and priorities).

3　*Now using the right-hand column of the attached sheet, consider how, in an ideal world, you would like to respond to these situations.*
Compare what you could actually do in your practice agency with what you would like to do by writing five key points that refer to each of these situations. Then, with your practice teacher, explore the reasons for any differences between the ideal and reality.

Reproduced from *Modern Social Work Practice* by Mark Doel and Steven M. Shardlow, Ashgate, Aldershot, 2005

| *The ideal* | *The actual* |
|---|---|
| Zoë Benner | Zoë Benner |
| 1 | 1 |
| 2 | 2 |
| 3 | 3 |
| 4 | 4 |
| 5 | 5 |
| Sam Weiner | Sam Weiner |
| 1 | 1 |
| 2 | 2 |
| 3 | 3 |
| 4 | 4 |
| 5 | 5 |
| Avis Jenkins | Avis Jenkins |
| 1 | 1 |
| 2 | 2 |
| 3 | 3 |
| 4 | 4 |
| 5 | 5 |

Reproduced from *Modern Social Work Practice* by Mark Doel and Steven M. Shardlow, Ashgate, Aldershot, 2005

# Teaching notes: *Accountability*

Addressing issues of accountability at an early stage of the period of practice learning may seem premature, and you certainly need to avoid frightening the student unnecessarily. Nonetheless, students will want to advise people accurately about their rights in relation to the agency's responsibilities. There is a parallel with the preparations for the student's own placement: is everybody clear about the procedures if there is disagreement or things go wrong? For example, if you have concerns about the student's competence, or your student is dissatisfied with your availability to give supervision, is there a clear path to be followed? Similarly, students need to be able to advise service users and carers.

One way to encourage students to think about accountability is to encourage them to consider how they keep records – a very visible sign of being accountable. A good way for students to test whether they are making fair, accurate and concise records of their work is to share these with service users and carers (Doel and Lawson, 1986). Through the dynamic use of records, students can demonstrate their accountability (except in a few of the most sensitive cases, usually concerning child protection investigations or mental health assessments for formal admission to hospital where agency policy may preclude the explicit sharing). The student receives immediate feedback from the service user and carer, both about the recording (use of language and so on) and the work itself. In this way, both the student and the service user/carer are able to check out whether they are working along the same lines, because it is hard to fudge the record. They are therefore demonstrating mutual accountability.

## Opportunities

Initially, many students may think about 'accountability' in terms of themselves – that is, for what can they be held to account. To introduce students to the complex notion of 'accountability' it is helpful to take a 'real-world' approach that can be used to illustrate the interaction between personal and institutional accountability. From the point of registration as a social work student to the point of qualification, issues of accountability arise through, for example, direct practice, the need to know about legislation such as the Data Protection Act (1984), and the professional requirements of the licensing bodies (such as CCW, GSCC, NISCC and SSSC).

# Learning notes: *Accountability*

There is broad consensus about how to define and understand the notion of accountability. Clark states that:

> Accountability is an intrinsic part of collaboration. It refers first to the requirement upon a professional to perform her duties, in collaboration with colleagues, to the expected standard. Second it requires the professional to demonstrate the performance to the appropriate individuals, colleagues and authorities. (Clark, 2000: 60)

Helpfully, Bamford (1982: 125) identifies five different forms of accountability in the context of social work:

- personal accountability
- accountability to the employer
- accountability to other agencies
- public accountability
- accountability to the client.

To which might be added the notion of 'professional accountability' and 'legal accountability'. We will use these different forms of accountability as a framework to explore the notion further.

## Personal accountability

We are accountable to ourselves and to others for the way in which we conduct our affairs: this accountability may be expressed through religious commitment to a moral code or through a secular commitment to treat others as they would wish to be treated themselves (perhaps most famously expressed in the categorical imperative – Kant, 1785). Alternatively, our behaviour may also depend on the outcomes (for example, as in Utilitarianism) rather than on motive or adherence to a moral code.

## Accountability to the employer

Employees are accountable to their employers for work undertaken as part of their role and duties. It is for the employee to maintain any codes of conduct that the employer may require. A range of employment legislation, different in all countries, exists to protect employers from abusing the position that they hold. Employers may not require or expect employees to perform illegal or immoral acts as part of their employment. When joining an organization, as a student for a period of practice learning, it is essential to keep to the rules and requirements expected of employees. Accountability to the employer is perhaps the most visible form of accountability.

## Accountability to other organizations

The development of the 'mixed economy of welfare' has had many consequences for practitioners, service users and carers alike. One of the most clearly evident has been the fragmentation of service delivery. There are now many more service providers than previously, both in the not-for-profit and the private sectors. At an institutional or governmental level the 'fragmented' character of service delivery, whatever the desired ideological characteristics, is problematic in the context of ensuring that service providers are publicly accountable for the quality of service they provide. Sullivan (2003) has suggested that it is necessary to move away from traditional notions of public accountability where one central body (i.e. government) holds others to account – so-called 'vertical accountability' – and instead to adopt 'horizontal' accountability mechanisms, whereby locally-based organizations 'join up' in mutually interactive accountability structures – something that, nonetheless, requires local government to adopt a strong coordination role. An example of how to develop a 'horizontal' approach to 'neighbourhood-based governance' through the relationships and participatory mechanisms evident in various community organizations in three cities has been examined by Chaskin (2003). You might like to consider the extent to which organizations within the area in which your practice is based are part of 'horizontal' systems of accountability. To what extent are the organizations able to hold each other to account?

## Public accountability

In the past ten years, across the public sector in the UK, there have been many attempts to improve the performance of public-sector organizations. Most notably this has centred on the creation of league tables denoting the performance of hospitals, schools, universities and so on. In the field of social care in England, 2002 saw the creation of a ranking system for local authority social services through the creation of *performance indicators* – a list of fifty key targets on which local authorities are ranked and cumulatively graded with either one, two or three stars – the worst authorities receiving no stars.[1]

The impact has been significant – to the extent that some Directors of Social Services have lost their jobs because their authority failed to achieve a high ranking. Even more importantly, these indicators have been used to control the way in which staff behave in relation to service users and carers. Hence, meeting the performance target becomes more important than meeting the needs of the service user or carer. This regulatory framework generates its own set of imperatives which, perversely,

---

[1] Details at http://www.doh.gov.uk/pssratings/index.htm

Reproduced from *Modern Social Work Practice* by Mark Doel and Steven M. Shardlow, Ashgate, Aldershot, 2005

may lead to a worse service for service users and carers. There is considerable criticism about the effectiveness of the 'star system' as a mechanism for improving public accountability (see, for example, Cutler and Waine, 2003).

Recent public disasters (in particular, the recent rail crashes in the UK at Potters Bar and Paddington) have raised questions about the adequacy of the law in respect to corporate accountability. This has raised the question of the need for a new offence to be added to the statute book – corporate manslaughter. A similar question has been raised in relation to the protection of vulnerable adults and children; the Home Office has recently announced that it intends to draft new legislation which could see local authorities on trial for manslaughter where there was evidence of a dereliction of duty leading to the death of a vulnerable adult or child (King, 2003).

## Accountability to service users and carers

High-quality social work practice is founded on the notion that the social worker is accountable to service users and carers for the work done with them or on their behalf. In many professions, this accountability is direct, immediate and individualized through the payment of fees. In such circumstances a service user or carer who is not satisfied with the service they receive may go elsewhere. In many countries, however, the nature of social work is such that service users and carers do not pay social workers, although there are some notable exceptions (such as the US where there is a significant volume of private social work practice). Nevertheless, irrespective of whether accountability to service users and carers is mediated by money, the social worker must *feel* and *is* accountable to the service user or carer for the work done.

The mechanisms to provide for accountability to service users and carers are:

- appeal mechanisms (the ability to appeal against a decision that has been made, such as not being awarded a place in a home for older people)
- complaints procedures (the ability to complain about the maladministration or delivery of services, such as a social worker repeatedly failing to make visits)
- the provision of high-quality information (if service users and carers receive full and detailed information about what is done on their behalf and records are truly open, they are enabled to challenge the social worker and hold the social worker to account)
- statutory review mechanisms enacted through bodies such as a children's rights commissioner (often termed an ombudsman) who will investigate complaints if these cannot be resolved at lower organizational levels. Such a commissioner exists for Wales, and there is agreement to appoint one for England (Children's Rights Alliance for England, 2003).

Reproduced from *Modern Social Work Practice* by Mark Doel and Steven M. Shardlow, Ashgate, Aldershot, 2005

We should be cautious in assuming that these mechanisms deliver anything but a flawed accountability to service users and carers. Preston-Shoot, for example, has criticized the impact of complaints procedures in an article entitled 'A Triumph of Hope over Experience?' (Preston-Shoot, 2001). The availability of such mechanisms does not of itself entail that they are accessible or can be used by service users and carers; it is incumbent upon social work agencies to develop approaches that enable service users and carers to make use of these mechanisms.

---

**Me holding others to account**
To get a *feel* of the service user or carer perspective, you might like to consider how it feels to have records made about you. Your service users and carers are the subjects of the records that you write. You are the subject of many records, too. Make a note of all the different agencies that you know will have some form of written record about you (your doctor, your bank, and so on). Are there any agencies which you suspect will have some record but about which you are not sure? How could you find out what is written about you in these files? How could you hold these agencies to account?

---

## Professional accountability

Professional codes of ethics have been adopted by many national professional social work associations: for example, in Australia by the AASW (2000), in the US by the NASW (1996) and, at an international level, by the International Federation of Social Workers (IFSW, 1994). Likewise the National Organisation of Practice Teachers (NOPT, 2000) has a *Code of Practice* for practice teachers (student supervisors). Such codes present, to the external world, a consensus about how the organization's membership define the nature and purpose of social work and the professional obligation to the broader society. Moreover, such codes indicate desired behaviour by professional social workers and specify prohibited behaviour. As such, they provide a form of accountability, if they are enforceable. In respect of social work such *enforceable* codes of ethics have not existed in most countries. Social work has been an aspirant profession,[2] one which has sought to claim professional status, responsibility and autonomy.

In England, the General Social Care Council (GSCC, 2002) has devised a *Code of Practice for Social Care Workers* (which applies to all social care staff not just social workers). According to the GSCC, the code has the following function:

---

[2] It is some considerable time since social work was characterized as a semi-profession, an idea associated with the work of Etzioni (see the chapter in Etzioni's book written by Toren, 1969).

Reproduced from *Modern Social Work Practice* by Mark Doel and Steven M. Shardlow, Ashgate, Aldershot, 2005

The Code of Practice for Social Care Workers is a list of statements that describe the standards of professional conduct and practice required of social care workers as they go about their daily work. Again, this is the first time that standards have been set in this way at national level, although many employers have similar standards in place at local level. The intention is to confirm the standards required in social care and ensure that workers know what standards of conduct employers, colleagues, service users, carers and the public expect of them. (GSCC, 2002)

This is not a code of ethics, nor a statement of professional values – it is, as it suggests, a list of standards for the individual practitioner and for the provider of services. It is designed as a regulatory mechanism to promote accountability, which will be enforced through compliance mechanisms. Students should read the relevant *Code of Practice* and consider the extent to which organizational behaviour and the professional behaviour of social workers conforms to the requirements of the code.

## Legal accountability

In the US there is considerable concern in professional circles about the extent to which social workers may be held legally liable. The NASW website[3] advertises professional liability insurance that covers the following eventualities:

- treatment without proper consent
- incorrect treatment /improper diagnosis
- failure to consult with, or refer a client to, a specialist
- failure to prevent a client's suicide
- causing a client's suicide
- failure to protect third parties from harm
- inappropriate release/detainment of a client in a hospital/confinement
- sexual involvement with clients or other sexual misconduct (subject to reduced limits)
- breach of confidentiality
- defamation
- false imprisonment
- failure to provide adequate care for clients in residential settings
- failure to be available when needed
- termination of treatment
- improper child placement

In other countries social workers may be less likely to be held legally liable and to be sued at law for professional actions that are taken in the course of their work. However, it behoves all practitioners to consider carefully the nature of the society

---

[3] http://www.naswinsurancetrust.org/types of insurance/swmi swpli.asp

Reproduced from *Modern Social Work Practice* by Mark Doel and Steven M. Shardlow, Ashgate, Aldershot, 2005

in which they practise and the extent of liability that they face. In the UK there is one area where the social worker can be held professionally liable, namely when acting as an ASW (Approved Social Worker) under the current Mental Health Act 1983 (under review at the time of writing).

## Assessment notes: *Accountability*

Accountability is about a commitment to connectedness with others and also a demonstration of the extent and nature of that commitment through a range of formal mechanisms.

If, as a student, you feel you can 'go it alone' or that you don't need much help from others, then you may be in danger of thinking that you are only accountable to yourself – to your own well-developed moral conscience. If you tend towards these feelings, you need to consider very carefully your commitment to being fully accountable to others.

Accountability is about engagement with others and your willingness to explain to others what you are doing and why you are doing it. This may be demonstrated through examples of your practice where you have made service users and carers fully aware of their rights – for example, by providing information about how decisions made by your organization may be legitimately reviewed.

Remember that, in terms of your practice as a student, your practice teacher may very well be legally liable and accountable for the actions that you perform in your direct work with service users or carers (Gelman *et al.*, 1996; Gelman and Wardell, 1988; Reamer, 1994; Shardlow, 2000) – not a matter to be taken lightly.

## Further reading

Banks, S. (2002), 'Professional Values and Accountabilities', in R. Adams, L. Dominelli and M. Payne (eds), *Critical Practice in Social Work*, Basingstoke: Palgrave, pp. 28–37.

Shardlow, S.M. (1995), 'Confidentiality, Accountability and the Boundaries of Client–Worker Relationships', in R. Hugman and D. Smith (eds), *Ethical Issues in Social Work*, London: Routledge, pp. 65–83.

# 12 Whistleblowing

## About Activity 12      *The myth of Sisyphus*

The problem of disclosure of information in the public interest is not new. According to Greek mythology (Homer), Sisyphus was the wisest of mortals, who disclosed to the public that the god Zeus had abducted and raped Aegina, the king's daughter. For this act, Sisyphus was condemned by the gods to perpetual punishment in the Underworld. This punishment was to roll a large boulder up a hill, only to have to watch it roll down again and endlessly repeat the cycle. Encapsulated in this myth are all the fears, worries and potential consequences for those who contemplate the disclosure of information.

*The myth of Sisyphus* consists of an exercise, completed in advance of a supervision session, which has been designed to provide an opportunity to explore some of the types of situation in which students and practitioners may consider 'blowing the whistle'.

This chapter should be read in conjunction with Chapter 11, 'Accountability'.

### Purpose

*The myth of Sisyphus* is designed to help students think about some of the pressures that might impinge upon their willingness to 'blow the whistle'. It is very easy to adopt an idealized stance – for example, in a supervision session – and to make extravagant claims about when and under what circumstances one would be willing to 'blow the whistle'. However, taking such an action in the real word is something different. In any situation where 'blowing the whistle' is a real possibility, managing your own stress is vital, and involvement in any whistleblowing situation will increase the stress

### Method

- Students should read this chapter one week before the completed activity, *The myth of Sisyphus*, is due to be discussed in a supervision session.
- It may be desirable to encourage the student to read some additional material about whistleblowing, such as Hunt (1998), *Whistleblowing in the Social Services*.

## Variations

The situations used in *The myth of Sisyphus* can be readily amended to fit any other specialist practice contexts. However, there is considerable virtue in encouraging social work students to think broadly and outside of their developing specialist interests. It is interesting to explore the extent to which tolerance for a particular behaviour is engendered by familiarity with, or proximity to, the performance of that behaviour.

Given the increasing importance of interprofessional practice, a highly desirable variation is to employ the activity with a mixed group of students from different professions. Such a context allows for the exploration of conflicting expectations among professions, as Hewison and Sim (1998) suggest professional codes of ethics which apply to different professional groups may tend to foster professional distinctiveness and exclusivity and may form a barrier to effective interprofessional working in areas such as disclosure of information. Such codes may strongly influence the willingness of any particular professional to 'blow the whistle'.

## Use by other professions

The concerns over whether or not to 'blow the whistle' are universal and affect all professional groups. In respect of the National Health Service see Hunt (1995). *The myth of Sisyphus* can be easily modified using different situations to meet the particular concerns of any professional group. It can be applied even more broadly, for example, to the research community. Wenger *et al.* (1999) found that, in the US, scientists infrequently disclosed unethical behaviour outside of the research team – raising the question of whether this behaviour constitutes a cover-up or self-regulation within the profession.

## National Occupational Standards for Social Work

The topics in this chapter relate to the following National Occupational Standards (see the Appendix):

  5:   Achieving change
  8:   Working with groups
 11:   Meetings and other decision-making forums.

In addition, this chapter is relevant to the whistleblowing requirements of the CCW, GSCC, NISCC and SSSC.

## *Activity 12      The myth of Sisyphus*

Consider each of the 'boulders' that are rolling down the hill in turn. Read the description of each boulder below and consider which factors push you towards disclosing and 'blowing the whistle' and which factors pull you back or restrain you from making a disclosure. Write *key words* in each of the boulder boxes on the activity sheet. When you have written all of the 'push' and 'pull' factors that come to mind:

1   Weigh the relative strength of the 'push' and 'pull' factors and decide which is the strongest.
2   Decide which action you would take in respect of each boulder.
3   Compare each of the five boulders and consider the different push and pull factors, and consider whether there are any differences in the way in which you would respond to each boulder.
4   Ask yourself: what are the reasons for these differences in behaviour?

Remember, it can be too easy to profess to be bold in a simulated learning experience!

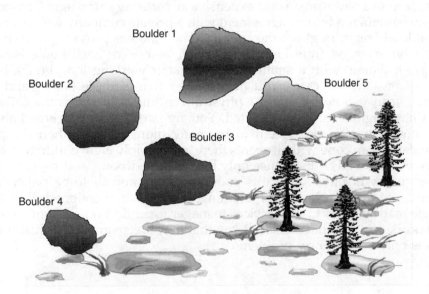

**Figure 12.1   The myth of Sisyphus – the boulders**

Reproduced from *Modern Social Work Practice* by Mark Doel and Steven M. Shardlow, Ashgate, Aldershot, 2005

### 'Boulder' 1

A carer, the parent of a person with learning difficulties, informs you that people with learning difficulties are being systematically abused in a residential unit owned and managed by your employer. You bring this to the attention of senior managers who seem unwilling to take action. Some six months later, you are visiting the unit and you witness an incident of a person with learning difficulties being verbally abused. You inform senior management, who thank you for your information. A further six months later you learn from a friend that nothing has happened.

### 'Boulder' 2

Your practice teacher 'jokes' that it is very easy to claim for expenses that have not been made. About a week later you hear him in the kitchen area saying much the same to another colleague. You think you hear him say that he has claimed several hundred pounds over the last few years. He sees you come in and notices your expression. At the next practice tutorial he explains that, over the years, he has run a number of user groups and has been completely unsuccessful in getting the agency to fund them, so he 'robs Peter to pay Paul'.

### 'Boulder' 3

The social work agency that you work for is desperately short of placements for children, despite a widespread and expensive advertising campaign. Consequently, the agency has entered into an agreement with a private company who provide care in several locations throughout the country. These homes provide group living for children who are aged from eight to fourteen years old. Each home is run as a 'family group home' with a small number of staff working long hours, but who provide a 'constancy of care'. You have visited two of these homes and, over a period of a year, you notice that the physical conditions in which the children are cared for have significantly deteriorated. You are particularly concerned about one of these homes where there seem to be many more children than the physical accommodation can cope with: it seems there are possibly eight children sleeping in one room in bunk beds – the house only has three bedrooms and two are used for staff. The quality of physical care is poor, and there appear to be rather 'scratch' meals and not much change of clothing. You have mentioned this to your immediate manager and to the services manager for children and families services. On both occasions, they have assured you that they are aware of the difficulties and that this is only a temporary problem.

Reproduced from *Modern Social Work Practice* by Mark Doel and Steven M. Shardlow, Ashgate, Aldershot, 2005

## 'Boulder' 4

You witness a colleague from another profession who appears to be unwell while conducting a joint assessment with you and a service user. However, you smell his breath and suspect that he is under the influence of alcohol. The behaviour of the colleague is rude and demeaning towards the service user, but his seniority, your newness to the team (you have only just started your placement) and your embarrassment in front of the service user means you feel unable to act there and then. You mention your concerns to your work-based supervisor who says that he is 'a bit of a maverick', but is really well respected. Another says she's heard he has some personal problems at present and tells you that it was probably a one-off. However, a third colleague tells you that it's about time something was done about him, but she's not going to stick her neck out because he's got friends in the right places.

   Despite reservations, you decide to follow this advice. In the final weeks of your placement, you go on three separate visits with this colleague. On the first two visits he is fine, but he turns up drunk to the third (four days before you leave the placement) and is offensive towards the service user.

## 'Boulder' 5

You have just been appointed to your first post as a qualified social worker in a statutory agency (a social services department). It is early March, and your new supervisor informs you that you must perform a certain number of assessments before 31 March (the end of the financial year), otherwise the authority is liable to lose a large amount of grant. Indeed, if the department does not meet its target, it is likely to be be penalized by £1 million, which would have a devastating impact on services. The supervisor explains that staff vacancies and the inadequacies of the person you are replacing have led to this situation. She realizes that you will not be able to complete the assessments together with the user but, as long as the forms are filled in before the 31st, 'you can do the proper work and do joint assessments together with the service users and carers after then, when there's more time'. She realizes that this is not good practice, 'but we are all between a rock and a hard place'.

Reproduced from *Modern Social Work Practice* by Mark Doel and Steven M. Shardlow, Ashgate, Aldershot, 2005

# Push and pull activity sheet

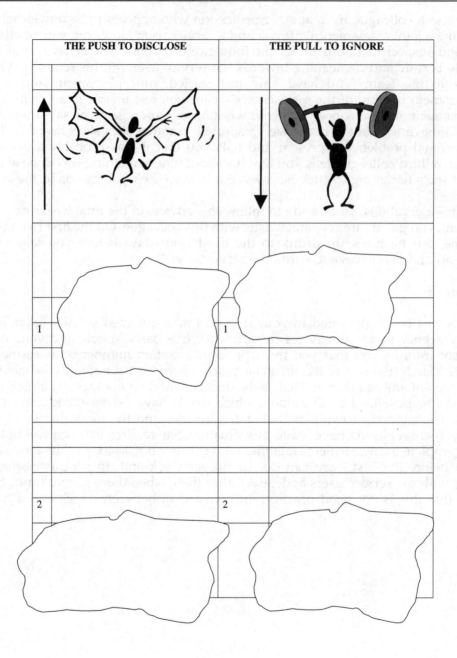

| THE PUSH TO DISCLOSE | THE PULL TO IGNORE |
|---|---|
| 1 | 1 |
| 2 | 2 |

# Push and pull activity sheet continued

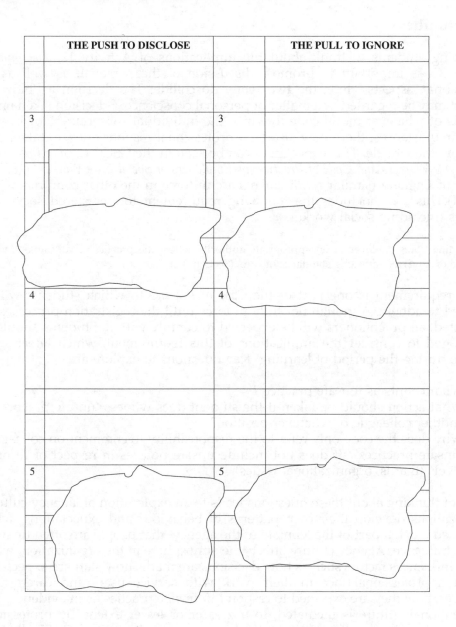

| | THE PUSH TO DISCLOSE | | THE PULL TO IGNORE |
|---|---|---|---|
| | | | |
| | | | |
| 3 | | 3 | |
| | | | |
| | | | |
| | | | |
| | | | |
| 4 | | 4 | |
| | | | |
| | | | |
| | | | |
| | | | |
| 5 | | 5 | |
| | | | |
| | | | |
| | | | |

Reproduced from *Modern Social Work Practice* by Mark Doel and Steven M. Shardlow, Ashgate, Aldershot, 2005

# Teaching notes: *Whistleblowing*

## Opportunities

In helping students to think about the implications of Activity 12, *The myth of Sisyphus*, it is important to promote discussion of the personal, as well as the professional, aspects. Here, the two really do collide. The decision to 'blow the whistle' may be regarded as a matter of personal conscience: a decision taken on the grounds of whatever moral code to which the individual subscribes. However, in some circumstances, there may also be a professional responsibility to take action and blow the whistle. This expectation can be seen in the GSCC *Code of Practice for Social Care Workers and Code of Practice for Employers of Social Care Workers* (2002) in respect of England (similar requirements are in force in the other countries within the UK).This code includes the following requirement for registered social care workers (including social workers):

> Informing your employer or an appropriate authority where the practice of colleagues may be unsafe or adversely affecting standards of care. (Section 3.2)

This requirement is one part of the *Code of Practice* to which students will be expected to adhere. Although not fully in force until the registration processes are completed, all practitioners will be expected to comply with it. Students should be encouraged to consider the implications of this requirement, which affects their practice during the period of learning. Key questions to explore are:

- What counts as 'unsafe practice'?
- What action should be taken if the student does witness 'unsafe practice' by another colleague of whatever position?
- Why does the code only refer to the responsibility to comment on colleagues' 'unsafe practices'? It does not include unsafe policies in respect of resource levels (that is, organizational issues).

Part of thinking about these questions leads to an exploration of 'agency culture'. Organizations develop their own patterns of behaviour and expectations, which become so much a part of the 'climate of the agency' that people are often unaware of their influence. Agency culture affects the atmosphere in the organization, which in turn influences factors such as how decisions are made, how staff are expected to present a professional face in their work with service users and carers, and, moreover, how they are expected to respond if 'unsafe practice' is in evidence. This organizational culture is mediated, to a greater or lesser extent, by professional culture and by local culture (the particular team or unit or similar). Finally, it is shaped by *your* own individual style.

In some work settings, there is little opportunity for individual expression: for example, airline cabin crew all wear identical clothing, and they are trained to provide a uniform response to passengers. The similarity of clothing between crew members symbolizes the uniformity of service. The delivery of a common standard is to be welcomed, but uniformity may promote conformity and the willingness to accept low standards or 'unsafe practice'.

Working in some agencies may feel woolly, like 'knitting fog', because of the lack of clear pathways for decisions, whereas other agencies may have very centralized, policy-driven cultures with very clear expectations about professional behaviour. Where there is no clear agency expectation, practitioners have little option but to rely on their own personal values and beliefs about how to present themselves to people. Using our own personal beliefs is made more difficult because agency practice is fluid and constantly changing. These shifts and changes interact with our professional and personal values; it can be difficult for the practitioner to feel firmly grounded and confident that any proposed action is soundly based (Shardlow, 1989). Increasingly, greater reliance is placed on external benchmarks of good practice, such as the GSCC *Code of Practice* or the National Occupational Standards, which define expectations. In the context of 'whistleblowing', students can be encouraged to consider their own orientation towards the agency culture and whether or not this encourages openness and disclosure of difficulty.

Some organizations have a culture of no-fault reporting of errors and problems, which allows for anonymous disclosure. Where an organization adopts such an approach, it is clearly committed to the evolution of better practice.

The examples in the activity, *The myth of Sisyphus*, are primarily concerned with examples of professional practice that concern service users and carers. However, there are, of course, many other potential 'boulders' that the student should consider, most notably those that relate to workplace harassment and bullying on grounds such as sexual harassment (see for example, Thompson, 2000a).

# Learning notes: *Whistleblowing*

According to Vernon, whistleblowing can be defined using the US Federal Whistleblower Act 1989:

> ...which describes the concept and practice as encompassing the disclosure of information by an employee or ex-employee which they reasonably believe 'evidences a violation of any law, rule or regulation, or gross mismanagement or gross waste of funds, an abuse of authority or a substantial and specific danger to public health and safety'. (Vernon, 1998: 222)

From this definition, key questions to consider are:

- When might it be appropriate to blow the whistle?
- Is whistleblowing a virtue or a vice?

The answers to both questions are likely to be highly situation-specific.

## The legal position

In the UK, the Public Interest Disclosure Act (PIDA)[1] introduced in 1998, provided legal protection for those who 'blow the whistle'. The Act defined the extent of legal protection, specifying: those people who are protected; the kinds of disclosure that may be made; and circumstances in which disclosure is legally permissible.

### *Protected employees*

Employees who 'blow the whistle' are protected from being subjected to a 'detriment' by their employer (this can include being denied promotion or training opportunities, or being unfairly dismissed – they may be able, for example, to claim for unfair dismissal).[2]

*So, what can be disclosed and when is disclosure protected?*

Disclosures called *qualifying disclosures* (disclosures that fall under the legislation – a necessary, but not sufficient, condition for the disclosure to be protected) are those where employees are convinced that they can demonstrate that they have information to reasonably believe that one of the following has occurred, is occurring or is very likely to occur:

- a criminal offence
- the breach of a legal obligation
- a miscarriage of justice
- a danger to the health or safety of any individual

---

[1] The full text of the Act can be found at: http://www.hmso.gov.uk/acts/acts1998/19980023.htm; the Act makes significant amendments to the Employment Rights Act (1996).

[2] National Health Service practitioners such as GPs and dentists are included in these provisions despite the fact they are self-employed within the health service structure.

- damage to the environment
- deliberate covering up of information tending to show any of the above.

As might be expected, there are some restrictions on what may count as a qualifying disclosure. For example, it is not a qualifying disclosure if to make such a disclosure would:

- break the law – for example, breach the Official Secrets Act 1989 – then that is not a qualifying disclosure (as in the case of Michael Shayler, who disclosed MI5 intelligence secrets)
- breach professionally privileged information – for example, as in the case of a lawyer to disclose information obtained in the course of legal consultation with a client.

A qualifying disclosure becomes a *protected disclosure* where it is made:

a   to the worker's employer
b   to another person whom the worker reasonably believes to be responsible for the problem.

In these circumstances, a disclosure made in good faith by an employee is protected under the PIDA. There are circumstances in which the employee can make a more general disclosure (that is, not to his/her employer but to someone else in a particularly serious case) – namely if:

- the disclosure is made in *good faith*
- it is reasonable to believe that the information, and any allegation contained in it, are *substantially true*, and
- the disclosure does *not* result in *personal gain*.

In addition, at least two of these conditions must apply – the worker must believe that he/she would be subjected to a detriment by his/her employer, that destruction or concealment of information had taken place, or that the same or very similar information had been disclosed previously.

In other countries, the forms of legislation will vary. In the US, for example whistleblowers had limited protection under a range of federal statutes prior to the passing of the Sarbanes-Oxley Act of 2002. Even now, US law is primarily concerned with covering criminal behaviour in relation to fraud and other financial matters. By contrast, in the UK, the PIDA covers environmental damage, health and safety, and in fact any legal obligation to which the employer is subject.

## The good, the bad and the ugly

The following are all examples of whistleblowing.
*What are the common factors in each of these examples?*

Reproduced from *Modern Social Work Practice* by Mark Doel and Steven M. Shardlow, Ashgate, Aldershot, 2005

---

**Gary Brown, Abbey National**

In 1993, Gary Brown was working in Abbey National's marketing department when he noticed some potentially fraudulent activities. He reported them internally in May 1994, and the man suspected of wrongdoing was suspended. In 1997, the suspect was found guilty of stealing £2m. Brown was commended by the judge, received £25 000 from Abbey National and an invitation to rejoin the bank. Since his return in March 1998, Brown has been promoted three times.

---

**Dr Stephen Bolsin, Bristol Royal Infirmary**

Dr Stephen Bolsin worked as a consultant anaesthetist at the Bristol Royal Infirmary in the UK, but during the 1980s and 1990s he became concerned about the higher than normal death rate following open-heart surgery on babies. He raised his concerns with fellow colleagues and hospital managers, but they were not addressed. After the death in 1995 of Joshua Loveday after an open-heart operation, his parents complained to the General Medical Council. Bolsin supported their complaint. Consequently, three members of the hospital staff were found guilty of professional misconduct.

---

**Sherron Watkins, Enron**

Sherron Watkins was vice-president of corporate development at the US energy company, Enron. In August 2001, she sent a memo to Enron chairman Kenneth Lay warning him about accounting practices in the company. Lay instigated a limited investigation by Enron's lawyers, which found that there was no major problem. Watkins also raised her concerns with people at Andersen, Enron's auditors. Last month, Enron admitted it had overstated its profits dating back to 1997 by $600 m.

---

(All extracts from Horn, 2002)

## Whistleblowing in social work

By virtue of the very powerful position that many social workers have over other people's lives, social work is a discipline in which situations that require someone to 'blow the whistle' are likely to arise (Ells and Dehn, 2001). In his introductory chapter to the book *Whistleblowing in the Social Services*, Hunt (1998) comments that organizational failure is by no means confined to health and social care, but that what is required is a 'reform of accountabilities throughout national life' (see Chapter 11, Accountability). The book contains accounts of situations where chronic abuse of service users and carers has only been prevented by the willingness of someone to blow the whistle. Notable is the chapter by Fairweather (1998), describing how, from 1992 to 1995, working as an investigative journalist for the

London *Evening Standard*, she investigated (with a co-journalist, Payne) a string of abuses, related to Islington Borough Council, that, prompted some sixteen governmental inquiries.[3] She comments on the difficulties of finding anyone who would listen, the lies of the council, as well as the half-hearted response of the Department of Health, the police and the local authority. Furthermore, in her opinion, had it not been for the actions of one persistent whistleblower, 'Islington's Children's Homes would still be controlled by paedophiles, pornographers and pimps' (Fairweather, 1998: 20). The views and actions of the whistleblower were vindicated in the White report (White and Hart, 1995). Of equal importance in the book is the chapter by Taylor, who describes the experience of being a whistleblower (Taylor, 1998). As a consequence of seeking to expose the abuse of children in North Wales children's homes, Taylor lost her job. In the chapter she reports a similar experience to Fairweather, that of official indifference or a willingness not to believe allegations, or, if believed, not to take action; the indifference of the authorities even attracted the interest of *Private Eye* (Foot, 1997).[4] As Taylor comments:

> Modern social work appears to bend to whatever social, penal and economic ideologies are dominant. Its purpose is unclear, it has no independent goals or standards and its responses are reactive and crisis driven. (Taylor, 1998: 45)

These characteristics, when coupled with the core tasks that social workers undertake, such as the provision of care for, and protection of, vulnerable people, make clear why it is so important that service users and carers be adequately protected. Whistleblowing is one way of protecting them and has official government support and active encouragement, in respect of vulnerable adults, for example (Department of Health, 2003).

## Assessment notes: *Whistleblowing*

In an idealized world, it is easy to 'paint' a self-portrait in which we see ourselves as champions in the battle against injustice and deprivation. However, self-delusion about our capabilities to challenge organizations and 'blow the whistle' is dangerous. The assessment of the ability to blow the whistle must temper an idealized commitment to social justice with a recognition of the other commitments that individuals have to their families. These are often financial and militate the drive to challenge injustice. Hence, the assessment of the ability to 'blow the whistle' is not merely a matter of identifying those situations where it would be appropriate; it is also about motivation, commitment, support and personal strength. These factors will be very different for each individual.

---

[3] This period in Islington remains both topical and controversial. The leader of Islington Council during this period was Margaret Hodge, later to become an MP and, in 2003, Minister for Children as part of Tony Blair's government. Her appointment to the ministerial post led to a campaign in the national press for her removal; at the time of writing she remains in post.

[4] A national satirical fortnightly magazine.

## Further reading

Hunt, G. (ed.) (1998), *Whistleblowing in the Social Services: public accountability and professional practice*, London: Edward Arnold.

Martin, B. (1999), *The Whistleblower's Handbook: How to be an effective resister*, Charlebury: John Carpenter.

Thompson, N. (2000), *Tackling Bullying and Harrassment in the Workplace*, Birmingham: Pepar Publications.

# Part IV

## Themes of Practice

# CONTEXT: Evidence-based practice

Over the last ten years or thereabouts, 'evidence-based practice' has become a 'cornerstone concept' both of social work policy and practice – i.e. a concept that underpins the very notion of what policy-makers and practitioners believe makes for 'good' social work practice. Immediately, on reflecting about the significance of this statement, some questions flash speedily to mind. For example:

1 Is it really the case that only in the last ten years has evidence-based practice been important?
2 If this is so, upon what was social work based previously?
3 Why did it take so long to ground social work in evidence – if indeed 'evidence' has only figured for the last ten years?
4 Whose evidence counts?
5 What would social work *not* based on evidence look like?

To answer the last question first, social work, by intuition, is alive and well and thriving in some places. Moreover, the concept of 'evidence-based practice' is not as straightforward as it may seem. To begin to understand this concept it is perhaps easiest to turn to a commonly accepted and rather well-used definition, first put forward by Sackett *et al.* (1996). This was originally advanced in the context of 'evidence-based medicine' and has been adapted for use in the context of social welfare, notably by Sheldon:

> Evidence-based social care is the conscientious, explicit and judicious use of current best evidence in making decisions regarding the welfare of those in need of social services. (Sheldon, 1998: 16)

According to Sheldon, there are some key words in this definition:

- 'conscientious', which implies a rejection of the notion of subjectivity – in particular, adherence to ideas or practices on the grounds that they have become our favourites
- 'explicit', which implies that the justification is made evident to others
- 'judicious', which implies that the evidence must be cautiously and carefully applied.

179

This definition prompts us to ask these questions:

1   What is evidence-based practice?
2   What is the best way to begin to explore the nature and importance of 'evidence-based practice'?
3   How might evidence-based practice be applied by the practitioner in their day-to-day work?

To answer these questions, we should begin by attempting to understand what 'evidence-based practice' might be in the context of social work. The recognition of the need for a rational approach to the delivery of social care, based upon reviewing outcomes, has been present from the very inception of unified local authority social services departments in England and Wales (social work departments in Scotland). As a testament to this commitment to develop services based according to rational policy-making processes, the following comment from the Seebohm Report provides the philosophical grounding for these departments:

> The personal social services are large-scale experiments in helping those in need. It is both wasteful and irresponsible to set experiments in motion and to omit to record and analyse what happens. It makes no sense in terms of administrative efficiency, and however little intended, indicates a careless attitude towards human welfare. (*Report of the Committee on Local Authority and Allied Personal Social Services*, 1968: 142)

From this statement we should not draw the erroneous conclusion that the call to evaluate social work was suddenly discovered in the 1960s, as Sheldon and Chilvers comment:

> ... the first president of the National Association of Social Workers (NASW) made this [evaluation] the subject of his inaugural address in 1931 ...
> I appeal to you, measure, evaluate, estimate, appraise your results in some form, in any terms that rest on anything beyond faith, assertion, and the 'illustrative case'. Let us do this for ourselves before some less knowledgeable and gentle body takes us by the shoulders and pushes us into the street. (Cabot, 1931, cited in Sheldon and Chilvers, 2000: 6)

As Sheldon and Chilvers note, the *old* can be quite shocking! The *idea* of using information gained from the evaluation of past practice to inform future approaches is not of itself new or novel. It is sometimes claimed that the origins of the concept of 'evidence-based practice' are to be found in a book by Cochrane (1972), *Random Reflections on Health Services*. This may be the earliest use in the literature of the term 'evidence-based practice' but it is a concept with a much longer history.

Gray (2001) suggests that the call for 'evidence-based practice' arose in relation to the medical profession for the following reasons: differences between the intervention suggested by research findings and actual interventions; variations in clinical practice; economic pressure; and the impact of the information revolution (given that much more material can now be effectively disseminated to a much larger group of people). In social work discourse, there has been a strand of academic analysis and writing since the 1960s that has posed questions about which interventions work and which do not[1] (see, for example, Fischer, 1976; Macdonald *et al.*, 1992; Mullen and Dumpson, 1972; Reid and Hanrahan, 1980; Sheldon and Macdonald, 1999) and the importance of adopting a scientific approach to practice (Reid, 2001; Sheppard, 1995). Despite these concerns, the term 'evidence-based practice' is not found in a social work context until the 1990s.

## Putting evidence-based practice into effect

The central idea underpinning evidence-based practice is, in essence, a simple one: *to find and use the best knowledge available and to apply that knowledge in your work.* Yet, despite the apparent simplicity of the idea, the application to practice is less than straightforward. According to Trinder (2000), there are two emergent strands of evidence-based practice – the *empirical* and the *pragmatic*. We suggest that there are at least three orientations that students might develop towards the use of research in their practice, as well as the possibility that no use is made of evidence-based practice at all. We do not claim that each of these are of equal merit.

Figure IV.1 represents these three different orientations to the use and application of research by social work practitioners and managers. The higher up the pyramid, the greater the prescription in the way in which research evidence is used. These different orientations are described fully below. Students (and others) can ask themselves which position they favour and why. We have used the word 'orientation' to signify that students and practitioners can decide how they position themselves in relation to research-based knowledge. A person may not always occupy the same position on the pyramid[2] – it may be determined by their practice context, changing preferences or the availability of research evidence.

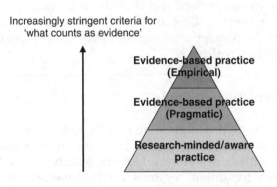

Increasingly stringent criteria for 'what counts as evidence'

Evidence-based practice (Empirical)

Evidence-based practice (Pragmatic)

Research-minded/aware practice

**Figure IV.1   A categorization of differing orientations towards research**

---

[1] It was through such research-based investigations that Task Centred Social Work developed.

[2] We should always be wary of inviting students to locate themselves in perpetuity in the confines of a given conceptual framework.

## The empirical orientation

The empirical orientation takes its name from Munro's flagship book *Understanding Social Work: an empirical approach* (2001). This orientation is characterized by: the most rigorous approach to the derivation of evidence (ideally through randomized control trials); the nature and quality of evidence that may be used; and the processes used to apply this evidence to practice. Philosophically, this orientation is grounded in the epistemology of Karl Popper (1959). In addition, there is a significant technical literature on how to achieve evidence-based practice. Sackett and colleagues list the following five steps necessary to apply evidence-based practice, as reported by Gibbs and Gambrill:

1   Convert information needs into answerable questions. Such questions are stated specifically enough to guide a computer search, concern the client's welfare, relate to a problem that has some chance of a solution, and ideally, formed in collaboration with the client. A well-formed question describes the client, course of action, alternate course(s) of action and intended result.
2   Track down, with maximum efficiency, the best evidence with which to answer the question. (This requires electronic access to bibliographic databases and skill in searching them efficiently and quickly enough to guide practice.)
3   Critically appraise the evidence for its validly and usefulness. (This entails applying a hierarchy relevant to several question/evidence types.)
4   Apply the results of this appraisal to policy/practice decisions. This requires deciding whether the evidence applies to the decision at hand, based on whether a client is similar enough to those studied, access to interventions described in the literature, weighing anticipated outcomes relative to concerns such as number, need to treat, practical, matters, and client's preferences.
5   Evaluate outcome. 'This may entail record-keeping including single-case designs.' (Sackett *et al.*, 1997: 3, as cited in Gibbs and Gambrill, 2002: 453–54)

The successful application of these steps requires that, amongst other things, social workers have access to computers and that there is readily available information that summarizes the current best evidence. The first of these matters is for employers to ensure. In respect of the codification of evidence, developments are underway to make this a reality.

---

### The empirical orientation: example

Covina Kauri is a student due to visit **Zoë Benner**. From reviewing the case materials before visiting (with a particular focus upon Kylie, Zoë's daughter, and her problem with bed-wetting). Covina searches for evidence about the impact of different treatment regimes for bed-wetting and identifies their relative success. Armed with this knowledge in advance of the visit to the family, Covina has a clear idea of what the options are and how these can be systematically implemented.

## What counts as evidence?

There is a supposed 'gold standard' for best available evidence, produced according to the Cochrane standards:

> The Cochrane Collaboration [founded in 1993] is an international non-profit and independent organisation, dedicated to making up-to-date, accurate information about the effects of healthcare readily available worldwide. It produces and disseminates systematic reviews of healthcare interventions and promotes the search for evidence in the form of clinical trials and other studies of interventions ...
>
> Those who prepare the reviews are mostly healthcare professionals who volunteer to work in one of the many Collaborative Review Groups, with editorial teams overseeing the preparation and maintenance of the reviews, as well as application of the rigorous quality standards for which Cochrane Reviews have become known. (Cochrane Collaboration, 2003)

There are strict rules governing how evidence should be weighed and then reported as part of a 'Cochrane-style' systematic review. Unsurprisingly perhaps, the medical world has a larger number of such reviews to draw upon than does the field of social care. In respect of social care, the Campbell Collaboration, (which mirrors the Cochrane Collaboration) was formally established in 2000 to produce systematic reviews of research evidence on behavioural interventions and public policy – in particular, education, criminal justice and social welfare. In addition, there are a growing number of resources that collect and disseminate evidence, notably: the Social Care Institute for Excellence (SCIE); Making Research Count (MRC); Research in Practice (RIP); the Centre for Evidence-Based Social Services (CEBSS) at the University of Exeter; the ESRC Evidence-Based Policy and Practice unit.[3] These initiatives represent an attempt to institutionalize decisions about 'current best evidence', so that the practitioner can be aware of the available knowledge and then apply given knowledge to a specific situation.

## Applying evidence to practice

Assuming that there is evidence and that this can be retrieved, it is then necessary to apply the knowledge to a given situation. This is perhaps the most challenging aspect of the evidence-based orientation. It is one matter to apply best evidence in a clinical environment where the process of differential diagnosis reveals the most likely explanation for any given set of symptoms. Once these are known, a particular treatment can be identified, implemented and evaluated. This is not the case in respect of social work, as Shaw and Shaw (1997) confirmed in their study of social workers, who were acutely aware of the ambiguity of social work evidence. As a response to some of these ambiguities and uncertainties, Webb has suggested that attention should be paid to models of decision-making which distinguish:

---

[3] Details can be found at the following websites: SCIE – www.scie.org.uk; MRC – www. makingresearchcount.org.uk/swk/research/mrc/welcome.html; RIP – www.rip.org.uk; CEBSS – www.ex.ac.uk/cebss; ESRC Evidence-Based Policy and Practice unit – www.evidencenetwork.org

1　the decision to be made
2　the chance of unknown events which can affect the result
3　the result itself. (Webb, 2002: 53)

He further suggests that that there is a range of decision-making models such as 'decision tree analysis' which have been used in clinical medicine and nursing but not, as yet, in social work. Whether the answer lies in the use of such decision modelling techniques, some of which are computer-based, or other approaches to decision-making, it is clear that there is a need for further exploration of how to apply best available evidence to the real world of social work.

## The pragmatic orientation

Many of the key elements of the empirical orientation above are derived by direct assimilation into social work from 'evidence-based practice' in clinical medicine and in clinical professions allied to medicine. As Trinder (2000) suggests, there are significant differences in the encounters between social workers and service users and those between the various healthcare clinicians and their patients. These differences are summarized in Table IV.1.

In healthcare practice, a patient may present with a single symptom that has a single cause. In this case, the patient can be effectively treated after understanding the nature of this cause and the subsequent application of a proven intervention – often some form of drug. This is a very different form of practice to that found in social work, where most problems experienced by service users and carers are the consequence of the interaction of many causal events and, moreover, where many modalities of intervention are possible! The key question is whether such differences entail that the application of evidence-based practice should be of a different kind or character to that in the clinical medical disciplines. This is a fundamental question. Trinder (2000) suggests that a pragmatic approach is one that draws upon current research evidence and does not depend on a hierarchy of types or sources of evidence. It is, in essence, about using evidence derived from a variety of research sources to inform social work practice. Humphries (2003) develops this position by suggesting that knowledge derived from sources such as different stakeholder perspectives (including service users and carers) and research

**Table IV.1　Simplified representation of some key differences between health and social care**

|  | Healthcare | Social work |
|---|---|---|
| Nature of patient/ service user problems | Sometimes multifactorial | Always multifactorial |
| Nature of intervention | Linear | Diffuse |
| Primary mode of intervention | Physical/pharmacological | Human relationship |

approaches, such as participatory research, should be valued and used. She rejects the privileging of knowledge derived from positivist research methodologies, just as she rejects the privileging of knowledge derived from service users and carers.

> It is a worthy aim to end the hegemony of positivist-inspired social science and the arrogance of some of its adherents in deriding other ways of knowing, sometimes cloaking their recommendations in a 'specious certainty' instead of the more humble language of 'wise conjectures' (Campbell, 1988: 298) ...
>
> At the same time, there is a tendency in some of the social work literature both to homogenise and to idealise service users' knowledge (Beresford and Croft, 2001), risking reversing the hierarchy, so that 'lay' knowledges may come to be viewed as superior to scientific knowledge. (Humphries, 2003: 89)

---

**The pragmatic orientation: example**

Janet McArthur is a student due to visit **Zoë Benner**. From reviewing the case materials before visiting (with a particular focus on Tilly, Zoë's daughter currently in foster care) Janet gleans all she can of the past history: she uses the SCIE website and identifies service-user knowledges about the experiences of foster care, materials about the impact of foster care on children, the importance of future planning and so on.

---

The pragmatic approach is grounded in notions of 'what works' and seeks to balance a range of different forms and types of knowledge. Hence, it is an inclusive approach, albeit one that might be seen by some to lack rigour. What is needed is some mechanism for weighing the values of respective knowledges.

This orientation would not be regarded as evidence-based practice by those advocating the empirical orientation.

## The research-minded / research-aware orientation

Research-mindedness/awareness (often known by either name), is represented in Figure IV.1 at the base of the pyramid, signifying that this is the least prescriptive orientation in respect of the use of evidence. The very term 'research mindedness/awareness' implies that the practitioner is aware of the existence and importance of research and positively oriented towards research. It is an orientation with two core dimensions:

1   a willingness and an ability to be able to make use of existing research
2   an interest in the implications of research findings for policy and practice.

This willingness to use research is suggestive of a pragmatic orientation to evidence-based practice. The research-aware practitioner will have familiarity with some research findings and will seek to apply those findings to practice wherever possible. Hence, knowledge gained from research provides a background to effective practice, which helps to inform decision-making. The application of research knowledge to practice is unsystematic, partial and occasional. For example, in July 2003 the ESRC released the following notices of forthcoming research reports[4] which would be of interest to the research-aware practitioner:

- The government's current policy of allowing state pensions to decline, while increasing reliance on occupational and other private pensions, will perpetuate the disadvantage that women face in providing adequately for their retirement (7 July).
- Difficulties that children with autism have in pointing and showing objects to other people may emerge from earlier problems with simple face-to-face interaction (10 July).
- Seven out of ten older people in deprived areas are vulnerable to or experience at least some form of social exclusion (16 July).
- Despite the expectations that surround it, eLearning is still an uncertain market, particularly when it comes to children in the home (20 July).
- According to new research, if one eyewitness to a crime recalls a rogue piece of information, it can seriously distort other witnesses' accounts (23 July).

These reports provide interesting and pertinent material that *could* be used by social workers to inform their practice. The question is: *how* would the information be used by the research-aware practitioner and on what grounds would useful or constructive research be selected? Hence, there is no expectation of the *systematic* use of research by the research-minded or research-aware practitioner. If the practitioner is willing to use research, the question remains as to what guides that usage – is it personal preference or is it some process external to the practitioner, which validates the quality of that research and has something to say about the situations in which it might be applied? As Bacon (1605) stated, 'What is known depends on how it is known'. In *The Salmon of Doubt*, Douglas Adams wrote:

> First he glanced at some of the entries under other birth signs, just to get a feel for the kind of mood the Great Zaganza was in. Mellow, it seemed at first sight. 'Your ability to take the long view will help you through some of the minor difficulties you experience when Mercury...' 'Past weeks have strained your patience, but new possibilities will now start to emerge as the Sun ...' 'Beware of allowing others to take advantage of your good nature...' He then read his own horoscope. 'Today you will meet a three-ton rhinoceros called Desmond.' (Adams, 2003)

Not surprisingly, astrologers do not allow themselves to be so specific; if they were, and they were right, we would be more impressed and wish to know more about their methods.

---

[4] Details at: http://www.esrc.ac.uk/esrccontent/news/forthcoming_notices.asp

---

**The Research-minded/aware orientation: example**

Atkinson Pendle is a student due to visit **Zoë Benner**. From reviewing the case materials before visiting he notices that there has been a suggestion that Kylie may be autistic. Atkinson remembers reading an ESRC research briefing about autism (see above). He reads this, as it is easily accessible on his computer, before visiting Zoë. This helps Atkinson feel more confident about understanding Kylie and her possible problems.

---

An additional aspect of being research-minded/aware is a willingness to undertake research, formulate a research purpose and design, and conduct and evaluate the research. Much of the knowledge and the technology in social work practice is created to solve immediate problems; a practitioner–researcher aims to *build* research knowledge and to add to our understanding of what is sometimes called 'intervention technology'. The practitioner–researcher's activities can also help combat practice fatigue and the dangers of work becoming routine. Research-mindedness/awareness has much to contribute to the practitioner's orientation towards the creation of knowledge. Whitaker and Archer (1989) cite Norah Dixon's parallel processes, between the activity of 'doing social work' and of 'doing research'. These are summarized in Figure IV.2.

Figure IV.2 clearly illustrates the similarity of the social work process to the research process. It is imperative that this similarity is harnessed for the development of research within social work, for example, by practitioners using skills developed through practice to engage in research and vice versa. Help and guidance exists for the practitioner who wants an understanding of research (Mark,

| Social work processes | Research processes |
| --- | --- |
| 1  Social worker / project worker is presented with a problem. | 1  Researcher is presented with a problem or question. |
| 2  Social worker collects facts which illuminate the nature and purpose of the problem. | 2  Researcher searches the literature on the problem or question. |
| 3  Social worker makes a plan of action. | 3  Researcher designs a study. |
| 4  Social worker attempts to carry out action plan, noting progress. | 4  Researcher collects material and collates it. |
| 5  Social worker reviews work and may make new plans. | 5  Researcher analyses material and produces conclusions, and possibly recommendations, for future action. |

*Source*: Whitaker and Archer (1989).

**Figure IV.2   The parallel processes of 'doing social work' and 'doing research'**

1996). In addition, there are many good examples of practitioner research (see, for example, Durham, 2003; Fuller and Petch, 1995; Whitaker and Archer, 1989) and service user research (Rowntree Research Findings) from which to draw.

## Critical appraisal: using evidence from research in practice

Whichever of the three orientations is selected, the following quotation from a social worker's post-qualifying portfolio perhaps summarizes one of the problematic aspects of social work theory and practice, both in terms of the conceptualization of an orientation to research and the presentation of such an orientation:

> The theoretical paradigms most commonly informing my practice are Psychodynamic and Psychosocial Casework Theories, Behavioural, Learning and Attachment Theories along with a combination of interventions such as Crisis Intervention and Task Centred and Network Analysis approaches. Additionally I look to models focusing on Poverty, Exclusion and Racism, which help me to understand the effects they have upon individuals and their families. (Post-qualifying portfolio, 2003)

This 'pick-n-mix' or 'cafeteria approach'[5] would seem ludicrous if applied, say, to political persuasion. For example, the statement 'The theoretical paradigms which most commonly inform my voting are state communism, libertarianism, nationalism, liberalism, democratic socialism and Christian Democracy' would make little sense because there are fundamental inconsistencies between these differing paradigms. Are there, perhaps, similar inconsistencies across the range of paradigms referred to in the social work practitioner's portfolio?

The justification (from the same portfolio) is that:

> I believe that an eclectic approach in social work is essential in that merging several theories has benefits for service users allowing customised approaches to problems, thus avoiding the dogma of one theory fits all. Such an eclectic approach also enhances my ability to work alongside professionals coming from other theoretical bases. (Post-qualifying portfolio, 2003)

Since all bases appear to be covered, it is difficult to know what 'other theoretical bases' might be. This portfolio is founded on the notion of the 'knowledge pile': so long as I dip into the pile of relevant knowledge about social work it does not matter if some elements of knowledge are incompatible. They can be melded together under the banner of 'eclecticism'. Are all forms of knowledge equally valid, useful and applicable? In the light of the comments in this portfolio, it is difficult to understand how the accumulation of such knowledge might steer the social worker towards any particular action.

By contrast, consider the following comment from Caspi and Reid:

---

[5] An approach based on unrestricted consumer choice – the kind of choice offered in a self-serivce food outlet.

Since we know that HIV can be transmitted through sharing infected needles, we would want to help an intravenous drug user who believed that AIDS was the result of bad karma to develop whatever perspective about AIDS might be necessary to convince them to use clean needles. (Caspi and Reid, 2002: 117–18)

This comment, provided it is grounded in well-evidenced empirical research, gives both a policy and practice imperative to the actions of policy-makers and social work practitioners if they are basing their actions on evidence. Sheldon and Macdonald, in a forthcoming book, state that there are three major difficulties faced by social workers in developing an evidenced-based approach:

1 There is a large body of potentially useful knowledge from fields as diverse as psychology, sociology, literature and information technology, and, unless we carefully control the way in which it is used, it becomes a pile of knowledge rather than a critical appraised knowledge foundation.
2 Social workers are largely taught that the approach they should adopt to practice is a matter of personal choice – a viewpoint that flies in the face of a considerable body of empirical research which suggests that certain approaches work better than others with regard to specific problems.
3 What shall count as evidence and what should be excluded has not been satisfactorily resolved.

Until these issues are resolved within the profession, the adoption of an evidenced-based approach to practice will remain problematic. As an approach it may carry ideological conviction at policy level but, until the 'practitioner on the Clapham Omnibus'[6] is convinced, progress towards the effective implementation of an evidence-based approach will be hindered. In conclusion, is the choice of which orientation to research to adopt a matter for the individual practitioner or not?

---

[6] A colloquialism denoting the average person.

# 13 Working with risk

*Dial 'D' for Danger* consists of six different scenarios, which students rank according to the perceived level of risk for the service user or others. By taking account of this ranking of levels and types of risk, students can explore their propensity to intervene in given types of professional situation.

*Dial 'D' for Danger* is best completed by a group of students and a practice teacher working together, although it can be used by a practice teacher and a student working as a pair.

## Purpose

*Dial 'D' for Danger* is intended to help students explore the complex issues involved where social work practice is at the crossroads of caring for people and/or seeking to control some aspects of their lives.

## Method

Before undertaking this activity, you will need to copy the dials on page 194. This consists of six 'dials of danger' and six 'dials of intervention'.

- Give the students the list of case scenarios (page 193), and ask them to rank these vignettes according to the 'dial of danger'. Then, ask the students to indicate their propensity to intervene.
- If you are working with a group of students, you can encourage them to discuss why they have made their particular risk-ranking decisions, and to explore the reasons for their propensity to intervene in any given situation.

## Variations

Although you could use the scenarios in Derby Street (Activity 1, *Licensed to learn*) you may find it is better to devise your own distinctive scenarios to fit with the nature of practice in your own agency. For example, if the student is placed in a children and families team, you may wish to create vignettes that relate only to these kinds of situation. However, as we have stated before, the value of a variety of situations cannot be overemphasized.

Alternatively, *Dial 'D' for Danger* can be completed independently by students and used as an exercise for discussion in a practice tutorial.

## Use by other professions

All professionals have to engage with risk: the airline pilot must decide whether the plane is safe to fly; the midwife must assess the level of risk involved in a particular birth plan chosen by an expectant mother. The nature and extent of risk encountered by each profession is different. Similarly, new developments in technological achievement, government policy or social expectations change our conceptions of risk. For example, in England, the government's White Paper, *Our Inheritance, Our Future: realising the potential of genetics in the NHS* (Department of Health, 2003c) explores how genetics will affect our notions of illness and health through 'a more personalised prediction of risk, more precise diagnosis, more targeted and effective use of existing drugs, new gene-based drugs and therapies, and prevention and treatment regimes tailored according to a person's individual genetic profile'.[1]

## National Occupational Standards for Social Work

The topics in this chapter relate to the following National Occupational Standards (see the Appendix):

  9:  Working with challenging behaviour
12:  Risks to other people
13:  Risks to self and colleagues
20:  Dilemmas and conflicts.

---

[1] At: http://www.doh.gov.uk/genetics/whitepaper.htm

## *Activity 13* *Dial 'D' for Danger*

### Degree of risk

Think about the following six vignettes and consider:

1 how dangerous the situation is for the service user or for others
2 your own willingness to intervene in each case.

#### Vignette **1**

Gillandi is a forty-nine-year-old woman who is a chronic alcoholic (and has been so for at least ten years). She has a husband (who is self-employed as a painter-decorator) and two children, both young women aged seventeen and nineteen. Recently, she has been drinking particularly heavily. There have been a series of incidents in which she has almost injured herself or others. A week ago, she was almost run over by a car; two weeks ago, she allowed food to burn on the cooker in the kitchen, causing a small fire in the kitchen.

#### Vignette **2**

Winston, a British African-Caribbean male aged nineteen, has been found guilty of several different crimes (including burglary and taking and driving cars) by the courts. He has been sentenced to a six months' home-based curfew between the hours of 8 p.m. and 8 a.m. for six nights per week. During the first three months, he does not seek to break the curfew and spends the one night that his curfew is not in force working at a youth project for offenders. He is very well liked by everyone at the youth project. In the second part of the sentence, Winston continues with the work at the youth project and maintains his curfew except for one night each week. He is evasive and will not tell you what he is doing during that time. In all other respects, Winston is conforming to all the court's expectations.

#### Vignette **3**

Howard is a well-educated white man in his thirties. About two years ago, he lost his job – one carrying considerable responsibilities with a large commercial enterprise. Since then, he has experienced financial difficulties leading to the break-up of his marriage and the loss of his family home. He now lives on benefit in social housing. He is adamant that he can care for the two children, a boy aged six and a girl aged eight. The school has expressed some concerns about the children not being fed properly and arriving at school hungry.

#### Vignette **4**

In the area served by your office, there is a large block of high-rise flats run by the local authority. These flats are in a poor state of repair and decoration. Many of them suffer from damp. No facilities exist for children to play, and there have been many muggings and attacks on local residents in the lifts and communal areas. There are several residents who wish to take action to improve the state of the flats. One of these asks you to organize a public meeting to bring people together to take action about the condition of the flats, but some of the other residents are not enthusiastic about involving social services.

#### Vignette **5**

Bob is a white eighty-five-year-old, living on his own in a small flat provided by the local authority. For the last year he has encountered difficulties in living on his own. Neighbours have complained to the local authority that his flat is smelly and that there is rubbish accumulating inside and outside the flat. On one of your visits to his flat, he allows you to see the inside; it is in a chaotic and filthy condition. Bob is obviously not eating properly, and the kitchen is in a filthy state. His clothes are dirty and he smells. In conversation, his memory appears to you to be failing. Yet he says he is content.

#### Vignette **6**

Two people, Robert and Sally, with moderate learning difficulties, both in their twenties, have married and set up home together in a local authority flat. They are determined to be as independent as possible. They decide to have a baby and, just before the baby is due, tell their social worker that they do not need the help of social services any longer now that they are to become parents.

Reproduced from *Modern Social Work Practice* by Mark Doel and Steven M. Shardlow, Ashgate, Aldershot, 2005

## Dials of danger

Without consulting with any of your colleagues, complete the following rankings for each of the vignettes listed in *Dial 'D' for danger*.

The more dangerous you consider the example, the higher the ranking on the dial of danger, (mimimal risk = 1; mild risk = 2/3; moderate risk = 5/6; considerable risk = 9/10; maximum risk = 12). The numbers in the centre of the dials refer to the vignettes described.

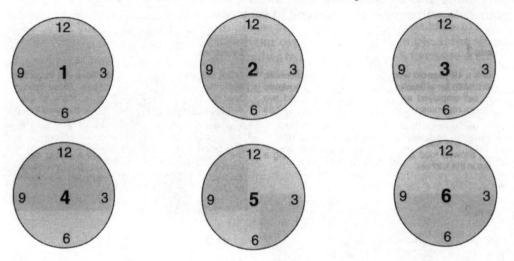

## Dials of intervention

Taking account of your perception of the degree of risk in the situation, you should now grade your willingness to intervene, by rating from 1 (= no inclination to intervene) to 12 (= no option but to intervene).

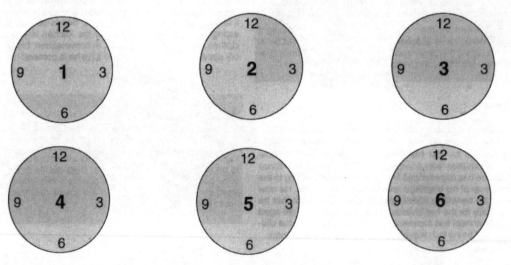

Reproduced from *Modern Social Work Practice* by Mark Doel and Steven M. Shardlow, Ashgate, Aldershot, 2005

# Teaching notes: *Working with risk*

*Dial 'D' for Danger* presents students with an apparently simple task, to categorize their propensity to intervene in a series of situations according to their perception of the degree of danger in a range of situations involving service users and carers. The 'propensity to intervene' and the 'degree of dangerousness' encourages students to compare two different dimensions of response to these situations. It might be assumed that a high degree of danger would have a correlation with a high propensity to intervene and therefore lead to intervention. However, we know that this is not the case (many women are in situations of extreme danger in domestic disputes, but this does not necessarily lead to a police presence), and there are many other factors which come into play. Encourage students to explore the reasons for their responses, using the following prompts if needed:

- attitudes to taking control
- cultural views about acceptable behaviour
- fears of making mistakes
- fears about own safety
- beliefs about the role of the social worker
- confidence about professional judgement
- knowledge of the legal context of social work practice.

Ascertaining levels of risk is always a complex issue (see Adams, 1995; Singleton and Holden, 1994). Students may identify that a situation has a high level of risk for one or more individuals, but may be unsure of the grounds upon which they might intervene. Usually, powers of intervention will be defined by statute (see Chapter 15, 'Law-informed practice'). Students can be encouraged to think about whether intervention in these situations is likely to be perceived by others as a demonstration of care or the imposition of control over the way in which individuals conduct their lives – or a combination of both.

**Example**

**Sue Shuk Wan** had achieved a high level of competence on her first practice learning site with children and families. Her second site in an adults' team was proving a little more difficult. Sue's Chinese parents had moved to Britain when she was only two. Brenda, her practice teacher, noticed that Sue found great difficulty in deciding when to intervene in the lives of older people. When Sue completed *Dial 'D' for Danger* she gave a very high danger ranking to Vignette 5, yet demonstrated a very low propensity to intervene. In discussion, she was reluctant to discuss her reasons, but it was clear to Brenda that Sue had difficulty with this scenario. No more was said at this point. A few weeks later, Brenda asked Sue to repeat the exercise with some specially created vignettes, all about older people. One of these concerned the situation of an older Chinese woman living alone, which by chance mirrored Sue's grandmother's situation. Using this example, she found it possible to discuss her own attitudes to old age, and intervening in the lives of older people, which were located in her own personal and cultural identity.

Intervening in the lives of other people may curtail their rights to live independently and may challenge a central notion of social work practice – the commitment to promoting empowerment. Students should be encouraged to reflect upon the tensions between intervention and the promotion of empowerment.

## Opportunities

There may be a tendency to try to protect students from exposure to risk. Unnecessary risks can be minimized, yet risk is inherent in all forms of social work. We serve students, and the people they will work with, best if we honestly acknowledge levels of risk and enable students to work with, and manage, those risks effectively.

# Learning notes: *Working with risk*

It is sometimes suggested that we live in a society in which levels of risk are increasing (Beck, 1990). In the UK social work literature, the idea of 'risk' hardly figured until the early 1980s when Brearley (1982) defined the notion of 'risk' in terms of the possible negative outcomes of any action or event. Risk is a complicated notion; it is not, for example, a legally defined concept (so we cannot base our professional practice upon the law and legal precedent). However, 'risk' is now a central concept in professional practice and is the subject of considerable interest (Stalker, 2003). We therefore need to explore ways of effectively deploying the concept of 'risk' in practice.

## Risk assessment

According to Manthorpe, *risk assessment* is the 'process of identifying hazards which may cause accident, disaster or harm' (2000: 298). Predicting risk is inherently problematic as it involves making a judgement about the likely future outcomes. There is always uncertainty about whether a particular event will occur, and chance plays a part in the outcome of any course of actions or events. There are two broad approaches to the assessment of risk:

1  *Clinical*. Here, a clinician or practitioner in a given field estimates the likelihood of a particular occurrence – for example, a depressed individual committing a serious act of self-harm.
2  *Actuarial*. Here, statistical methods are used to identify risk to general situations or groups. For example, we can predict with some certainty the proportion of smokers within a given population who will have died from smoking-related illness by a certain age (but not necessarily which particular individuals).

If it is possible to estimate the level of risk with some degree of accuracy, then a professionally balanced decision about whether it is necessary to intervene is also possible. The estimation of level of risk depends on detailed knowledge about the potential causes of risk and how to apply that knowledge to a particular situation. Reviewing the available evidence at the time, Kemshall suggests that clinical prediction of risk has 'a poor record of accuracy' in respect of mental health (Kemshall, 1996: 136). Corby (1996) notes that, in the field of child protection, there has been a considerable growth in the number of risk assessment instruments, especially in the US.[2]

Assessing risk is very difficult when people have a number of different risk factors in their lives: the identification of risk that a child might be abused by its

---

[2] One of the most widely used is Milner's *Child Abuse Potential Inventory* (Milner, 1986) for which a very high success rate is claimed. For a review of some of these assessment instruments, see Doueck, *et al.* (1993).

Reproduced from *Modern Social Work Practice* by Mark Doel and Steven M. Shardlow, Ashgate, Aldershot, 2005

parents requires different knowledge from the estimation of risk that people with mental illness will harm themselves or others; different again are the associated risks for some people with physical disabilities in performing certain tasks. Kemshall and Pritchard (1996) have collected details of how to assess risk for particular types of service user. However, in each case there are common questions to be considered when making a judgement:

- What is the nature of the risk – is it life-threatening or a minor inconvenience? For example, there is some risk attached to crossing the road, yet, for many people, it is a risk they choose to take every day because the incidence of accidents is low relative to the number of people crossing roads.
- Is there a risk to a minor or a vulnerable person? For example, is it a risk to a person who is able to judge the level of risk for themselves, or are they prevented or unable to do so, for whatever reason?
- Is this a subjective or objective definition of risk – is there agreement among those involved about the determination of the risk?
- What protective measures can people take themselves against the risk?
- Are there risks if you do intervene, and how are these weighed against non-intervention?

The answers to such questions have been collected into a matrix model proposed by O'Sullivan (1999). This graphically makes visible the strengths and weaknesses of a particular course of action, in this case whether or not to allow a child to remain in a foster home. The strengths and weaknesses might be identified as illustrated in Table 13.1.

Such a diagrammatic approach can be used in other situations to aid decision-making.

**Table 13.1    Strengths/hazards analysis**

| 'Staying in foster home' option | |
| --- | --- |
| **Present** | **Future** |
| *Hazards* <br> Difficulties in relationship between foster parents <br> Zena's history of running away | *Danger* <br> Foster home will suddenly break down |
| *Strengths* <br> Experienced foster family <br> Foster family from same ethnic background | *Benefit* <br> A caring and stable base to work towards Zena's reconciliation with her family |

*Source*: O'Sullivan (1999: 141).

Reproduced from *Modern Social Work Practice* by Mark Doel and Steven M. Shardlow, Ashgate, Aldershot, 2005

# Typology of risks

When making an assessment of risk it can be helpful to think about different types of risk (Manthorpe, 2000). For example, Stevenson and Parsloe (1993) identify three categories where intervention may be required:

*Physical risk*
Circumstances where the individual may harm themselves or cause harm to others; in these cases social workers may have to decide, either alone or in conjunction with others on the extent of that risk, as in the case of somebody who is mentally ill and threatening harm to themselves or others.

*Social risk*
Individuals whose behaviour isolates and alienates themselves from others should be encouraged to behave in a more socially acceptable fashion; in addition neighbours and family can also be encouraged to understand and manage these behaviours.

*Emotional risk*
Where the physical health or emotional well-being of people is put at risk by the role that they occupy; for example, where a person has the sole care of another highly dependent individual.

It is worth remembering that all human action carries some risk. Try doing a risk assessment on yourself for the day, then making recommendations about how your life should be limited to lessen all these risks. Helpful? Probably not. (See the anecdote about the 'soft-boiled egg syndrome' in the Introduction to Part III). De Bono calls risk assessment 'black hat thinking', with statements that are often preceded by 'I see a danger of ...' (de Bono, 2000: 83). A focus on degrees of risk has potential for disempowerment.

# Risk management

Risk management is the tension between allowing individuals autonomy and protecting them from themselves or ensuring the protection of others (Gurney, 2000). A difficulty for social work has always been to determine when to intervene, even if there are legal grounds for so doing; in other words, what standards of risk are acceptable and what risks prompt social workers to intervene? The problem of determining socially acceptable standards for intervention remains a complex problem for society in general and social work practice in particular. As Stalker suggests:

> ... risk management moves along a continuum between control, legitimate authority and empowerment. Between the controlling ends of the continuum lie models of risk management which seek to reduce harms and maximise benefits. (Stalker, 2003: 218)

A problem may arise when social workers have almost complete control over the lives of vulnerable individuals, as in group care, and there have been several well-

Reproduced from *Modern Social Work Practice* by Mark Doel and Steven M. Shardlow, Ashgate, Aldershot, 2005

reported examples of that power being abused (Clough, 1996). Yet there is no reason to suppose that autonomy and protection cannot be balanced. Being a parent involves both caring for a child and controlling the child's behaviour, and successful parents are able to demonstrate both love and control – if not without tensions!

> It seems as if there's no happy medium. You either let them out and you're careless, or you keep them in and you're over protective, and your lad's gonnae have an accident because you cannae teach it to be street wise if you've got him in the house. (Roberts *et al.*, 1995: 66 – from a study by Brown and Harris)

This parent expresses well some of the dilemmas implicit in both caring for somebody and seeking to put limits on their behaviour. People may value their autonomy more highly than they value being protected from harm; they may be happy to accept the risks of everyday life. However, a sharp distinction must be made where there is a risk to others. In such cases, action must be taken to minimize the risk of harm to others, where potential harm is significant and the 'other' is a person in a vulnerable situation. Professional codes of practice for social workers may be of some help in providing guidance about such matters (see for example, GSCC, 2002; NASW, 1996).

There is a range of different tools available to identify the nature and extent of risk. Table 13.2 gives details of a young man with Asperger's syndrome. Using this format it is possible to both identify potential risks and also specify how these are managed. It is not necessary to have a narrative to describe the situation – the relevant professional information can be gleaned from the schedule.

You can encourage your student to produce a similar schedule in respect of one service user or carer. Alternatively, invite the student to construct a similar schedule in respect of one of the Derby Street residents (Activity 1, *Licensed to learn*, page 13).

## Risk avoidance

Risk avoidance may either lead to desirable professional behaviour through enabling service people to avoid behaviour that carries a high level of detrimental risk[3] or it may result in overcautious professional practice that places people in more danger. For example, it would be unthinkable to allow children in group care to behave as they pleased, yet there must be acceptable limits to the ways in which behaviour is controlled (Department of Health, 1993). The protection of one individual, whether child or adult, may entail a restriction of their rights to behave as they choose or it may restrict others. In such situations, social workers are placed in an invidious position in having to meet two contradictory imperatives. This is exemplified by the cartoon in Figure 13.1. The social worker is placed in a difficult

---

[3] It should not be forgotten that some individuals enjoy a 'high-risk' lifestyle – for example, mountaineers.

Reproduced from *Modern Social Work Practice* by Mark Doel and Steven M. Shardlow, Ashgate, Aldershot, 2005

**Table 13.2   An example of a risk assessment harm–benefit analysis**[*]

| Risk factors | Harms | Benefits |
|---|---|---|
| **Financial**<br><br>Potential for abuse? | • Increased cost of care package.<br>• Vulnerability to exploitation due to Asperger's syndrome and his inability to understand financial matters. | • He is able to remain in his home environment.<br>• Chandler's parents collect his benefits and manage his finances.<br>• He always has enough money to purchase items. |
| **Social**<br><br>Who does he live with? Live alone?<br><br>The ability/inability of people to continue caring.<br><br>The presence/lack of home/social support.<br><br>Ability/inability to cope alone in own home. | • Lives with mother and father in family home.<br>• There are tensions between his parents, which increase Chandler's anxieties and lead to behavioural outbursts.<br>• Chandler's mother struggles to cope with aggressive behaviours. She provides most of the care for Chandler.<br>• She has little support from her husband or extended family.<br>• Risk of carer breakdown and consequential need for 24-hour residential care for Chandler. | • He is very close to his family.<br>• This is a familiar environment where he feels comfortable.<br>• He does not respond well to change and needs predictability in his life.<br>• He has regular respite care at a local not-for-profit facility, which gives his parents frequent breaks from caring. |
| **Environmental**<br><br>Home conditions – for example, gas, fires, obstacles, etc.<br><br>Neighbours, friends – support/lack of. | • He dislikes large, crowded and noisy environments that heighten his anxiety and result in behavioural outbursts.<br>• He places heavy demands on his carers who are frequently the subject of physical assaults. | • He has many friends/acquaintances at his day service.<br>• He receives regular respite care to maintain the family situation.<br>• He has a number of staff who support him at day services and are experienced in meeting his needs. |

*continued*

Reproduced from *Modern Social Work Practice* by Mark Doel and Steven M. Shardlow, Ashgate, Aldershot, 2005

| | | |
|---|---|---|
| The threat of removal of care networks. | • He requires support from staff who are experienced in meeting the needs of individuals with severe challenging behaviours. | |
| The nature and extent of hospitalizations. | | |
| **Psychological** | • He becomes anxious when he experiences unplanned change, busy environments or people invading his space. | • He has his day presented to him in picture format so that his day is as structured and predictable as possible. |
| The anxieties of significant others. | | |
| Significant cognitive impairment. | • He has Asperger's syndrome and severe challenging behaviour. | |
| Mental health issues? | • His behaviours include repetitive speech, verbal threats and physical assaults on staff/service users. | |
| Threats to safety of self/ others. | | |
| **Familial** | • Chandler's family are at risk of physical injury. | • He has a high degree of structure and routine in his day. |
| The impact of the risk upon carers/family members. | • There is a risk of carer breakdown. | • He has regular respite care to facilitate breaks from caring. |
| The lack of home/social support. | | |
| The anxieties of significant others. | | |
| High levels of conflict with relatives. | | |
| **Physical** | • There is a risk of physical injury to self and others. | • The least restrictive alternative is always employed when supporting through behavioural difficulties. |
| High levels of disability. | | |
| Older age. | | |
| General health. | | *continued* |

Reproduced from *Modern Social Work Practice* by Mark Doel and Steven M. Shardlow, Ashgate, Aldershot, 2005

| Other | • There is a risk of physical injury to support staff and other service users at the day service.<br>• There is a risk of physical injury to staff/service users on transport.<br>• There is a risk of injury to Chandler's sister who transports him. | • Chandler's sister transports him in her car without any incidents yet reported. |
|---|---|---|

* This assessment is a live example used by one local authority in the UK.

*Note*: It is important to make explicit an estimate of the scale of the harm, the potential for future harm, the strengths of a situation, and the manageability of the risks.

position and seems to be in a lose-lose situation.

The microscope of potential public scrutiny can be a very effective inhibitor to appropriate professional risk taking. There is a very real danger that the avoidance of risk becomes the primary determinant of the social worker's actions. It may be that the overwhelming sense of risk perceived by the social worker is not the risk to the child, service user or carer, but the risk to the practitioner. This sense of risk can then tip the balance in favour of a professional practice that is designed first and foremost to protect the individual practitioner – a defensive practice (Thompson, 2000).

Social workers can be subject to a range of risks through engaging in professional practice: for example, in some contexts the risk of contracting highly infectious and potentially life-threatening illnesses; or the potential risk of violence from some service users and carers (see, for example, Littlechild, 1996). You should identify these risks with your practice tutor or supervisor and determine strategies to minimize and manage their level.

## Assessment notes: *Working with risk*

When working with risk, you may tend to respond, as a novice practitioner, either by being overcautious – leading to unnecessary and unjustified intervention – or by being overtolerant of risk – leading to interventions not being made when required. Of course, there is no absolute measure of the extent to which risk and judgements about the nature of 'risk' are likely to vary between individuals. The extent of that variance and the reasons for such judgements are central to determining whether you have fully understood the notion of working with 'risk'. This is an ability that you need to be able to demonstrate in your assignments and through your practice. Until you have been through the process of professional socialization, you are likely to be at variance with commonly held *professional* norms about working with risk. If your view is significantly at variance with other professionals, you need to consider carefully why this may be the case and be able to produce a convincing and persuasive reason. Variance does not automatically mean that your views are incorrect.

Reproduced from *Modern Social Work Practice* by Mark Doel and Steven M. Shardlow, Ashgate, Aldershot, 2005

Figure 13.1   'The social worker cannot win?' by Kevin Kallaugher

This is one area of practice where simulation can provide excellent opportunities for assessment, as it does not place you, the student, in a vulnerable position where you have to make actual decisions which could be prejudicial to the safety of the service user or carer, but still allows you to experience the potential gravity of some situations. You may want to discuss possible simulation options, which assess risk, with your practice teacher.

## Further reading

Alaszewski, A., Harrison, L. and Manthorpe, J. (1998), *Risk, Health and Welfare*, Buckingham: Open University Press.

Kemshall, H. and Pritchard, J. (eds) (1996), *Good Practice in Risk Assessment and Risk Management*, London: Jessica Kingsley.

Parsloe, P. (ed.) (1999), *Risk Assessment in Social Care*, London: Jessica Kingsley.

# 14 Anti-oppressive practice

## About Activity 14    *The drawbridge*

*The drawbridge* is taken from Judy Katz's (1978) book, *White Awareness: handbook for anti-racist training*, though its use has been adapted for our current purposes. It asks the student to make fine-tuned moral judgements about responsibility. From their response to this story, the student can learn more about where they are located in terms of their understanding of power, oppression and social structures.

This activity is suited to small groups, where there is a better chance of a variety of opinions arising. It gains from dissent, rather than consensus, itself illustrating the value of diversity.

### Purpose

A relatively neutral device can be very effective in exploring loaded subjects. An apparent distance in place and time can free people to consider issues of power and oppression much closer to home. *The drawbridge* helps students to consider how service users and other colleagues may have very different perspectives and power bases, and the impact this can have on the work.

### Method

- In advance of the activity familiarize yourself with the Teaching notes on pages 210–213.
- *The drawbridge* is best done without preparation, since discussing the exercise beforehand defeats some of its purpose. Everybody involved should have a copy of the exercise and it is most effective if it is read out loud.
- Once the story has been concluded, ask the students to spend three to five minutes rating each of the six characters according to how responsible they think each is for the death of the Baroness. Emphasize that there are no specifically 'right' or 'wrong' ratings for responsibility. This will prevent students from 'second-guessing' what they think you want to hear.
- Next lead a discussion on why the participants have made their particular decisions.

- Guide any further discussion using the Teaching notes which follow.

## Variations

*The drawbridge* can also be used with groups of service users, as well as students and colleagues.

## Use by other professions

This activity can readily be used by different professional groups. It would be interesting to compare the range of opinions across disciplines. As you can see from Table 14.1 on page 215, social work students reflect great differences in their views.

## National Occupational Standards for Social Work

The topics in this chapter relate to the following National Occupational Standards (see the Appendix):

 2:   Making informed decisions
 9:   Working with risk
20:   Managing complex ethical issues, dilemmas and conflicts.

## *Activity 14:* *The drawbridge*

As he left for a visit to his outlying districts, the jealous **Baron** warned his pretty wife: 'Do not leave the castle while I am gone, or I will punish you severely when I return!'

But as the hours passed, the young **Baroness** grew lonely; despite her husband's warning she decided to visit her **Lover**, who lived in the countryside nearby.

The castle was situated on an island in a wide, fast-flowing river. A drawbridge linked the island to the mainland at the narrowest point in the river.

'Surely my husband will not return before dawn,' she thought, and ordered her servants to lower the drawbridge and leave it down until she returned.

After spending several pleasant hours with her Lover, the Baroness returned to the drawbridge, only to find it blocked by a **Gateman** wildly waving a long, cruel knife. 'Do not attempt to cross this bridge, Baroness, or I will have to kill you,' the Gateman cried. 'The Baron ordered me to do so.'

Fearing for her life, the Baroness returned to her Lover and asked for help. 'Our relationship is only a romantic one,' the Lover said. 'I will not help.'

The Baroness then sought out a **Boatman** on the river, explaining her plight to him, and asked him to take her across the river in his boat. 'I will do it, but only if you can pay my fee of five marks,' he responded.

'But I have no money with me,' the Baroness protested.

'That is too bad. No money, no ride,' the Boatman said flatly.

Her fear growing, the Baroness ran crying to a **Friend**'s home and, after explaining her desperate situation, begged for enough money to pay the Boatman his fee.

'If you had not disobeyed your husband, this would not have happened,' the Friend said. 'I will give you no money.'

With dawn approaching and her last resource exhausted, the Baroness returned to the drawbridge in desperation, attempted to cross to the castle, and was slain by the Gateman.

In order of priorities, who is most responsible for the death of the Baroness?

Use the boxes below to rank the six characters: 6 for most responsible; 5 for next most responsible, down to 1 for least responsible.

*Ranking*

Baron
Baroness
Gateman
Lover
Boatman
Friend

*Source*: Taken from Katz (1978: 70–1)

Reproduced from *Modern Social Work Practice* by Mark Doel and Steven M. Shardlow, Ashgate, Aldershot, 2005

# Teaching notes: *Anti-oppressive practice*

You should familiarize yourself with the material in this section before you embark on *The drawbridge* with students. What follows will assist you in helping the students relate their particular responses to a wider canvas. The Learning notes (pages 214–218) introduce the students to some of the central issues in anti-oppressive practice.

## Helping the student to learn from *The drawbridge*

There can be no clear right or wrong in the moral debate about responsibility in the story of *The drawbridge* because it depends on what system of beliefs is used to measure and weigh 'responsibility'. Although students may feel that the idea of theory is something rather distant and obscure, in fact they draw on their own personal theories to explain this story. They may not formalize this into a fully coherent theory but they nevertheless use a conceptual framework, a *paradigm*, to begin to make sense and meaning of the world.

There are many paradigms, and individual students using the same paradigm may still come to different conclusions about responsibility. The examples below are collected from numerous occasions when *The drawbridge* has been used with new social work students in their very first week of training. All the quotes are taken from students' own statements.

### Psychological paradigm

*'I think the Baroness has poor self-esteem'; 'the Friend was too frightened to help'; 'the Baron has a power complex'; 'the Baron is really very insecure'; 'the Baroness didn't think he really meant it'.*

These statements are characteristic of a set of explanations which seek to explain the behaviours of the players in motivational terms, and look for psychological causes for their actions.

### Legal paradigm

*'Although he was acting under duress, the Gateman actually murdered her, so it's obvious that he was most responsible'; 'there was an employment contract between the Gateman and the Baron'.*

For some people, it is the legal framework that is the ultimate arbiter. When applying levels of responsibility, the current laws are used as the yardstick.

### Cultural relativism paradigm

*'In those days that was how things were done and the Baron was only doing what he did because that's all he knew'; 'if it was now, I'd think differently'.*

Most significant in this paradigm are the indications that the events are somehow not of this time or place, so it is considered right to apply a different set of moral standards which take this context into account.

## Individualism paradigm

*'Everybody is responsible for their own actions, and the Baroness knew what the consequences would be'*; *'he may have been acting under duress, but the Gateman is responsible for his own actions'*; *'the Lover chose not to help'*.

Western philosophy lays great emphasis on our rights, duties and obligations as autonomous individuals. We are moral agents with free will and the ability to exercise choice. This overrides collective responsibilities or social determinants. This philosophy was expressed in its extreme by Margaret Thatcher's declaration that there was no such thing as society.

## Class paradigm

*'Why should the Boatman give her a free ride? That's his livelihood and who's she to be going around with no money?'*; *'the Gateman will be scapegoated because he's just one of the workers'*.

As a worker, the Boatman is near the bottom of the social order and the Baroness is a member of the oppressive ruling class, so why should he not rejoice at her downfall? The Gateman, too, is a member of the oppressed working class, even if he is its unwitting agent.

## Feminism paradigm

*'The Baroness was the victim of a patriarchal society'*; *'she was subject to male abuse'*; *'the men let her down at every turn'*.

Apart from the Baroness, all the players are male (except the Lover, whose gender is not determined). The woman is killed by a man on the orders of a man, and no man comes to her aid. However, there is an alternative feminist paradigm that would claim that it is patronizing to see the Baroness as a victim; in this case, feminism leads them to conclude that she was the author of her own downfall.

## Fundamentalist paradigm

*'The Baroness broke her wedding vows'*; *'no matter what the reason, she has sinned against the promises sanctioned by marriage in the eyes of God'*.

There are many different religious paradigms, but a conservative one would measure responsibility against some churchs' teaching that adultery is a sin.

## Power paradigm

*'The Baron had the power of life and death and, in using that power, he is the most responsible'*; *'no-one else had that kind of power'*.

Using a paradigm of power, the Baron is seen as an instrument of an oppressive society in which power is unequally distributed and cruelly enforced, with others in relatively powerless positions coerced into obedience.

Relating the students' ratings for *The drawbridge* to broader paradigms is important in three ways. First, it begins to demystify the idea of theory. The notion of paradigm is more readily grasped, and students can begin to see how what they have often viewed as unassembled or disconnected ideas are, in fact, part of a more coherent belief and value system. Second, it becomes apparent that other people *really* do see the world in very different ways, especially if the student has the opportunity to discuss *The drawbridge* with a significant number of other people. Students can appreciate how easy it would be to become stuck or oppositional with colleagues and service users who may be observing and explaining the world from very different paradigms.

Finally, in addition to learning to value the difference and diversity which is apparent from the responses to *The drawbridge*, students also begin to paint these personal beliefs on a broader canvas. The bigger picture is one where not all paradigms are considered equal. Some paradigms are seen as 'normal', and those who hold different paradigms are marginalized, pathologized or trivialized. This first level of awareness is essential to anti-oppressive practice.

## Opportunities

Looking for opportunities for the student to learn about anti-oppressive practice is like looking for opportunities to breathe, yet, if it is not labelled 'opportunity for anti-oppressive practice', then, like breathing, students tend to be unaware of its existence.

Starting with your own relationship with the student, as a practice teacher or worksite supervisor, in what ways do your biographies differ and in what ways are they similar? Discussing the potential impact of difference and similarity in this core relationship is a first step towards students considering difference and similarity between themselves and the various people with whom they work. What is your mutual commitment to promoting equality as an ethical stance (Loewenberg and Dolgoff, 2000)? Consider your own commitment to modelling anti-oppressive practice teaching. You will find the exercises and direct dialogue in Dalrymple and Burke (1998) very useful in this respect.

You might also want students to explore policy development in the agency. In the area of race, for example, the amended Race Relations Act (2000) now makes it a duty of all local authorities to consider all areas of racial equality:

> In practice, this means that listed public authorities must take account of racial equality in the day to day work of policy-making, service delivery, employment practice and other functions. (Commission for Racial Equality, 2003)

Indeed, the Macpherson Report (1999) has brought the notion of institutional racism to a wider, near-universal audience.

## Anti-oppressive practice teaching

As well as teaching about anti-oppressive practice, it is important to demonstrate anti-oppressive practice teaching. Lefevre (1998) focuses on the importance of recognizing and addressing imbalances of power between the practice teacher and student to achieve a partnership approach to practice learning which exemplifies anti-discriminatory practice. The complex relationship between teacher and learner, assessor and student mirrors the complexities in the wider world. A simple analysis would suggest that the supervisor is more powerful than the student, and in some important dimensions this is true; however, in addition to the possible complexities of race, gender and so on (say, a black female practice teacher with a white, male student) good practice teaching requires a willingness to expose one's work to a scrutiny which other practitioners do not experience. When it works well, the relationship between student and supervisor is a powerful one for all concerned, demonstrating the fact that power is not a question of 'if you have more, I have less'.

For a useful preparation for practice, see West and Watson's (2002: 50) personal learning audit. They contend that empowered students become empowered workers, and we would add that they become empower*ing* workers, too.

# Learning notes: *Anti-oppressive practice*

## Language

It is important to remember that anti-oppressive practice equates with the fundamentals of good social work practice: the pursuit of equality and justice. Anti-oppressive practice requires an understanding of social structures and their impact on individuals and communities; in addition, it requires a commitment to ethical principles which value difference and diversity, and to a form of practice which is both *self*-aware and *others*-aware.

Anxiety about language is sometimes a barrier to learning, especially the fear that you have to learn what it is 'right' to say or believe. Often this is related to a belief that anti-oppressive practice is about knowing the right terminology (Chand *et al.*, 1999). This is often referred to as 'political correctness', which is an insidious attempt to trivialize important issues and has too often been successful in diverting attention from the serious issues which lie behind the use of language. We should not produce a list of taboo words, but develop 'a sensitivity to the complex role of language' (Thompson, 2002: 52).

It is the issues which lie behind the use of language which are important, not learning by rote a supposed list of right and wrong terms. Addressing these potential concerns very early in your studies with your practice teacher is the best way to free up discussion; this is not to give the green light to insensitive language, but to open the door to a genuine dialogue about the impact and sensitivity of language.

For a very clear explanation of terms such as diversity, difference, discrimination, oppression, and the like, see Thompson (2002).

## Using your learning from *The drawbridge*

We hope you have had the chance to work on *The drawbridge* with others and to experience a wide range of opinion. We have used the exercise with many different groups, including social work students at the beginning of their training, and the results of the group of social work students shown in Table 14.1 is typical of the diversity of the responses. What is your response to this?

The issue of responsibility is important. For instance, one of the most powerful weapons used by insider groups against outsider groups is guilt and blame. To the practical burden of poverty add the moral burden of guilt for not being able to find work or support a family adequately. It is important for social work to help people untangle responsibilities, and to challenge ideas of blame which the in-groups (in work, in money, in luck) attribute to the out-groups.

One of the most virulent examples of blaming out-groups is that attributed to people with positive HIV/AIDS status. Blaming somebody for catching a disease through sexual contact is as ridiculous as castigating a cholera victim for drinking

Reproduced from *Modern Social Work Practice* by Mark Doel and Steven M. Shardlow, Ashgate, Aldershot, 2005

**Table 14.1** **Student responses to *The drawbridge* at the start of their social work training (n = 25). Numbers of rankings by each character in the story**

| | Ranking[1] | | | | | |
| | 6 | 5 | 4 | 3 | 2 | 1 |
|---|---|---|---|---|---|---|
| Baron | 10[2] | 7 | 5 | 0 | 0 | 3 |
| Baroness | 10 | 8 | 2 | 2 | 0 | 3 |
| Gateman | 4 | 6 | 6 | 4 | 3 | 2 |
| Lover | 1 | 3 | 12 | 8 | 1 | 0 |
| Boatman | 0 | 0 | 0 | 4 | 12 | 9 |
| Friend | 0 | 1 | 0 | 7 | 9 | 8 |

[1] 6 = most responsible for the Baroness' death; 1 = least responsible.
[2] That is, 10 students gave the Baron a '6' ranking

contaminated water. With more knowledge of risks, of course individuals have increasing responsibility for their own behaviour (witness the prosecution of individuals who knowingly infect others), but the attribution of blame to those with the virus is a typical example of the insider–outsider phenomenon.

The notion of insider–outsider groups reflects the general subtleties of anti-oppressive practice. Within insider and outsider groups there are yet more insider and outsider groups, sometimes called subcultures. For example:

> ...the Asian communities provide a bulwark against racism, a means of mutual protection and solidarity. They are very antagonistic towards anything seen as a threat to Asian values ... Being gay or lesbian is interpreted as having been seduced or infected by Western culture. This leads to denial or calls for treatment. (Khan, 1992:19)

Social work is perhaps unique amongst professions in that it works largely with people who, in some way or another, are outsiders. Often, it is their very status as outsiders which brings them into contact with social work.

Although boundaries between insider and outsider groups are permeable, there is often special mention when this occurs. For instance, when Baroness Amos became International Development Secretary, it was remarked that she was the first black woman to serve in the Cabinet, and the report noted a denial that 'Lady Amos, a 49-year old Guyanan, was selected because of her race' (*Metro*, 2003).

Identification is often felt most strongly by outsider groups. We rarely hear about 'a white perspective' or 'the heterosexual community'. It can be illuminating to reverse the situation, and ask insider groups to subject themselves to the scrutiny to which outsider groups are subjected:

- What do you think is the cause of your heterosexuality?
- When did you first realize you might be heterosexual?

Reproduced from *Modern Social Work Practice* by Mark Doel and Steven M. Shardlow, Ashgate, Aldershot, 2005

- Have you told your parents? What do they think?
- Would you say that you had an inadequate mother or father figure?
- Don't you think your heterosexuality might be a phase you are going through?
- Isn't it possible that what you need is a good gay partner?
- More than 90 per cent of child molesters are heterosexuals. Would you feel comfortable about entrusting your children's education to heterosexual teachers? (Taken from *New Internationalist*, 1989.)

People who resist or bend their identification arouse strong feelings in some others. This is especially true for gender and sexuality, as witnessed by the heated controversy over 'outing' homosexuals, the ridicule which transsexuals experience, and the public fascination for transvestism as an entertainment. The strength which both in-groups and out-groups derive from identifying themselves in relation to each other (that is, heterosexual as 'not gay' and homosexual as 'not straight') is shown by the particular hostility reserved for groups which challenge this polarization, such as bisexual people and people of dual heritage.

## Power and empowerment

There is a growing literature which examines social work practice using a paradigm of power, and we particularly direct you to Thompson (2003: 13–20), who analyses the way in which inequalities of power and opportunity operate at three levels – personal, cultural and societal. The personal includes individual practice and personal prejudice; the cultural relates to commonalities, consensus and conformity; and the structural refers to social divisions and oppression at a socio-political and institutional level (for example, the fact that women are more likely to be imprisoned for a first offence).

At all three levels it is necessary to consider how issues of social justice and equality can be advanced. As a student, and subsequently as a qualified social worker, you are likely to have most opportunity at the personal level, some opportunity at the cultural and less at the structural, to promote equality. However, your impact on the day-to-day experience of many individuals, families and their communities is considerable, and you have regular opportunities to confront injustice and to increase people's sense of power. These opportunities are almost always dilemmas, too. How far to confront agency policies which disempower? How to sensitize an individual to their own sense of internalized oppression while not adding to that oppression? How to recognize and use your own power in ways that empower others? This is a lifelong quest.

## Diversity and difference

The commitment to promote social justice and equality is not new, and anti-oppressive practice, therefore, has historical roots. There is not enough space to

Reproduced from *Modern Social Work Practice* by Mark Doel and Steven M. Shardlow, Ashgate, Aldershot, 2005

explore this issue here (see Thompson, 2003: 147–81), but let us remember that the notion of diversity and difference is a current manifestation and that it, too, will evolve. From a situation in which differences in society were considered to be a threat to social cohesion, there is now a much greater recognition of the enormous changes in Britain and that the differences in British society should be celebrated as a national asset. For example, 'creativity' indexes of various British cities use ethnic variation and the size of the gay community as significant positive indicators. Anti-discriminatory and anti-oppressive practice means promoting the value of diversity.

The fact is that differences more often to lead to discrimination than to celebration, and as a social work student you need to work with this. Indeed, social work is, itself, an out-group. It will always make itself unpopular by its constant reminder of the out-groups' existence and disadvantage. Despite a general sense of malaise in the social work profession, if we look at the vast changes in British society over the past few decades, social work could be said to be achieving its mission. It will receive no thanks nor recognition (and, of course, it is but one small player in these changes), and there is still huge inequality and discrimination. Nevertheless, it is important not to internalize feelings of powerlessness as a profession, and to celebrate those things that make our profession different.

In North America, the commitment to social justice and equality expresses itself in the notion of ethnic-sensitive and culturally competent practice. Devore and Schlesinger use the example of a Jewish hospital social worker who doubted the doctors' concern that an infected rash on a child's leg was exacerbated by dirt; as an insider she knew that 'Jewish mothers fuss and bathe their children a lot'. However, in this case it turned out that the child's rash was, indeed, exacerbated by a lack of hygiene. The social worker's insider knowledge of 'proper Jewish behaviour' misled her, and she subsequently described herself as feeling insulted by this mother's behaviour. Her assumptions as an insider slowed down the process of helping the mother come to grips with the problem (Devore and Schlesinger, 1999: 191). This is an interesting example not only of how easy it is to internalize stereotypes from *within* an outsider group, but also of the potential for oppressive practice. Notions of ethnic-sensitive and culturally competent practice are valuable, but they can neglect the structural levels of power and oppression.

In highlighting difference it is also important not to overlook similarities. The notion of a cultural inventory (Flood, 1988) values what brings people together and what they have in common – what makes them 'a community'.

## Assessment notes: *Anti-oppressive practice*

The opportunities to assess anti-oppressive practice are as ubiquitous as those to learn about it. A key hurdle to overcome is the idea that it is something special and discrete that might occur on Tuesdays. Every encounter offers opportunities to promote equality and work with diversity.

Reproduced from *Modern Social Work Practice* by Mark Doel and Steven M. Shardlow, Ashgate, Aldershot, 2005

General statements of good intent are especially common in the area of anti-oppressive practice, so avoid statements such as 'I worked with Jean Smith in an anti-oppressive way'. It is much more illuminating for you, as well as for any assessor, to be specific about how you promoted equality or, indeed, to be upfront about the dilemmas you have faced in terms of power, discrimination, diversity and difference. As we have already noted, it is not a question of being able to write the 'right phrases', whatever these might be, but to exemplify your own small part in the uneven struggle towards social justice and equality.

## Further reading

Devore, W. and Schlesinger, E.G. (1999), *Ethnic-Sensitive Social Work Practice* (5th edn), Boston, MA: Allyn and Bacon.
GSCC (2002), *Codes of Practice for Social Care Workers and Employers*, London: GSCC.
Thompson, N. (2003), *Promoting Equality*, London: Palgrave Macmillan.

# 15 Law-informed practice

## About Activity 15   A–Z of the law – spirit and letter

*A–Z of the law* consists of twenty-six situations in which there is a possibility that a law has been broken. Students are not being tested on their knowledge of the law, but are asked to judge how *confident* they are that a law has been broken or not, and to consider their own attitudes to the law.

   *A–Z of the law* can be undertaken either by a practice teacher and student together, or in a small group.

### Purpose

This chapter is designed to help students understand the legal context and framework of law that governs their practice. In speaking of 'law-informed practice', the activity recognizes that it is not possible to have detailed knowledge of all the laws which are significant to social work practice, and that students need to be as aware of what they don't know as of what they do know. The activity aims to start a process that demystifies the law and legal processes.

### Method

- Make the activity available to the students beforehand, so that they can prepare answers to the questions on the activity sheet. Students should indicate against each item those situations where they are confident that a law has been broken; those where they are confident that it has not been broken; and those where they are uncertain.
- Discuss each item in turn, looking at the further question: if a law has been broken, should it be invoked?
- Follow the students' own interests in pursuing two or three of the situations further.
- Ask the students to do some follow-up work in relation to a couple of the scenarios which relate to the kind of work done during the placement.

219

If working with small groups, they can each work on five or six of the situations and share their findings. A deliberately wide range of situations is included so that the students get an understanding that law-informed practice is significant in a variety of settings – disability (Cooper, 2000), childcare (Cullen and Lane, 2003) or mental health (Rashid *et al.*, 2002) specialisms.

## Variations

Once the student has been sensitized by this activity to the importance of law-informed practice, it is helpful to provide case material tailored to the placement setting as examples of the ways in which specific laws can influence, guide or determine practice. A case example which is set at different stages in its development helps the student to look at the legal options at various steps in the 'career' of the case, and the consequences of choosing or not choosing particular paths. An example of this kind of build-on exercise is provided by Braye and Preston-Shoot (1990). CCETSW Paper 7 (1991c) also has examples of exercises to use with students.

## Use by other professions

Other professional groups are likely to operate within different legal contexts depending on the nature of their role and function. The scope of the questions can be adapted to fit with those responsibilities, for example the administration of drugs, housing law and so on obtaining consent to a particular procedure.

## National Occupational Standards for Social Work

The topics in this chapter relate to the following National Occupational Standards (see the Appendix):

16:   Managing information
20:   Dilemmas and conflicts
21:   Contributing to best social work practice.

# Activity 15    A–Z of the law – spirit and letter

| Has a law been broken? | Yes ✓ | No ✓ | Unsure ✓ |
|---|---|---|---|
| Sixteen-year-old **A**rnie has been sniffing glue in the toilets at school. | ■ | ■ | ■ |
| The **B**enner family have had their electricity disconnected because of non-payment of bills. | ■ | ■ | ■ |
| The **C**arters have parked their van in a disabled-only car parking space. They do not have a disabled badge. | ■ | ■ | ■ |
| Jason **D**ean does not declare his voluntary work to the unemployment benefits office. | ■ | ■ | ■ |
| Social worker **E**ve claims fifty extra miles on her car allowance to subsidize a trip for the members of her substance abuse group. | ■ | ■ | ■ |
| Landlord Mr **F**inch has locked a tenant out of a furnished bedsit, complaining of 'filth and squalor'. | ■ | ■ | ■ |
| The local authority has failed to provide a stairlift for Ms **G**arthwaite, who suffers from multiple sclerosis and lives in her own two-storey house. | ■ | ■ | ■ |
| Eighteen-year-old **H**oward, who is severely disabled, asks his key worker to masturbate him. | ■ | ■ | ■ |
| His key worker **I**an agrees to do this. | ■ | ■ | ■ |
| **J**ackson reveals he had sexual intercourse with a fourteen-year-old girl three years ago. | ■ | ■ | ■ |
| There is no leaflet available in **K**urdish for Stefan **K**iyani to read about social services in his area. | ■ | ■ | ■ |
| Mrs **L**ehry is not registered as a childminder, but she minds two children after school twice a week. | ■ | ■ | ■ |

Reproduced from *Modern Social Work Practice* by Mark Doel and Steven M. Shardlow, Ashgate, Aldershot, 2005

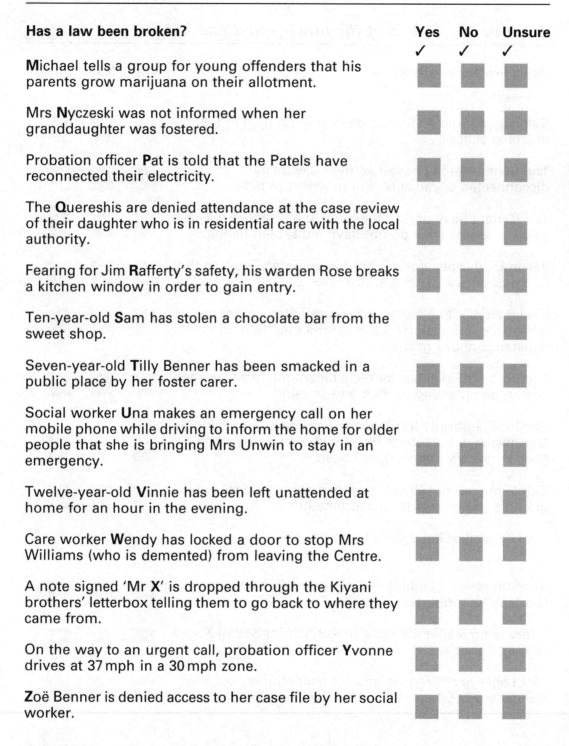

**Has a law been broken?**

|  | Yes ✓ | No ✓ | Unsure ✓ |
|---|---|---|---|
| **M**ichael tells a group for young offenders that his parents grow marijuana on their allotment. | ▢ | ▢ | ▢ |
| Mrs **N**yczeski was not informed when her granddaughter was fostered. | ▢ | ▢ | ▢ |
| Probation officer **P**at is told that the Patels have reconnected their electricity. | ▢ | ▢ | ▢ |
| The **Q**uereshis are denied attendance at the case review of their daughter who is in residential care with the local authority. | ▢ | ▢ | ▢ |
| Fearing for Jim **R**afferty's safety, his warden Rose breaks a kitchen window in order to gain entry. | ▢ | ▢ | ▢ |
| Ten-year-old **S**am has stolen a chocolate bar from the sweet shop. | ▢ | ▢ | ▢ |
| Seven-year-old **T**illy Benner has been smacked in a public place by her foster carer. | ▢ | ▢ | ▢ |
| Social worker **U**na makes an emergency call on her mobile phone while driving to inform the home for older people that she is bringing Mrs Unwin to stay in an emergency. | ▢ | ▢ | ▢ |
| Twelve-year-old **V**innie has been left unattended at home for an hour in the evening. | ▢ | ▢ | ▢ |
| Care worker **W**endy has locked a door to stop Mrs Williams (who is demented) from leaving the Centre. | ▢ | ▢ | ▢ |
| A note signed 'Mr **X**' is dropped through the Kiyani brothers' letterbox telling them to go back to where they came from. | ▢ | ▢ | ▢ |
| On the way to an urgent call, probation officer **Y**vonne drives at 37 mph in a 30 mph zone. | ▢ | ▢ | ▢ |
| **Z**oë Benner is denied access to her case file by her social worker. | ▢ | ▢ | ▢ |

Reproduced from *Modern Social Work Practice* by Mark Doel and Steven M. Shardlow, Ashgate, Aldershot, 2005

- *If a law has been broken, should it be invoked?*

- *If so, what steps would you take to invoke it?*

*Note:* Answers are not given, both because the law does change – it applies differently in different countries – and because, in not providing answers, further opportunities for students to undertake follow-up work to check the current legal position becomes possible.

# Teaching notes: *Law-informed practice*

The *A–Z of the law* activity has two main purposes. The first is to sensitize the student to the importance of the legal context of social work practice, and the second is to dispel some of the mystique that the law offers clear, hard and fast rules. These two purposes may seem paradoxical – the one elevating the profile of law and the other diminishing it – but, in fact, the activity is an opportunity for the student to develop law-informed practice, tuning in to the connections between social work and a legal framework. Ball *et al.* (1988) compare the social work student who does not understand the legal framework to 'a brick-layer without a plumbline'. The law offers not one, but many, plumblines which can be used to very different effects: guaranteeing service users' and carers' rights; securing service users' and carers' protection; enforcing social control.

Students need to be honest with themselves about their attitude towards the law. For example, where would the student rate the following statements on a scale of 1 to 10 (strongly disagree to strongly agree)?[1]

The law is:

- a weapon the powerful use to keep the powerless in their place
- a safeguard for the individual against the state
- relatively arbitrary in the way it is applied
- a reflection of social tensions and dilemmas
- something that can only be created by a religious body
- an intrusion into the lives of individuals
- slow to catch up with social changes
- white, male and middle-class
- an ass
- a mechanism to regulate social exchange
- something that should never be broken.

## Linking social work and the law

Helping students to understand the relationship between social work and the law can be aided by encouraging them to discuss three distinctions, which help to expose different aspects of law and its relationship to social work:

*Distinction 1: the relationship of law and social work*

According to Braye and Preston-Shoot (2002: 62) the complex relationship between social work and the law can be characterized in three different ways:

---

[1] This could be developed and used as an exercise with students, as well as helping to inform the teacher's approach to promoting learning.

1 Law provides the 'defining mandate' for practice – that is, it provides a specification of what must be done.
2 Law describes a generalized 'ethical duty of care' which determines the responsibilities of the social worker.
3 Both of these polarities (1 and 2) are key determinants of social work and it is for practitioners and managers to 'determine the balance to be struck' in any given situation.

*Ask the student to consider the implications of each of these three characteristics.*

## Distinction 2: domains of law

Braye and Preston-Shoot also helpfully draw a distinction between the different domains of *social work law* and *social welfare law*:

> ...*social work law*, which included powers and duties that expressly mandate social work activity, and *social welfare law*, comprising statues with which social workers must be familiar if they are to respond appropriately to service users' needs but which do not permit or require specific actions by them. (Braye and Preston-Shoot; 2002: 63)

*Ask the student to relate the notion of domains to a situation with which they have been working.*

## Distinction 3: types of legal instrument

There are various types of legal requirement that derive from different forms of legal instrument:

1 *Common law*. This is a body of commonly accepted laws, which are interpreted by the judiciary, based on precedent; that is, the common law is modified by judicial judgements and forms a body of case law.
2 *Statute law (sometimes called primary legislation)*. These are Acts of Parliament[2] (Edinburgh, Northern Ireland Assembly, Welsh Assembly, Westminster). Statutes, if relevant to the case, always takes precedence over common law.
3 *Statutory Instruments (sometimes called secondary legislation)*. These are rules, regulations and schedules issued by the relevant ministry or government department. They can be harder to identify than primary legislation, but often contain specific statements about practice requirements.
4 *Circulars[3] and other guidance issued by government departments*. These indicate how a law should be interpreted they are not as enforceable as statutory instruments.

---

[2] Available at: www.hmso.gov.uk/acts.html
[3] Available at: www.doh.gov.uk/publications/index.html

5    *Quasi-legal statements.* These are documents produced by various non-governmental bodies that provide for the setting of standards and regulations. The
National Occupational Standards for Social Work and National Service Frameworks for Mental Health or Older People are examples.

*Ask the students to consider an aspect of practice and to identify the various forms of legal
instrument that govern their practice in this field.*

When organizing learning opportunities for students it is helpful to encourage
students to be clear about the way in which they conceptualize the relationship of
social work to the law in these and other ways. Whatever the practice teacher's or
student's views on this matter, the teaching of law for social workers has come
under considerable and sustained criticism in the UK (criticisms which added fuel
to the fire which carried probation training out of social work in 1996) because social
workers have been seen as neither knowledgeable about, nor able to make effective
use of, the law (Ball *et al.*, 1988; Ball, *et al.*, 1991; Blom-Cooper, 1985). These critics of
law teaching, whose criticisms were as valid then as now, state that law must be a
central part of social work teaching and pivotal to professional practice – in other
words, that law is the 'defining mandate' of social work. However, there are also
critics of the prescriptive approach to teaching law. Braye and Preston-Shoot (1990;
1992) assert that teaching law and its subsequent application 'must be considered in
a conceptual frame of practice dilemmas which confront every practitioner and
create role conflict, uncertainty, ambiguity, and insecurity'. These dilemmas, 'posed
by taking account both of the law and the ethical duty of care in professional
practice, lead social workers into the eye of the storm'. The authors look at the
tensions between rights versus risk; care versus control; needs versus resources;
duty versus power; legalism versus professionalism, amongst others. They suggest
that it is not just knowledge of the law which must be conveyed, 'but the problems
and the dilemmas in applying it'.

## The growing importance of the law for professional education

In documents regulating social work education there has been a growing emphasis
on the importance of teaching and learning about law. The origins of this process
can be seen in relation to the DipSW in Section 2.1 of CCETSW Paper 30 (1991a),
which *outlined* the core areas of legal knowledge to be studied by all students, and
the Review of the Diploma in Social Work which required a working knowledge of
legal and statutory requirements (CCETSW, 1995). Most recently, as part of the
Reform of Social Work Education initiative and the creation of an undergraduate
level basic professional qualification, the Department of Health for England has
placed special emphasis on law, which is singled out[4] as a key element on which all
students must be taught and assessed (Department of Health, 2002a: 8). It is

---

[4] Along with: partnership working; communication skills; assessment planning intervention and
review; human growth; development; mental health and disability for special attention.

important to draw the student's attention to the ever-increasing importance of law for social work practice.

## Opportunities

Of particular interest to practice teachers are Braye and Preston-Shoot's findings about ways to help students learn, retain and apply law teaching. The group of students with whom they worked had reservations about the lack of practice opportunities, feeling that it is difficult to retain knowledge of the law without putting it to use. Practice-led methods of learning, where a case example was used to trigger discussion and subsequent teaching inputs linked directly to concerns arising from the discussion, were preferred by two-thirds of the student group. It is interesting that Braye and Preston-Shoot (1992) saw evidence of 'an unsettling effect' as some of the students moved from a state of blissful ignorance to a realization of what they did not know.

Eadie and Ward (1995) took this approach further, focusing all the learning around students' work on case examples presented to them. This 'scenario approach' arose out of the findings of an earlier study (Hogg *et al.*, 1992) of law teaching on placements, which they describe as 'profoundly disturbing'. The findings revealed:

- a widespread lack of accurate substantive knowledge of legislation, precedent and legal structure, processes and concepts
- a confusion about the nature of the law (what is a legal issue?) and the relationship of the law to social work activity
- an inconsistent approach to teaching both in college and on placement
- little awareness of how gender and race issues affect teaching and learning.

The law scenarios enabled small groups of students to develop their inquiry and investigative skills to find out what they needed to know in a number of different areas, such as 'through-care' in probation work. At the end of their investigations, the students gave presentations, so that they could all learn from each other's researches (Eadie and Ward, 1995). Although the different areas produced different details, the processes of the research were very similar, as were themes such as issues of racism and discrimination institutionalized in legislation.

It would be useful to use a scenario approach on an individual basis with a student, or perhaps by gathering a small group of students placed in your agency. As an approach that focuses as much on the processes of learning about the law and the context for its application, as on the content of the law, it has more likelihood of 'sticking'.

Approaches to teaching law have been developed in a range of ways: for example, Duncan *et al.* (2003) describe how an ecological approach to practice can be used to develop an understanding of the ever-widening circles of law that may be relevant. They conclude that a deep and purposeful engagement by practitioners with the legal implications of professional practice is fundamental to ecologically grounded theories. Braye and a group of students comment on the benefit of using enquiry action methods for learning about the law (Braye *et al.*, 2003); while Broadbent and White (2003) explore how 'decision making' techniques can be used to promote student's appreciation of the law.

## Seeking legal expertise

In 1991, CCETSW Paper 7 (1991c) listed thirty-seven different Acts of Parliament relating to social work practice in England and Wales, forty-four in Northern Ireland and forty-four in Scotland.[5] This number will be much greater now, due to the ever-increasing volume of new legislation, the rate of amendment of existing legislation (for example, a plethora of new Criminal Justice Acts), devolutionary trends across the UK which are increasing the differences in legislation across the four countries, and the application of EU legislation to the UK. However, legislation is more accessible than previously, and can be accessed online.[6] It would be a feat to remember the titles of all these Acts, never mind the details of their provisions. Remembering them all is even more problematic as, to our knowledge, no organization has maintained a running tally of the legislation applicable to social work. Even when the details of Acts are learnt and tested, it is questionable how much of this detail is retained. How much legal knowledge have you retained from your own qualifying training? It is frequent use of the law that determines how well it is remembered.

Writing some time ago, Stevenson (1988) doubted whether it is desirable or feasible to acquire factual legal knowledge during basic professional education and questions the reliability of such knowledge. Inaccurate legal advice given to a service user or carer is worse than no advice at all – but the function of a social worker is not to provide definitive legal advice. Even so, students do need to recognize that social work sits within a legal framework and they should know how that framework constructs their work. It is important that students cultivate both an understanding of what they don't know and the skills to know when and how to seek additional expertise. Increasingly, there is an expectation that, at the point of qualification, students will have more than a generalized familiarity with the way in which social work is constructed by the law – that they will have a working knowledge of some aspects relevant to particular areas of practice.

Initially, students need to develop a clear picture of the practice goals in a particular piece of work, with the people involved and *within a legal framework*. Once they have this picture, they should know how and where to seek the advice which will help them to achieve those practice goals; detailed legal advice will, in turn, reshape some aspects of those practice goals, but it is a myth to believe that 'application of the law' will by itself bring clarity to the picture. The law is not 'cut and dried'; it seldom offers concrete conclusions, because – like social work practice – it, too, reflects the dilemmas in society. Braye and Preston-Shoot (1997) expose

---

[5] The law in relation to social work is different in the different countries of the UK. For a comparison of law in respect of children and families, see for example, Tisdal *et al.* (1997).

[6] Acts of the Westminster Parliament are available at: http://www.hmso.gov.uk/acts.htm

other myths about the law: that it is helpful, neutral, confers substantial powers, and provides good and right solutions.

In conclusion, knowledge probably sticks when it is related to specific practice examples, and when the student has used it personally. It needs consistent reinforcement. Students need some detailed legal knowledge within the context of developing law-informed practice, so that they know which questions to ask and where and how to seek legal expertise to provide the detail.

# Learning notes: *Law-informed practice*

> Social workers have been criticized for being over-zealous in their use of the law and for failing to use available legal powers. (Preston-Shoot, 1993: 65)

This quotation neatly encapsulates the *actual* response of social work to the law. It is extremely difficult for social workers to achieve a balance in the way that the law is deployed in social work on account of the complex situations with which they have to deal.

In addition to having a knowledge of the legal framework, it is also important for you to be aware of your own feelings about how the law should be invoked. This involves careful consideration of the legal consequences of professional actions as well as an understanding of what is legally permissible. In some countries, the individual practitioner can be legally held to account for actions taken. For example, in the US there is a growing interest in liability issues in relation to social work practice (see, for example, Houston-Vega *et al.*, 1996). This may become a growing feature of social work practice in the UK as the registration and regulation of practitioners takes effect (GSCC, 2002).

As Johns states, it should be borne in mind that the law does not provide definitive answers for practice:

> The law cannot tell social workers what to do in every circumstance: it can only set out a framework. The law cannot resolve the everyday tensions and dilemmas of social work practice, since there is no ready prescription for resolving the complex problems that sometimes confront social workers. Above all the law cannot substitute for sound professional practice. (Johns, 2003: 7)

In the UK, there are certain situations where the practitioner has personal liability. According to Jones (2003), in respect of section 114(2) of the Mental Health Act 1983:

> [an] approved social worker is therefore personally liable for his[7] actions whilst carrying out functions under this Act. He should exercise his own judgement, based upon social and medical evidence, and not act at the behest of his employers, medical practitioners or other persons who might be involved with the patient's welfare. (Jones, 2003: 96)

This position is supported by case law (*St George's Healthcare NHS Trust v. S* [1998] 3 All ER 673). However, despite the fact that the social worker acts in a personal capacity, Jones states that:

> Although an approved social worker acts in a personal capacity when carrying out his functions under this act [Mental Health Act] . . . as an employee he will be protected by the doctrine of

---

[7] Gender-specific language in original.

Reproduced from *Modern Social Work Practice* by Mark Doel and Steven M. Shardlow, Ashgate, Aldershot, 2005

vicarious liability and the local authority will be liable for wrongs done by him while acting in the course of his employment. (Jones, 2003: 439)

## The approval–disapproval continuum

Return to the scenarios in *A–Z of the law*. Your response to the law in different situations is an important influence on your actions. How strongly do you feel about each of them? Take your three lists (one where you think a law has been broken, one where you think it has not, and one where you are uncertain), and draw a *continuum line* for each list. Using one end for strongly approve of the action taken (1) and one end for strongly disapprove (10), place each scenario on its continuum:

| | | |
|---|---|---|
| **A LAW HAS BEEN BROKEN** | | |
| strongly approve | neutral response | strongly disapprove |
| (1) | (5) | (10) |
| **A LAW HAS NOT BEEN BROKEN** | | |
| strongly approve | neutral response | strongly disapprove |
| (1) | (5) | (10) |
| **UNCERTAIN WHETHER A LAW HAS BEEN BROKEN** | | |
| strongly approve | neutral response | strongly disapprove |
| (1) | (5) | (10) |

Are there situations where you are confident that a law has been broken, but where you feel less disapproval than situations where a law has not been broken?
    Ball *et al.* (1988) define the following categories of legal activity:

- enforcing the rights of service users and carers
- protecting the vulnerable
- protecting society
- enforcing compliance.

Which category do you think each of the situations in *A–Z of the law* might fall into?

## Assessment notes: *Law-informed practice*

The assessment of law can focus on two broad areas:

1   the extent to which students understand the relationship of social work practice to the law – in other words, the context and importance of law in a particular site for social work practice
2   legal knowledge and the ability to apply elements of the law in practice (for example, childcare law, mental health law, the law that relates to residential care).

You need to be very clear about which is required. Other professions engage in rote learning of law pertinent to their practice. So far, social work has resisted this, but the increased importance given to this aspect of practice by government suggests that there should be a stronger emphasis on assessing students' abilities to work effectively with the law in day-to-day practice. The law can be examined in very creative ways; for example Henderson, Scott and Lloyd report an experiment to examine Approved Social Workers (ASWs) using oral methods (Henderson, Scott and Lloyd, 2003) – something that is more usual in some other professions such as medicine or psychiatry and is frequently used on mainland Europe. There is no reason not to be innovative in the assessment of law – you can encourage your practice teacher or programme to explore alternative methods.

## Further reading

Brayne, H. and Carr, H. (2003), *Law for Social Workers* (8th edn), Oxford: Oxford University Press.
Cull, L-A. and Roche, J. (2001), *The Law and Social Work: contemporary issues for practice*, Basingstoke: Palgrave.
Johns, R. (2003), *Using the Law in Social Work*, Exeter: Learning Matters.

# 16 Generalist and specialist practice

## About Activity 16    *Essence of social work*

*Essence of social work* is designed to trigger a consideration of what is different about, and what is common to, the various manifestations of social work. In this activity, students are encouraged to look for the 'core' of social work practice.

### Purpose

One of the major continuing shifts in the construction of social work practice is the emphasis given to generic, generalist and specialist practice. This activity explores some of the differences between these different kinds of practice and the chapter will help to clarify some of the confusion in understanding these terms.

### Method

- Ask the students to read the advertisements in the *Essence of social work* activity. They are all taken from the back pages of the same issue of *Community Care*[1] published in the autumn of 2003. The names of employing agencies have been changed, contacts and addresses have been omitted, but in all other respects the advertisements are unaltered.
- Ask them to consider what are the main similarities and what are the main differences in the work which these job adverts reveal. What is the 'social worker' in them?
- Discuss with the students what they think the job adverts tell them about current social work practice. Suggest that they ask five people who are not connected with social work (friends and relatives, for instance) what social work is.

---

[1] A weekly social work journal published in the UK.

233

## Variations

Five or six detailed job descriptions from your own agency might draw out the commonalities and differences even more clearly. Try comparing these with adverts from other non-social work journals for related posts (for example, health visitors, probation officers) – how different and how similar are they?

Specialist practice is currently the dominant form of practice in the UK (see 'Teaching notes' for more details). In order to begin to understand the great diversity in the way specialisms are represented, you could ask students to make a note of all the different specialist social work practice they are aware of. The harder task is to identify what is the 'social work' function in these different forms of practice.

## Use by other professions

'Specialisms' are well-developed in medical practice. In addition to the 'territorial' approach or functional approach to medical specialisms, there are other kinds of demarcation. Acupuncturists, chiropractors and homeopaths specialize in alternative *methods* of practice. By contrast, social work does not have a strong base in practice methodology. It seems that everyone is either eclectic (code for agnostic), or claims to practise in a task-centred way, despite the absence of all the formal elements of the task-centred model. Indeed, agencies would tend to be suspicious of practitioners declaring that they are to be method specialists; seeking a position as a 'Brief Solution Specialist' or a 'Cognitive Behaviourist Specialist' would be unlikely to carry much weight.

The nature and desirability of specialist practice is a matter of debate within many professional disciplines. In respect of occupational therapy, Harries and Gilhooly (2003: 396) found that generic working tended to give more importance to those service users and carers who presented high risk of violence or suicide; in health visiting, Salmon, Hook and Hayward (2003) reported a modest study which revealed that parents preferred the services of an innovative and specialist health visitor in infant mental health. This post was specifically designed to work with families with children under four years of age who showed signs of early mental health problems; in nursing, Hill *et al.* (2002) showed better outcomes from specialist nurse-led assessment in respect of looked-after children.

## National Occupational Standards for Social Work

The topics in this chapter relate to most of the National Occupational Standards (see the Appendix) and the following in particular:

  2:   Making informed decisions together
 17:   Working interprofessionally
 19:   Professional development
 21:   Promoting best social work practice.

# Activity 16    *Essence of social work*

## Head of Care
## Bettleheim
## Residential School

**Grade Residential Social Worker 'F'**
**£32,682–£35,974 p.a. inc.**
**41 hours per week,**
**40 weeks per year**

We seek a qualified, experienced, dedicated Senior Manager (CQSW, Dip SW NVQ level, Management Qualification) to run a highly successful Residential Department in this nationally recognized specialist VI (Visually impaired)/MDVI (Multi-disabled Visually Impaired) school. The school is founded on the principles of commitment, honest, integrity and the dedication of our experienced, motivated and trained staff teams. We require a manager who has confidence, experience and knowledge to ensure that high standards of practice continue to exceed National Care Standards requirements. You will have leadership skills and be able to promote a culture in the school which is responsive to the needs of our pupils and be able to demonstrate a proven track record in residential care at senior level.

The appointment is subject to a CRB check.

*We are an Equal Opportunity Employer and welcome applications regardless of race, colour, nationality, ethnic origin, sex, marital status, disability or age. All applications are considered on the basis of their merits and abilities for the job.*

Positive About Disabled People

## Cymru Care
## Service Manager
## £27,420 35 hours

Cymru Care provides services throughout Wales and has a proven track record in developing and managing services to single vulnerable people.

Anglefan is a ground-breaking project that provides high quality support for people who have complex mental health needs. Based in Mid-Wales, Anglefan is a highly valued and influential development within the local authority strategy and will inform future philosophy and practice around supporting people in a non-institutional, therapeutic setting. The core house comprises five flats and will have a crisis bed. In addition, floating support is provided to 20 clients in their own homes.

This post offers a rare opportunity for a highly-motivated and dynamic mental health professional to be at the cutting edge of innovative and sustainable service development. You will lead an enthusiastic team and the community in directing the learning, development and values of Anglefan. Candidates should have an excellent working knowledge of good practice in the field of mental health, have highly developed interpersonal and communication skills and be committed to creativity in service enhancement. In addition you will be flexible, enthusiastic and able to evidence excellent leadership skills.

We offer: good terms and conditions of employment, 22 days' annual leave, rising to 29 after 3 years' service, 6% contribution to pension fund.

*We are committed to Equal Opportunities.*

**Butler Council**
**Restorative Justice Development Officer**
**£30,267 to £32,682 p.a. inc.**

An exciting opportunity has arisen for a dynamic individual to develop effective practice in restorative justice processes for children and young people aged 8–13 and their families. You will work to expand capacity in the voluntary and statutory sector for early intervention work and develop a range of approaches that lead to reparation; look at innovative ways of preventing offending behaviour; commission services and ensure participation of children and young people and their carers. You will be based in the Youth Offending Team and have strong links to the Children's Fund Partnership.

You will need:
- A minimum of three years' experience of working with young people and their families in a diverse inner city area
- An understanding of restorative justice, the criminal justice system and child development as well as issues relating to children of this age group and their families
- Experience of developing services in the voluntary and statutory sector

Butler Council values the diversity of its community and aims to have a workforce that reflects this. We therefore encourage applications from all sections of the community.

*Investor in People*

*Suffragette City*
*Senior Practitioners*
*Fostering and Adoption*

**Up to £35,100 p.a. inc.**

We require two senior practitioners in the Fostering Support Team, one providing support specifically to kinship carers. We also need one full-time senior in the Adoption Family Finding Team and one half-time post in the Adoption Support Team.

You will have at least two years' post-qualifying experience in children and families work and preferably experience in either fostering or adoption.

*Positive About Disabled People*

Reproduced from *Modern Social Work Practice* by Mark Doel and Steven M. Shardlow, Ashgate, Aldershot, 2005

---

## *East Hollishire*
## *Joint Commissioning Manager*
## *£34,000–£37,000 p.a. Full time*

*This post presents an exciting opportunity to lead the development of joint commissioning and service improvement for mental health and possibly other joint services in the future. You will take forward the agenda set out in the National Service Framework and other key national and local priorities, working with voluntary agencies and user and carer groups. We are looking for an enthusiastic and innovative manager with experience in commissioning or providing mental health services and other adult services. You will be educated to degree level and have at least two years' management experience in the health service or local authority. You will have a successful track record of planning and implementing service change.*

*Positive About Disabled People*
*Investor in People*

---

### Meyer and Timms County Council

**SOCIAL SERVICES**
Children and families

*Supervising Social Workers (Task-Centred Team)*
*SW1/2 £19,824–£21,993/£22,689–£25,911*
*pro rata for part time*
*1 × 37 hrs per week. 1 × 11.10 hrs per week*
*(Thurs. p.m. and Fri. all day)*

Committed to best practice and achieving good outcomes for Looked-After Children? Working as part of an established team to provide a high quality supervision and support to foster carers to meet National Standards? If you are looking for a challenge and have the required skills for this role we would like to hear from you.

We have two opportunities in the Task-Centred Team Family Placement Service. In **Meyer and Timms County Council** we are highly motivated to meet the challenges of National Care Standards.

We are looking for an enthusiastic worker committed to implementing National Care Standards in Foster Care and meeting the needs of children requiring emergency and short-term placements. Your work will include the assessment and supervision of Task-Centred carers, contributing to providing an office duty service and making placements.

Our Family Placement Service offers:
- a permanent full-time and a part-time post
- the chance to work in an authority committed to meeting the National Care standards
- regular supervision
- training opportunities including PQ/PQCCA
- a friendly settled team in a pleasant city centre environment.

We require:
- a DipSW or equivalent qualification
- preferably two years' previous experience in a children and families social work setting.

We particularly welcome applications from ethnic minority communities as they are under-represented in this area of work: Section 38(1)b of the Race Relations Act 1976 applies. All applications will be considered on their merits alone. The successful candidates will be required to complete a CRD form in line with Section 115 of The Police Act 1997.

*Positive About Disabled People*
*Investor in People*

---

*St Marcus and St Stefan's Hospice*
*BEREAVEMENT SERVICE COORDINATOR/SOCIAL WORKER*

**20 hrs per week**
**Salary scale: £20,000–£22,000**
**Rising by four annual increments pro rata**

St Marcus and St Stefan's Hospice provides In-Patient Care, Day Care and an Out-Patient Department for people with advanced progressive disease. We want to develop and expand the current bereavement support that is offered to families and carers.

Working closely with the Multidisciplinary team, you will offer practical and emotional support to patients and their families. You may be working with children and young people, providing individual and groupwork with bereaved families. You will also be required to train, coordinate and supervise a committed group of Bereavement Volunteers and participate in any activities that involve bereavement support.

You will have at least 3 years' experience in a healthcare-related discipline involving work within a multidisciplinary setting. A professional qualification (either Social Care or Healthcare) with counselling or family therapy is essential.

---

**Faithful Social Services**
**Child Care Social Workers**

**Up to £30,420 (including market supplement)**

Full/part-time positions available. Generous relocation package applies.

We are committed to building a supportive, cross-agency team that provides the very highest standards of Child Care Practice. That's why we're increasing the number of Social Workers in our team.

You'll be part of a district-based, very supportive Child Care Team. Locally we work with a Children's Fund, a Sure Start programme and Resource Centres at Faithful. Our supervision programme will help you develop (there are also opportunities for further education). We actively promote the PQ and Child Care Award programmes, which is recognised in the pay structure. Last, but by no means least, you'll receive your own laptop and our highly organised computer systems.

Working towards equal opportunities
Positive About Disabled People
Investor in People

---

Reproduced from *Modern Social Work Practice* by Mark Doel and Steven M. Shardlow, Ashgate, Aldershot, 2005

**London Borough of Barclay/Barclay Care NHS Trust**
**Assertive Outreach Service Practitioners**
**Grade F/G Social Worker/Approved Social Worker or Senior I/II Occupational Therapist**

**Competitive salary dependent upon experience and qualifications**

Barclay Care NHS Trust and The London Borough of Barclay Social Services are working in partnership to develop a range of integrated Mental Health services. We are looking to appoint several Mental Health practitioners who have the skills and experience to work closely with individuals with complex needs and an enduring and severe mental illness.

You will have a professional qualification in nursing, social work or occupational therapy, supported by a commitment to this challenging client group. Evidence of professional development and a high level of clinical skill are essential, and these will be supported by the ability to work as part of a multidisciplinary team.

The Trust is committed to Equal Opportunities and improving working lives. A No Smoking Policy operates on all sites.

*Positive About Disabled People*

- *What do you think these job adverts tell you about current social work practice?*
- *Try asking five people who are not connected with social work (friends and relatives, for instance) what social work is.*

Reproduced from *Modern Social Work Practice* by Mark Doel and Steven M. Shardlow, Ashgate, Aldershot, 2005

## Teaching notes: *Generalist and specialist practice*

### What is generalist practice?

Students are likely to come with a reasonable understanding of the notion of 'specialist' practice, though we will see later how complex the notion of speciality is. However, the notion of 'generalist' practice, whilst better understood in North America, is not particularly current in the UK. Moreover, it is often confused with 'generic' practice, to which we will turn later.

Writing about social work in the 1960s, in a book entitled *The Creative Generalist*, Heus and Pincus noted that:

> ... in spite of the existence of a single professional association, social work remained fragmented by method (casework, groupwork, and community organization), fields of practice (for example medical social work, child welfare, corrections) and divided purposes (for example individual change versus environmental change, service versus reform). (Heus and Pincus, 1986: 6)

The 1970s, however, were a time when the prominence of systems theory acted as a unifying force, leading to the development of an integrated social work method. Social work became conceptualized as planned change rather than individual therapy, and systems theory helped to integrate the profession, with a focus on the interaction between people and their environment. To use the language of systems theory, the service user was often assumed to be the 'target of change', although the target could also be other components of the system.

Allying systems thinking and a problem-solving approach with knowledge from the interdisciplinary field of creativity, Heus and Pincus (1986) developed a notion of the 'creative generalist' in an attempt to understand the *art* side of practice and to bring intuitive and rational thinking together (see the Introduction to Part III).

We may associate a generalist with an eclectic, 'master of none' approach, and a specialist with an expert. 'Since expertise is a hallmark of professionalism, the eclectic is (seen as) less than professional' (Heus and Pincus, 1986). Similarly, the tendency in North American universities to offer generalist practice at a beginning, bachelors, level has emphasized its place as a junior – the first level of professional education. However, a generalist and a specialist have different *kinds* of expertise, as the following illustration demonstrates.

If we return to Derby Street (*Licensed to learn*, page 13), we can see that there might be a variety of social work specialists involved with different people in the various households. Indeed, a useful supplementary activity to conduct with students would be to ask them to consider which workers from your own agency and others might be involved with the different residents, and what opportunities for interprofessional working there might be. Clearly, there is a social work *role* to be played in each and every household, and also with the neighbourhood as a whole.

If we were writing about 'modern' social work practice in 1980, we would have had a prominent chapter on neighbourhood work, sometimes called *patch work*, and a single (community) social worker would probably have been the first point of call for all of the residents of Derby Street. This social worker would have practised in a generalist way (though, just to confuse things, this would have been referred to as 'generic' in the UK, as explained later). The social worker would have had a broad knowledge of many different systems and would have been expected to refer to more specialist services if a situation stretched their expertise or resources. Whilst it was an advantage for service users to have a single point of call, there was an inherent disadvantage in attempting to acquire a depth of knowledge in so many different aspects of life. This way of organizing and conceptualizing social work practice has now all but disappeared, though history suggests that the fashion is cyclical, so it may yet return in some form. In practice, of course, it was often the team that was generalist, rather than the individual worker, with the team constituting a generalist system of service (each member of the team specializing to a certain extent), similar to Seebohm's (1968; 1989) vision for the reorganization of British social work services in the early 1970s.

In summary, *generalist* practice is, therefore, a concept which refers to the breadth and variety of systems with which the social worker is expected to work (Tolson *et al.*, 1994: 396). Using Derby Street as a reference point to discuss the pros and cons of generalist practice encourages students to think critically and creatively about social work practice.

## Generic social work practice

The term 'generic' is often used synonymously with generalist, as part of the 'jack of all trades, master of none' syndrome. However, this is mistaken. Generic social work is that which is common to all social work practice, however and wherever it is practised. In other words, what is the 'social work' in the work of a social worker in a residential childcare facility, and what does this have in common with the social work practised by a social worker in a community mental health team? Moreover, what do these both have in common with generalist social work as described in the previous section?

The *Essence of social work* activity which the student completed in preparation for this topic should begin to explore these issues. As the activity demonstrates, there are many posts which no longer carry the title 'social worker', such as the 'Restorative Justice Development Officer' and the 'Assertive Outreach Service Practitioner'. Those elements of their practice which we would recognize as social work is what we are terming 'generic' – a common core. By doing this activity, the student will begin to understand how social work practice is not confined to posts with 'social worker' in the title and, conversely, that some social work positions may actually involve relatively little 'social work'.

## The significance of the generalist–specialist debate

Students may consider the issue of generalist, specialist and generic social work to be of historical, rather than current, interest. However, it is important to help students see the continuing significance of these issues, as part of their enquiry into how social work is conceptualized. The heart-searching about *'What is social work?'*

and the repeated concerns about its ability to survive, point to at least two major issues:

1   The profession remains uncertain about how to conceptualize itself. We hope that the debates in this chapter will help students and practitioners alike to set their own practice in a wider, intellectual context.
2   Even when a conceptual map for social work has been agreed and understood, its generic core is by no means a given. What is it that is common to all forms of practice, which we call social work?

## Opportunities

The current organization of social work services means that the student is likely to have a series of experiences of different kinds of specialist practice (we look at how 'specialist' can be conceptualized in the 'Learning notes'). It is important for practice teachers and work-based supervisors to ensure that they enable the student to associate the particular experience of specialist practice to the core elements of generic social work. Students need to enquire what components of their current learning and practice are *social work*, as opposed to *mental health* or *childcare*. This may be something which you, as practice teacher or work-based supervisor, have not asked yourself for some time, too!

We continue this theme, *'What is social work?'*, in the 'Learning notes' which follow.

# Learning notes: *Generalist and specialist practice*

The note on the flysheet of Zofia Butrym's book, *The Nature of Social Work*, was written in 1976, but remains apt today:

> This book argues that the present lack of consensus about the nature and the functions of social work constitutes a serious problem which, if allowed to continue, will result in loss of purpose and usefulness by social workers. It therefore attempts to answer the question: 'What is social work?' (Butrym, 1976)

Twenty years on, the title of Malcolm Payne's book asks '*What is Professional Social Work?*' His narrative, which runs through the book, 'implies that being involved in education and management, being in the voluntary and statutory sectors and doing community, policy and development work can all be regarded as social work' (Payne, 1996: 9–10).

If experienced social workers in educational and practice settings are asking '*What is social work?*', students can be forgiven for pondering the same question. In this chapter we take one abiding tension in social work practice – that between general and specialist practice – as a specific illustration of the quest to define social work. We have rooted this central tension in its historical context; an understanding of the recurring nature of these themes will help you understand the present state of social work and better anticipate its future.

## The common base of social work practice

> The common base of social work practice consists of concepts, generalizations, and principles relating to knowledge, values and intervention – i.e. abstract ideas. (Bartlett, 1970: 129)

Writing in 1970, Harriet Bartlett made a distinction between generic practice and the common base of social work practice which is as useful now as it was then. Bartlett warns against what she refers to as 'bipolar thinking' – that is, a division which separates people from their contexts. She sees the need to direct attention to the nature of the exchange between individuals and their environment as a way of eliminating this separation. Activity 1, *Licensed to learn*, is central to this question of considering individuals and families in their environment.

Bartlett considers that the early focus in social work on 'feeling and doing', though useful in developing the skills base of the individual practitioner, deflected attention from 'thinking and knowing', so there was no equal momentum toward a comprehensive view of social work: 'Thus the relation between the practice of the individual social worker and the broad essentials of his [sic] profession's practice was not faced' (Bartlett, 1970: 134). Bartlett proposed the concept of social functioning as providing a common base for social work practice. Below we describe how, just at the time Bartlett was writing, methodologies were being

Reproduced from *Modern Social Work Practice* by Mark Doel and Steven M. Shardlow, Ashgate, Aldershot, 2005

developed, which would be forces for integration, rather than division, in social work practice. These forces continue to provide a conceptual map, both for the social work profession as a whole and for individual practice as a part.

## What is a specialism?

Going further back, almost half a century ago, Hollis and Taylor (1951) pointed to the 'lack of adequate criteria for determining what is *basic* and what is *specialized* in social work' and considered this to be the main reason for the inability to develop a satisfactory social work curriculum. Bartlett (1970: 94) noted that the concept of specialization is only valid 'when there is a concept of a whole that can be divided into parts' and that social work's peculiar origins as 'a profession growing *through* its parts' led to premature concepts of specialization. An aggregation can just as soon become a disaggregation. She declared that 'practitioners not long in practice cannot be regarded as specialists because specialization rests on extended study and experience from which true expertise develops' (Bartlett, 1970: 195). Bartlett would, therefore, have considered the idea of developing a specialist area of practice as a social work *student* as very premature.

Bartlett argued for greater discrimination in the use of the terms 'generic' and 'specific', and of 'basic' and 'specialized'. Papell (1996) reminds us that the term 'generic' first appeared in North American social work in the report of the Milford Conference in 1929, though only a single method (casework) was then involved. 'The recommendation was that education presented in the university was to be generic while the specialized knowledge needed in settings wherever casework was practised – such as psychiatric, medical, child welfare – was to be taught in the field' (Papell, 1996: 16).

The division between specialist and generic, specialism and generalism, remains far from clear. The distinctions can be drawn along many different lines, depending on time and place. A quarter of a century ago, Bartlett noted that social workers were accustomed to think of their practice in terms of agencies, fields and methods. She mused why it was proving so difficult for 'social workers to take the necessary steps toward a perception of their practice as no longer fragmented' (Bartlett, 1970: 130). At the beginning of the twenty-first century, the movement towards specialist practice in the UK is strong and is largely defined by age: children and families, or adult services. Traditionally, lines have been drawn according to service user groups defined by the nature of the 'problem' – mental health worker, child protection worker, mobility officer and so on.

## Forms of specialism

Notwithstanding the conceptual difficulty in defining specialist, generalist and generic social work, observation reveals that, in the real world, specialist practice

Reproduced from *Modern Social Work Practice* by Mark Doel and Steven M. Shardlow, Ashgate, Aldershot, 2005

comes in many shapes and sizes. Horwath and Shardlow (2003) have suggested that there are at least eight different 'territories'[2] of specialist practice, namely:

1 *Service user group*

The social worker works mainly or exclusively with one type or group of service user: this has become the dominant paradigm of professional practice in the UK at the time of writing, to the extent that the term 'specialist practice' has become synonymous with this type of specialism. Certainly, within England there is an apparently ever-widening gap, in terms of practice skills and knowledge, between those who work with children and families and those who work with adults. This has become the primary division in professional practice.

2 *Community*

One form of specialism was common in the UK during the late 1970s and 1980s, variously known as 'locally-based social work', 'neighbourhood work' and 'patch-based social work'. The core of a community focus lies in the geographical specialization around a particular neighbourhood: for a research-based appraisal of this approach see Hadley and McGrath (1981). The Barclay Report (1982) also advocated communities of interest as a form of specialism.

3 *Expertise*

Some social workers are recognized by others to have a particularly detailed knowledge or skill in some aspect of social work and become known as experts. Frequently, they are awarded that status informally by colleagues who will seek out such experts to consult. Some social workers also occupy specialist (senior practitioner) posts. However, in North America, the concept of specialist practice (sometimes called 'concentration' in the curriculum) is concerned more with depth, so that one can have a generalist knowledge or a specialist knowledge of the same 'territory', the difference being the depth of knowledge, not the 'territory' itself. This is more akin to the notion of specialism in medical practice, where the consultant is the expert.

4 *Method*

Practitioners themselves are often sceptical towards the idea of models and methods, seeing them as suspect and restrictive. The nearest approach to a methodological specialism is groupwork, which some probation services have adopted as the preferred method of service. However, groupwork is as much a context for practice as it is a single method of practice (there are, for instance, as many methods of groupwork practice as there are individual practice). Adopting a self-definition as a groupworker does allow practitioners to have an affinity with practitioners from other professional backgrounds.

---

[2] In this view of specialism, social work is a land of many territories (defined by age, service user group, nature of problem, setting and so on) and specialist workers become knowledgeable about their territory in more detail, rather like consultants carve up the territory of the human body – foot, heart, ear, nose and throat, and so on.

Reproduced from *Modern Social Work Practice* by Mark Doel and Steven M. Shardlow, Ashgate, Aldershot, 2005

5  *Mode*

Some thirty years ago, it was usual for social workers to define their orientation to their practice according to which 'mode' of practice they were engaged with: individuals, families, groups or communities. Whilst some social workers may have defined themselves as being generalists and working across several different modes, others would have specialized in one mode.

6  *Organizational form or structure*

Determining who works with a particular service user according to organisational form and structure has been a popular approach to specialization at various times; 'intake' or 'reception' teams consisted of social workers who dealt with the initial service user contact, with complementary 'long-term teams' of social workers who took over responsibility after a certain period of time. These are specialisms by time, as is the work of the emergency duty team which deals with service user needs outside of normal office hours.

7  *Qualification*

In the UK there are some areas of specialist practice that have a particular national post-qualifying award, notably in respect of specific areas of practice – childcare and mental health. There is also a more generalist qualification, the AASW (Advanced Award in Social Work) and the Practice Teaching Award, for those who specialize in teaching students in practice settings. It may become a requirement to have a specialist award to be able to practise in certain areas. This has long been the case in healthcare where practitioners have been subject to requirements to maintain their professional development as registered practitioners and, in addition, are required to have specified qualifications in order to be able to perform.

8  *Setting*

The setting in which the practitioner is based can also be seen as a specialism; field social worker, residential worker, day-centre worker. Historically, setting has been an important definer of salary and status, but the recent trend has been for settings to be merged in the education of social workers. In the 1960s in the UK there were Residential Child Care Officer courses, but an attempt to establish a Residential Child Care 'pathway' on the Diploma in Social Work programme was not considered viable, and it merged with the Child Care pathway.

In addition to setting, 'field' has also been used to demarcate areas of social work practice: hospital, school, court and so on. In these circumstances, social work is a *secondary activity* to the principal profession, such as medicine, education or the law. There is something to be said for the idea that social work practice in a secondary setting is itself a form of specialism. It is also one that seems likely to become increasingly common as new organizational arrangements, particularly those that integrate health and social care, are developed for the delivery of welfare. Interestingly, some areas of specialist practice are seldom considered specialisms. For example, is social work management a specialism? New forms of specialist

Reproduced from *Modern Social Work Practice* by Mark Doel and Steven M. Shardlow, Ashgate, Aldershot, 2005

practice are emerging: for example, in the US, rapid-response teams that provide immediate intervention in cases of financial abuse against elders – so-called FAST (Financial Abuse Specialist Team) teams (Allen, 2000; Malks *et al.* 2002).

The notion of specialization, though fashionable at present, is far from clear-cut. The terms of debate have been all but closed off by the assumption that the meaning of specialist work is defined by the current forms of practice.

## Generalism and specialism – the future

In the UK in the early years of the twenty-first century, the specialist tide is as high as it has ever been. The policy origins for this lie deeply embedded in the development of the mixed economy of welfare from 1989 onwards, particularly in respect of adults (Department of Health, 1989). In addition, there has been a strong belief that childcare practice is so complex that it can only be undertaken by a specialist, as evidenced through the manifest failures in the protection of children, from the death of Maria Colwell (*Report of the Committee of Inquiry ... in Relation to Maria Colwell*, 1974), to Jasmine Beckford (*A Child in Trust*, 1985) through to Victoria Climbié (Department of Health and Home Office, 2003).

However, there is no reason to suppose that the specialist–generalist cycle has come to an end. Looking back over the past fifty years, specialist practice has been the 'norm' and generalist practice the exception. The strength of social work is to be found in its diversity and its ability to extemporize as society changes and evolves. However, the failure to conceptualize notions of generic, specialist and generalist practice continues to leave social work exposed. The territorial model is implicit, adopted by default in the absence of clear thinking about alternatives, and it leaves professions in general, and social work in particular, vulnerable to colonization or disintegration. This is why it is very important to develop our conceptualization of social work practice, and your practice learning site is a good place to start.

## Assessment notes: *Generalist and specialist practice*

If you are working in a specialist practice environment, which in modern UK social work is the most likely, it is important to be able to demonstrate that you understand how much of your knowledge and skills are *specific* to your current practice environment. These may advantage you in working with some types of service user: however, they may equally disadvantage you with some other service users and carers. You must be able to demonstrate your awareness of your specialist strengths. Furthermore, you need to be aware, and be able to evidence, the extent of your understanding of the complex range of issues that have an impact on the ability of specialists from different areas of practice to work effectively together.

It is also important to be able to show that you understand how your specialist strengths relate to core social work practice; how does this specific experience of practice learning develop your general understanding of what is common to social work practice?

When faced with a choice of two options it is tempting to try to decide which is the best or most preferable. Yet there has been little empirical work to determine the real advantages and disadvantages of specialism and generalism (Davies, 2000: 145), and you need to demonstrate your understanding of the policy origins of the current forms of specialist practice. It is important, therefore, to demonstrate a broad understanding of the strengths and weaknesses of the various forms of practice.

## Further reading

Fuller, R. and Tulle-Winton, E. (1996), 'Specialism, Genericism and Others: does it make a difference? A study of social work services to elderly people', *British Journal of Social Work*, 26(5), 679–98.

Horwath, J. and Shardlow, S.M. (eds). (2003), *Making Links Across Specialisms: understanding modern social work practice*, Lyme Regis: Russell House.

# 17 Comparative practice

Being able to look at the world from the point of view of others is an essential aspect of social work – whether the others are service users, carers or social workers from other places, at other times. Taking two approaches to comparing different views – those of people in other countries, or changes in your view over time – *View from another place...another time* provides an opportunity for students to think about the key characteristics of social work in their own country and to consider how those characteristics could be presented to give an impression of social work to those from elsewhere or to compare practice learning experience from an earlier period of learning. Ideally, the activity is best undertaken with a group of two or three students – even better if they are from different countries or practice contexts.

## Purpose

If we do not understand the context within which we practise social work, our practice will be circumscribed by the moment and by the demands of the agency in which we work. To have a broad vision of how social work is practised elsewhere provides a grounding on which to develop a critical approach to social work practice.

## Method

- Give each student a copy of the activity, *View from another place ... another time*, about a week before a practice tutorial: they may complete either Part 1 or Part 2.[1]
- Ask the students to follow the guide notes for the activity and produce a written assignment before the session.

---

[1] Of course, students may also be asked to complete both parts – ideally at different times.

## Variations

This activity can be used either singly with one student or with several as part of a practice tutorial. The content of the activity can be modified to take account of other forms of comparison and by selecting different 'prompt' material for the students. It may be difficult to develop the idea of comparative practice in relation to social work overseas, but less so in respect of earlier practice learning. However, there are many other forms of comparison, many of which are frequently neglected, that can be used to develop an appreciation of 'comparative practice'. For example, a comparison with a different region, between an urban and a rural area, or another historical comparison could be engendered by identifying suitable materials. Employing these other forms of comparison is of particular importance in generating a rounded notion of what is entailed by a comparative perspective.

The exercise can also be used as an Internet-based activity if you have contacts with students based in other countries – discussion and comment can be structured through e-mail discussion or even, if resources allow, through some type of virtual learning environment (VLE).

## Use by other professions

*View from another place ... another time* lends itself to use by other professions. It can be modified to suit the needs of any profession by, for example, using a definition taken from an international body about the particular profession. Importantly, the exercise can be used to promote interprofessional learning (see page 53). A group of students from different professional backgrounds can be asked to prepare and present to each other their views about their own and other professions, thereby promoting a comparative dialogue about comparative professional practice. For example, this could be through a comparison of different approaches to the same issue, such as, how to interpret standards for professional practice (Shardlow *et al.*, 2004).

## National Occupational Standards for Social Work

The topics in this chapter relate to the following National Occupational Standards (see the Appendix):

19:   Professional development
21:   Contributing to best social work practice.

## *Activity 17 View from another place ... another time*

There are two parts to this activity corresponding to the two different views, in place and time. You may choose to focus on one or the other, or – if you have time – consider both.

## Part 1: View from another place ... international comparisons

Social work is an international activity; it takes place around the world in many different forms. Consider the definition of social work below, from the International Federation of Social Workers.

---

### *International Federation of Social Workers*
### *Definition of Social Work*

**DEFINITION**
*The social work profession promotes social change, problem solving in human relationships and the empowerment and liberation of people to enhance well-being. Utilising theories of human behaviour and social systems, social work intervenes at the points where people interact with their environments. Principles of human rights and social justice are fundamental to social work.*

**COMMENTARY**
Social work in its various forms addresses the multiple, complex transactions between people and their environments. Its mission is to enable all people to develop their full potential, enrich their lives, and prevent dysfunction. Professional social work is focused on problem solving and change. As such, social workers are change agents in society and in the lives of the individuals, families and communities they serve. Social work is an interrelated system of values, theory and practice.

**Values**
Social work grew out of humanitarian and democratic ideals, and its values are based on respect for the equality, worth, and dignity of all people. Since its beginnings over a century ago, social work practice has focused on meeting human needs and developing human potential. Human rights and social justice serve as the motivation and justification for social work action. In solidarity with those who are disadvantaged, the profession strives to alleviate poverty and to liberate vulnerable and oppressed people in order to promote social inclusion. Social work values are embodied in the profession's national and international codes of ethics.

*continued*

---

Reproduced from *Modern Social Work Practice* by Mark Doel and Steven M. Shardlow, Ashgate, Aldershot, 2005

**Theory**

Social work bases its methodology on a systematic body of evidence-based knowledge derived from research and practice evaluation, including local and indigenous knowledge specific to its context. It recognises the complexity of interactions between human beings and their environment, and the capacity of people both to be affected by and to alter the multiple influences upon them including bio-psychosocial factors. The social work profession draws on theories of human development and behaviour and social systems to analyse complex situations and to facilitate individual, organisational, social and cultural changes.

**Practice**

Social work addresses the barriers, inequities and injustices that exist in society. It responds to crises and emergencies as well as to everyday personal and social problems. Social work utilises a variety of skills, techniques, and activities consistent with its holistic focus on persons and their environments. Social work interventions range from primarily person-focused psychosocial processes to involvement in social policy, planning and development. These include counselling, clinical social work, groupwork, social pedagogical work, and family treatment and therapy as well as efforts to help people obtain services and resources in the community. Interventions also include agency administration, community organisation and engaging in social and political action to impact social policy and economic development. The holistic focus of social work is universal, but the priorities of social work practice will vary from country to country and from time to time depending on cultural, historical, and socio-economic conditions.

*\* This international definition of the social work profession replaces the IFSW definition adopted in 1982. It is understood that social work in the 21st century is dynamic and evolving, and therefore no definition should be regarded as exhaustive.*

*Adopted by the IFSW General Meeting in Montréal, Canada, July 2000*[2]

- *Does this definition highlight the key aspects of social work in your country – from your point of view? If not, how would you describe social work in your country to someone **from another place or another time?***

Like most abstract questions this is quite hard to answer. To help with this task, think about one or a group of the residents of Derby Street (Activity 1, *Licensed to learn*). Take one of the scenarios about the residents described in the book and think about how you would work with the individual or group. From this hypothesized practice example try to draw out the key themes that define good practice. These might form the elements of social work that you would use to describe social work in your country.

- Discuss in the practice tutorial.

---

[2] Found at http://www.ifsw.org/Publications/4.6e.pub.html. The definition is also available in Danish; Finnish; German; French; Norwegian; Portuguese; Spanish and Swedish.

- For homework find at least one published paper in a journal that discusses the same area of practice in another country and reflect upon the similarities and differences (in respect of child protection in England and France, see, for example, A. Cooper (1994), 'A Tale of Two Cultures – race, ideology and child protection in France and England', *Social Work in Europe*, 1(3): 53–60).
- This should give you the basis for describing social work – something that you could give to someone from another place.
- To complete the activity, draft an e-mail describing social work in your country to send to a group of students in another country. This can be a simulation or, ideally, sent to initiate a dialogue.

## Part 2: View from another time ... practice learning comparisons

Over the period of your practice learning, either on one site or over several sites and several periods of practice learning, your views will have developed and changed. Sometimes we find it difficult to be aware of such changes.

- Select one of the chapters from the book and re-read it – you may want to seek the advice of your practice teacher about which one to choose.

---

**Foundations of Practice**
*Context:*  New opportunities for practice learning

1   Knowing the service user and carer
2   Knowing your self
3   Knowing the role

**Direct Practice**
*Context:*  Interprofessional learning and practice

4   Preparation
5   Generating options
6   Making assessments in partnership
7   Working in and with groups
8   Working in difficult situations

**Agency Practice**
*Context:*  Creative practice and procedural requirements

9   Making priorities
10   Managing resources
11   Accountability
12   Whistleblowing

**Themes of Practice**
*Context:*  Evidence-based practice

13   Working with risk
14   Anti-oppressive practice
15   Law-informed practice
16   Generalist and specialist practice
17   Comparative practice

---

- Locate any notes that you made when completing the activity and reconsider them. When reviewing the notes, recall your response to the activity and try to identify the key principles of professional practice that informed your view at that time.
- Complete the activity again – using either the same or different material.

Reproduced from *Modern Social Work Practice* by Mark Doel and Steven M. Shardlow, Ashgate, Aldershot, 2005

- Compare your earlier response with your current response.
- Discuss in the practice tutorial and explore the reasons for any differences both between changes in your views and changes in the views of others. What is emphasized by one person may not be emphasized by another. Explore the scope and extent of the similarities of these different visions through discussion.

# Teaching notes: *Comparative practice*

In learning about how to 'do social work' we can draw a parallel with learning how to drive a car. In the early stages of driving, many learners find that there are too many actions to perform in a very short time period, and there can be a similar feeling of being overwhelmed when learning social work. In such situations learners may tend to focus on the minutiae of task performance rather than broader considerations about the meanings and significance of actions. The novice car driver may be unconcerned with asking questions about the mechanics of the car, the social symbolism of car ownership or the impact of the car on urban life. Likewise, the beginner social worker may be unconcerned with questions about the need for social work as an activity in society, the impact of social work on individuals and the state, or whether social work takes different forms in different countries, regions or societies and so on. Even so, students should be encouraged to ask these broader questions from an early stage in their professional development. To explore social work comparatively is one way to promote this broader thinking.

## Opportunities

Traditionally the term 'comparative practice' has been used to denote social work as it is practised in other countries. Here, we have used the term in a much broader context (although we have remained within the bounds of convention within the activity *View from another place...another time*). The term 'comparative social work' can and, we believe, should be used to denote any form of comparison: international, historical, interprofessional, and those based on the perspectives of different stakeholders. There are many opportunities to help students explore comparative approaches (see 'Dimensions of comparison' in Learning notes below) – if we adopt this broad conceptualization of the notion of 'comparative social work'.

# Learning notes: *Comparative practice*

Comparison may be motivated by the desire to find out more about the *other*, who may be perceived as exotic or strange. Increasing familiarity with the 'other' is likely to reduce this sense of 'otherness' and lead instead to a greater understanding not just of the other but also, surprisingly, of the self and one's own circumstances. Through comparison, the reasons and justifications for our own actions made within our own professional context are subject to challenge. We may be more inclined to ask questions such as 'Why do we do it this way?' Hence, focusing on the practice and policy of others may promote a greater sense of the possibilities of one's own practice, a desire for and a knowledge of other ways of working, than those that we see on a day-to-day basis. The boundaries of our imagination can be extended through comparison.

## Dimensions of comparison

As we have noted, there are several different dimensions of comparison.

### International comparison

Comparative social work may be regarded, erroneously, as being synonymous with international social work. Certainly, much of what is taken to be international social work has a comparative dimension. Midgely, in a review of current developments in international social work, described three different types of international social work, as follows:

1   specialist social work conducted by international agencies such as the International Red Cross
2   contacts and exchanges between social workers from different countries
3   a global awareness enabling social workers to transcend a concern for the local and particular (Midgley, 2001: 24–25).

Of these types of social work, the first two are self-explanatory, and the meaning of the third is less immediately obvious. The ability of social workers to 'transcend the local' implies an ability to appreciate, for example, the impact of global economic change on local communities and therefore to be able to frame realistic and achievable responses. Looking around the globe, social work is practised in a variety of different ways (in respect of Europe, see Adams *et al.*, 2000; 2001; Cannan *et al.*, 1992; Lorenz, 1994 and, for the rest of the world, see Lyons, 1999; Tan, 2004; Tan and Dodds, 2002; Tan and Envall, 2000). Likewise, there are considerable differences in the approach to practice learning. There are also examples of strong similarities between some countries (see Doel and Shardlow, 1996; Shardlow and Doel, 2002). An awareness of some of these differences and similarities will help

Reproduced from *Modern Social Work Practice* by Mark Doel and Steven M. Shardlow, Ashgate, Aldershot, 2005

you understand this wider context of social work and reflect critically on social work practice.

## Comparison across locality and region

Is good social work the same – in Bangor, Banochbrae, Belfast, Birmingham and Brighton, to mention but a few places in one state, the UK? In different localities and regions good practice in social work may be defined by the employer, through expectations that the employer places upon practitioners about what is a requirement for good practice. Hence, aspects of social work may differ between one region or locality and another. Where social workers depend on their *own* employer's definition of 'good' or 'desirable' practice, practice may become insular. This can lead to dangerous practice. In the UK there are increasingly strong pressures to define the nature of good practice at national level through various National Service Frameworks (NSF)[3] for particular groups of service users or carers or though a variety of national inspection mechanisms of social work providers.

## Rural and urban comparisons

There is a substantial literature in other countries, such as in the US, concerned with the nature of rural social work (Randall and Csikai, 2003; Shepherd, 2001). Rather less attention has been paid within the literature to rural social work practice in the UK, with the exception of Pugh (2000), who comments that, 'The social and economic realities of rural life are starkly different from those of urban life' (Pugh, 2000). He also suggests that there are few skills unique to the rural context, but that skills should be used in an informed way that are sensitive to the rural context. Some of the difficulties of providing social services in rural areas can be seen in the findings of the Social Services Inspectorate (1999), that most rural social services departments found difficulty with:

- arranging staff time efficiently
- staff recruitment and retention
- staff shortages leading to lack of choice for users
- providing replacements when staff were sick or on leave
- the high costs of travelling time and travel expenses
- meeting users' concerns about consistency of care – that is, being helped by a known and trusted person. (Pugh, 2000: 122)

If you are working in an urban area, you might like to consider how many of these factors also apply and whether the causes of problems of service delivery are different in rural and urban locations. The problems experienced by some

---

[3] These NSFs can be accessed through the Department of Health website at: www.doh.gov.uk.

communities, such as black people, travellers and those with a mental illness, may be different in a rural context. Dhalech has described a cycle that affects black people as follows:

- The isolation of living in rural communities with little or no support can exacerbate the experience of racism but maintain its invisibility.
- This in turn creates a lack of confidence to seek advice and information.
- As a result, minority ethnic community members are inclined to attempt to resolve the issues within the private circles of family and friends.
- This then emphasizes their lack of awareness of what services are available to the public.
- Underuse of services and underreporting of the needs of minority ethnic people are often reinforced by previous negative experiences with an agency.
- As a result, developing confidence in communities that have continually experienced disadvantage and discrimination is a lengthy process and requires long-term commitment of human and other resources. (Dhalech, 1999, p. 14)

There are no easy solutions to these issues. However, Pugh concluded by suggesting that there are some common themes which help to develop good practice in a rural setting:

> Good knowledge of the community and how it works is a prerequisite of success. Without an awareness of local dynamics and the personal politics of an area, workers will struggle to understand how people experience their problems. (Pugh, 2000: 150)

## Comparison of different stakeholders' opinions

The term 'stakeholder' became fashionable in political discourse during the 1990s and has been used to signify individuals or groups who have a 'stake' in a particular process or outcome. Social work practitioners should be able to compare and contrast the views of different stakeholders. For example, in the social work context the notion of stakeholding has been used to recognize that, in policy formulation, in decisions about the allocation of scarce resources or in the evaluation of services, there are different groups and individuals who have a right to be heard and, importantly, that their voices cannot accurately be represented by others who have a different perspective. The impact of this movement has been to gain greater recognition of the importance of voices that would not otherwise have been heard – for example, the voices of service users and carers (for a detailed articulation of this position, see Beresford and Croft, 2001). Exploring or examining a social work issue by comparing the actual or likely views of different stakeholders can, and should, be a most instructive experience.

## Historical comparisons

Social workers often seem to lack sufficient concern for the history of the discipline. The intensity and immediacy of current demand militates against an interest in the past. Yet, comparing past social work with present practice can be rewarding, interesting and, above all, highly informative – the only problem being that there are all too few possibilities for accurate comparison. One modest area where historical comparison is possible centres on knowledge about motivation to enter social work. In 1973, during the height of the influence of 'radical social work', Pearson (1973), in what has become a seminal study, asked a sample of social work students for two statements:

1   Through entering social work I hope to achieve ...
2   Through entering social work I hope to avoid ...

Pearson's analysis of the responses suggested that social work students were a sociologically 'deviant' group who rejected conventional social values and who, by adopting social work as an occupation, were seeking to reconcile private dissatisfactions through action in the public arena with the aim of social change. Pearson pejoratively characterized social work as the 'privatised solution of public ills'. This may have remained an interesting, albeit isolated, study had it not been replicated[4] several times in the UK (Holme and Maizels, 1978), in New Zealand (Uttley, 1981) and in Australia (Solas, 1994).[5] When Solas conducted his analysis, the political motivation of social work students seemed to be waning, although personal fulfilment was still a strong motivating factor for entering social work. It is interesting to note and speculate on the changes over time in the motivation of social work students based upon a detailed analysis of these studies. Perhaps the wisdom of time suggests, as do Christie and Kruck (1998), that uni-causal explanations of motivation are inherently flawed and that the drive to enter social work is to be found in a range of personal, political and professional motives (to mention but a few factors).

## Interprofessional comparison

Important comparisons can be made between the ways in which different professions respond to similar situations. Perhaps this is the most significant area for comparison given the importance of interprofessional working. A very fruitful

---

[4] It is interesting to speculate why this study has been replicated and so many others have not; perhaps it is the intriguing findings or possibly the simple methodology.
[5] It would, of course, be possible to attempt a geographical comparison based on the findings from these various studies. There are other studies such as that by Jovelin (2001), conducted in France, who posed the question whether entering social work was a choice or an accident. Such studies extend the possibility for trans-national comparison.

area of comparison can be found in the way in which different professions respond to ethical problems (see, for example, Banks, 1998). Alternatively, Parker and Merrylees (2002) conducted a study that explores the similarities and differences in the motivations of recruits who enter nursing and social work. Taking a detailed biographical approach, they found that experiences of care-giving were significant influences on the decision to enter social work and nursing. These and similar studies are invaluable in helping to situate social work in relation to other professions.

## Assessment notes: *Comparative practice*

When you seek to evidence your understanding of 'comparative social work', the primary concern should not be the details of your knowledge of social work practice in another country, location, time, place and so on. What is important is to understand the significance of 'comparison' as a technique to further our understanding about ourselves and others. Social work practice can be based on quite fundamentally different premises. For example, Sacco (1996) describes an African paradigm as a foundation for a spirituality in social work practice, which is in strong contrast to the Western materialist basis of social work. Through this understanding of difference, using comparison as a mechanism, it is possible to better understand ourselves. Demonstrating an appreciation of the importance of comparison throughout any practice learning opportunity and consistently across any assessment tasks is essential. It is not necessary always to seek out the complex or more exotic comparisons. Drawing upon comparisons, for example, between yourself and, say, your practice teacher, other students or the earlier and later parts of your practice learning experience can be a highly constructive mechanism to promote a deeper understanding both of yourself and 'the other'.

## Further reading

Payne, M. and Shardlow, S.M. (eds) (2002), *Social Work in the British Isles*, London: Jessica Kingsley.
Pugh, R. (2000), *Rural Social Work*, Lyme Regis: Russell House.
Tan, N-T. (ed.) (2004), *Social Work Around the World III*, Berne: International Federation of Social Workers.
Tan, N-T. and Envall, E. (eds) (2000), *Social Work Around the World*, Berne: International Federation of Social Workers.
Tan, N-T. and Envall, E. (eds) (2002), *Social Work Around the World: II*, Berne: International Federation of Social Workers.
Younghusband, E. (1981), *The Newest Profession: a short history of social work*, Sutton: Community Care/IPC Business Press.

# Appendix: National Occupational Standards

## Summary of the National Occupational Standards (NOS) for Social Work in England (TOPSS, 2002)

**Key Role 1  Prepare for, and work with individuals, families, carers, groups and communities to assess their needs and circumstances**

*Unit 1 Prepare for social work contact and involvement*

1.1  Review case notes and other relevant literature
1.2  Liaise with others to access additional information that can inform initial contact and involvement
1.3  Evaluate all the information to identify the best form of initial involvement.


*Unit 2 Work with individuals, families, carers, groups and communities to help them make informed decisions*

2.1  Inform people about your own and the organization's duties and responsibilities
2.2  Work with people to identify, gather, analyse and understand information
2.3  Work with people to identify, analyse, clarify and express their strengths, expectations and limitations
2.4  Work with people to assess and make informed decisions about their needs, circumstances, risks, preferred options and resources.

*Unit 3 Assess needs and options to recommend a course of action*

3.1  Assess and review the preferred options of people
3.2  Assess needs, risks and options taking into account legal and other requirements
3.3  Assess and recommend an appropriate course of action for people.

**Key Role 2   Plan, carry out, review and evaluate social work practice with individuals, families, carers, groups, communities and other professionals**

*Unit 4 Respond to crisis situations*

4.1   Assess the urgency of requests for action
4.2   Identify the need for legal and procedural intervention
4.3   Plan and implement action to meet the immediate needs and circumstances
4.4   Review the outcomes with people.


*Unit 5 Interact with individuals, families, carers, groups and communities to achieve change and development and to improve life opportunities*

5.1   Develop and maintain relationships with people
5.2   Work with people to avoid crisis situations and address problems and conflict
5.3   Apply and justify social work methods and models used to achieve change and development, and to improve life opportunities
5.4   Regularly monitor, review and evaluate changes in needs and circumstances
5.5   Reduce contact and withdraw from relationships appropriately.


*Unit 6 Prepare, produce, implement and evaluate plans with individuals, families, carers, groups, communities and professional colleagues*

6.1   Negotiate the provision to be included in the plans
6.2   Identify content and actions, and draft plans
6.3   Carry out your own responsibilities and monitor, coordinate and support the actions of others involved in implementing the plans
6.4   Review the effectiveness of the plans with the people involved
6.5   Renegotiate and revise plans to meet changing needs and circumstances.


*Unit 7 Support the development of networks to meet assessed needs and planned outcomes*

7.1   Examine with people the support networks which can be accessed and developed
7.2   Work with people to initiate and sustain support networks
7.3   Contribute to the development and evaluation of support networks.

*Unit 8 Work with groups to promote growth, development and independence*

8.1 Identify opportunities to form and support groups
8.2 Use group programmes, processes and dynamics to promote individual growth, development and independence, and to foster interpersonal skills
8.3 Help groups to achieve planned outcomes for their members and to evaluate the appropriateness of their work
8.4 Disengage from groups appropriately.

*Unit 9 Address behaviour which presents a risk to individuals, families, carers, groups and communities*

9.1 Take immediate action to deal with the behaviour that presents a risk
9.2 Work with people to identify and evaluate situations and circumstances that may trigger the behaviour
9.3 Work with people on strategies and support that could positively change the behaviour.

## Key Role 3   Support individuals to represent their needs, views and circumstances

*Unit 10 Advocate with, and on behalf of, individuals, families, carers, groups and communities*

10.1 Assess whether you should act as the advocate for the person or persons
10.2 Assist people to access independent advocacy
10.3 Advocate for, and with, people.

*Unit 11 Prepare for, and participate in decision-making forums*

11.1 Prepare reports and documents for decision-making forums
11.2 Work with people to select the best form of representation for decision-making forums
11.3 Present evidence to people, and help people to understand the procedures in decision-making forums, and the outcomes from them
11.4 Enable people to be involved in decision-making forums.

### Key Role 4   Manage risk to individuals, families, carers, groups, communities, self and colleagues

*Unit 12 Assess and manage risks to individuals, families, carers, groups and communities*

12.1   Identify and assess the nature of the risk
12.2   Balance the rights and responsibilities of people with associated risks
12.3   Regularly monitor, reassess and manage risk to people.

*Unit 13 Assess, minimize and manage risk to self and colleagues*

13.1   Assess potential risk to self and colleagues
13.2   Work within the risk assessment and management procedures of your own and other relevant organizations and professions
13.3   Plan, monitor and review outcomes and actions to minimize stress and risk.

### Key Role 5   Manage and be accountable, with supervision and support, for your own social work practice within your organization

*Unit 14 Manage and be accountable for your own work*

14.1   Manage and prioritise your workload within organizational policies and priorities
14.2   Carry out duties using professional judgement and the knowledge base of social work practice
14.3   Monitor and evaluate the effectiveness of your programme of work in meeting the organizational requirements and the needs of people
14.4   Use professional and managerial supervision and support to improve your practice.

*Unit 15 Contribute to the management of resources and services*

15.1   Contribute to the procedures involved in purchasing and commissioning services
15.2   Contribute to monitoring the effectiveness of services in meeting need
15.3   Contribute to monitoring the quality of the services provided
15.4   Contribute to managing information.

*Unit 16 Manage, present and share records and reports*

16.1   Maintain accurate, complete, accessible and up-to-date records and reports
16.2   Provide evidence for professional judgements and decisions
16.3   Implement legal and policy frameworks for access to records and reports
16.4   Share records with people, including professional colleagues.

*Unit 17 Work within multidisciplinary and multi-organizational teams, networks and systems*

17.1   Develop and maintain effective working relationships
17.2   Contribute to identifying and agreeing the goals, objectives and lifespan of the team, network or system
17.3   Contribute to evaluating the effectiveness of the team, network or system
17.4   Deal consistently with disagreements and conflict within relationships.

## Key Role 6   Demonstrate professional competence in social work practice

*Unit 18 Research, analyse, evaluate, and use current knowledge of best social work practice*

18.1   Review and update your own knowledge of legal, policy and procedural frameworks
18.2   Use professional and organizational supervision and support to research, critically analyse and review knowledge-based practice
18.3   Implement knowledge-based social work models and methods to develop and improve your own practice.

*Unit 19 Work within agreed standards of social work practice and ensure own professional development*

19.1   Exercise and justify professional judgements
19.2   Use professional assertiveness to justify decisions and uphold professional social work practice, values and ethics
19.3   Work within the principles and values underpinning social work practice
19.4   Critically reflect upon your own practice and performance using supervision and support systems
19.5   Use supervision and support to take action to meet continuing professional development needs.

## Unit 20 Manage complex ethical issues, dilemmas and conflicts

20.1   Identify and assess issues, dilemmas and conflicts that might affect your practice
20.2   Devise strategies to deal with ethical issues, dilemmas and conflicts
20.3   Reflect on outcomes.

## Unit 21 Contribute to the promotion of best social work practice

21.1   Contribute to policy review and development
21.2   Use supervision and organizational and professional systems to inform a course of action where practice falls below required standards
21.3   Work with colleagues to contribute to team development.

# Glossary of acronyms

The following acronyms are used in the book (some useful website addresses are also included):

**AASW**  Australian Association of Social Work. This body accredits Australian Schools of Social Work.  www.aasw.asn.au

**BASW**  British Association of Social Workers  www.basw.co.uk

**BSW**  Bachelor of Social Work (basic qualifying degree in social work at baccalaureate level)

**CASSW**  Canadian Association of Schools of Social Work. This body accredits Canadian social work programmes.  www.cassw-acess

**CCETSW**  Central Council for Education and Training in Social Work. This body accredited UK social work training programmes until 2001.

**CCW**  Cyngor Gofal Cymru/Care Council for Wales  www.ccwales.org.uk

**CSWE**  Council on Social Work Education. This body accredits social work programmes in the US.  www.cswe.org

**DfES**  Department for Education and Skills  www.dfes.gov.uk

**DH**  Department of Health (UK government at Westminster)  www.doh.gov.uk

**DipSW**  Diploma in Social Work (social work qualifying award in the UK being superceded by a new degree)

**GSCC**  General Social Care Council. The council operates as the regulator of social work education and the social care workforce in England.  www.gscc.org.uk

**HEFCE**  Higher Education Funding Council England  www.hefce.ac.uk

**HEFCW**  Higher Education Funding Council for Wales  www.wfc.ac.uk/hefcw

**MSW**  Masters in Social Work

**NISCC**  Northern Ireland Social Care Council  www.niscc.info

**PLTF**  Practice Learning Task Force  www.practicelearning.org.uk

| | |
|---|---|
| **PTA** | Practice Teaching Award (post-qualifying award in practice teaching in the UK) |
| **QAA** | Quality Assurance Agency for Higher Education   www.qaa.ac.uk |
| **SCIE** | Social Care Institute for Excellence   www.scie.org.uk. The organization collects knowledge about social care. See, for example, the electronic Library for Social Care www.elsc.org.uk |
| **SHEFC** | Scottish Higher Education Funding Council   www.shefc.ac.uk |
| **SSSC** | Scottish Social Services Council   www.sssc.uk |
| **SWAP/ltsn** | Social Policy and Social Work Learning and Teaching Support Network   www.swap.ac.uk |
| **TOPSS England** | Training Organisation for the Personal Social Services www.topss.org.uk |
| **World Wide Web Resources** | www.nyu.edu/socialwork/wwwrsw |

# Glossary of terms

The glossary has two purposes. First, it provides a quick guide to unfamiliar terms used in the book. The second purpose is to help overseas readers who may not be familiar with some technical words or phrases used in UK English, which relate to social work. We decided that it would be intrusive to have these explanations in brackets in the text, so have placed them in this separate glossary. If you come across a word or phrase in the text, please refer to this glossary in the hope that we have anticipated your confusion.

Rather than offer a definition of each and every word, we have decided to group similar terms together. These groupings follow the A–Z below. The words in any one group are not necessarily synonyms; they are linked in the way of a thesaurus. Even when different terms do appear to be synonymous by referring to the same activity or person (such as practice teacher; field instructor; student supervisor), very different meanings can be implied: the teaching of practice; instruction in fieldwork; a student supervised.

One term which seems to be universal is 'student'!

**Academic setting**     see *Class setting*
**Accreditation**     see *Competencies*
**Agency**     see *Practice setting*
**Alumni**     see *Class setting*
**Assessment**     see *Competencies*
**Block placement**     see *Placement*
**Classroom**     see *Class setting*
**Class setting**     see *Class setting*
**Class (-based) teacher**     see *Field liaison staff*
**Client**     see *Practice setting*
**College**     see *Class setting*
**College staff**     see *Field liaison staff*
**Competencies**     see *Competencies*
**Concurrent placement**     see *Placement*
**Consultant**     see *Consultant*
**Core competencies**     see *Competencies*
**Course**     see *Programme*
**Course teacher**     see *Field liaison staff*

**CRB**      see *Criminal Records Bureau*
**Curriculum**      see *Placement*
**Director of fieldwork**      see *Field liaison staff*
**Educational contract**      see *Placement*
**Education programme**      see *Programme*
**Employer**      see *Practice setting*
**Enterprise**      see *Practice setting*
**Establishment**      see *Practice setting*
**Evaluation**      see *Competencies*
**Faculty**      see *Field liaison staff*
**Field**      see *Practice setting*
**Field education**      see *Placement*
**Field educator**      see *Practice teacher / Field instructor*
**Field instruction**      see *Placement*
**Field instructor**      see *Practice teacher / Field instructor*
**Field liaison (staff)**      see *Field liaison staff*
**Field practice**      see *Placement*
**Field practicum manual**      see *Placement*
**Field program**      see *Placement*
**Field setting**      see *Practice setting*
**Field supervision**      see *Placement*
**Field supervisor**      see *Practice teacher / Field instructor*
**Field teacher**      see *Practice teacher / Field instructor*
**Fieldwork**      see *Placement*
**In-service training**      see *Programme*
**Institution**      see *Class setting; Practice setting*
**Joint appointment**      see *Field liaison staff*
**Laboratory setting**      see *Class setting*
**Learning contract**      see *Placement*
**Learning objectives**      see *Competencies*
**Lecturer**      see *Field liaison staff*
**Liaison staff**      see *Field liaison staff*
**Long-arm supervision**      see *Placement*
**Mentor**      see *Consultant*
**Off-site supervision/practice teaching**      see *Placement*
**Organization**      see *Practice setting*
**Outcomes**      see *Competencies*
**Pedagogue**      see *Pedagogue*
**Performance criteria**      see *Competencies*
**Placement**      see *Placement*
**Placement agreement**      see *Placement*
**Placement of particular practice**      sce *Placement*
**Placement team**      see *Field liaison staff*
**Polytechnic**      see *Class setting*
**Portfolio; practice assignment**      see *Competencies*
**Practice**      see *Practice*

**Practice assessor**    see *Practice teacher / Field instructor*
**Practice competence**    see *Competence*
**Practice curriculum**    see *Placement*
**Practice learning**    see *Placement*
**Practice learning opportunity**    see *Placement*
**Practice learning site**    see *Placement*
**Practice setting**    see *Practice setting*
**Practice teacher**    see *Practice teacher / Field instructor*
**Practice teaching / learning**    see *Placement*
**Practicum**    see *Placement*
**Practitioner**    see *Practice setting*
**Programme**    see *Programme*
**Programme provider**    see *Programme*
**Public welfare department**    see *Practice setting*
**School (of social work)**    see *Class setting*
**Service organization; service setting**    see *Practice setting*
**Service user**    see *Practice setting*
**Social department; social office; social welfare agency**    see *Practice setting*
**Specialist or semi-specialist practice teacher / field instructor**    see *Practice teacher / Field instructor*
**Statutory agency**    see *Practice setting*
**Student supervisor**    see *Practice teacher / Field instructor*
**Supervision**    see *Placement*
**Training**    see *Programme*
**Training institute**    see *Class setting*
**Tutor**    see *Field liaison staff*
**University**    see *Class setting*
**University staff / teacher**    see *Field liaison staff*
**User-led agency**    see *Practise setting*
**Voluntary (non-profit) agency**    see *Practice setting*
**Welfare agencies**    see *Practice setting*
**Workload**    see *Practice setting*

## Class setting

*academic setting; alumni; classroom; college; educational establishment/institution; laboratory setting; polytechnic; school of social work; training institute; university*

The class setting refers to the *educational establishment* or *institution* where students pursue their learning of social work. The learning in the class setting is associated with the *academic* content of the programme. This might take place in a *university, polytechnic, training institute* or *college,* and at postgraduate or undergraduate level. The word *college* is often used as a general term for the higher education setting. Graduates from any higher education course are sometimes referred to as *alumni.*

Colleges sometimes run classes which attempt to simulate the conditions found in practice in the agencies by creating a *laboratory setting*, often using skills training and video feedback.

## Competencies

*accreditation; assessment; core competencies; evaluation; learning goals or objectives; performance criteria; outcomes; portfolio; practice assignment; practice competence*

Social work students are *assessed* to see if they are competent to practise as a social worker. The most important, generic competencies are often referred to as *'core'*. The practice teacher/field instructor usually makes a recommendation of 'pass', 'fail' or 'refer' for further work, or 'satisfactory'/'unsatisfactory'. In the UK the notion of 'ready to practise' or 'not yet ready to practise' is developing.

Methods of assessment on placements vary. The most common has been a report written by the practice teacher/field instructor, which includes material and *practice assignments* by the student, such as case notes. There is an increasing move towards *competency-based assessment*, in which the *learning objectives* are carefully detailed, and the student is expected to provide evidence of achieving these objectives, using agreed *performance criteria*. In the UK, practice teachers also face an assessment if they wish to gain the Practice Teaching Award; they are assessed by means of a *portfolio*, which is a collection of evidence of ability collected over time. This system of *accreditation* is designed to guarantee the quality of practice learning available to the students.

The word *evaluation* has slightly different meanings; sometimes it may imply a formal measurement of a student's abilities at the end of placement, which is its most frequent use in North America. Alternatively, it may refer to the quality of the placement (and the whole programme), in terms of helping students to achieve their *learning goals*. This is its most frequent usage in the UK.

## Consultant

*mentor*
A consultant or *mentor* usually refers to a person with considerable experience and expertise who is able to provide consultation and teaching. On training programmes for practice teachers/field instructors, a consultant or mentor helps the trainee to develop skills in practice teaching/field instruction.

## Criminal Records Bureau (CRB)

All social work students and practitioners, and many other professions, must undergo a check to indicate whether they have any convictions. Social work courses must then decide whether any convictions prevent the individual from practising social work (and therefore from continuing their studies). CRB forms also document investigations which have not necessarily gone to court.

# Field liaison staff

*academic staff; class (-based) teachers; college staff; course teacher; director of fieldwork; educators; faculty; joint appointments; lecturer; placement team; tutor; university staff / teacher*

The members of the *academic staff* at the educational establishment (university, college and so on) who are responsible for communication with practice teachers/ field instructors are called field liaison staff. This responsibility might fall to one or two people, or be shared by a team of academic staff *(placement team)*. The person with primary responsibility is sometimes designated the director of fieldwork. The term *tutor* is used in the UK for the members of the *university staff* who are responsible for providing college support to the student while on placement.

There are other *class-based teachers*, members of the academic *faculty*, who are not involved in the student's learning outside the educational establishment. In the UK and Australasia the general term for all college-based teachers, whether involved in liaison or not, is *lecturer*.

Some educational establishments have set up *joint appointments* with social work agencies, so that one person (or sometimes a pair) works partly as a member of faculty at the university and partly as a practitioner in the agency.

# Pedagogue

In the Anglo-Saxon world there is no professional group known as pedagogues. In much of the European mainland this is a distinctive profession, working with people in ways that are analogous to social work, but with a greater emphasis on the educative functions.

# Placement

*block placement; concurrent placement; curriculum; educational contract; field education; field instruction; field practice; field practicum manual; field program; fieldwork; learning contract; long-arm supervision; off-site supervision / practice teaching; placement of particular practice; practice curriculum; practice learning; practice teaching; practicum; site; student supervision*

A placement is the period of learning that occurs when a student is located in a social work agency. What the practice teacher/field instructor does is referred to as *practice teaching, student supervision* or *field instruction*; what the student does is referred to as *practice learning*. Although these terms refer to the same activity, there are subtle differences between 'supervision', 'instruction' and 'teaching'.

*Practicum* is a North American term which brings together the notion of the placement and also what is to be learned on placement – the *practice curriculum*. The practice curriculum might be designed for general learning about social work, or for a *particular area of practice* (such as child protection or mental health).

Most programmes provide a placement handbook or *field practicum manual* to guide the placement, with information about the *educational contract* or *placement agreement* which spells out expectations for the placement and the areas of practice to be learned (the curriculum), the regulations for assessing the level of a student's practice competence, and the placement arrangements, such as the required number of meetings between university staff, practice teachers/field instructors and students during a placement.

Arrangements for placements differ; for example, the overall length and whether they are *block* (five days a week) or *concurrent* (some part of the week on placement and some part in the class setting). Some students receive *long-arm supervision* or *offsite practice-teaching* from a practitioner who is not their day-to-day supervisor.

The terminology of the new qualifying social work degree in the UK has changed in subtle ways. There is a tendency for the term 'placement' to be replaced by 'practice learning opportunity', 'practice learning setting' and we have coined the term practice learning *site*. In this book, we use all of these terms, though we consider practice learning to be possible not just in practice agencies, but also in class settings. In this respect, the older term 'placement' is more specific than 'practice learning opportunity' since it refers solely to the practice learning which takes place in an agency setting.

**Note:** the term 'placement' is also used by practitioners to refer to children placed in foster care, residential care, and so on.

## Practice

This word is used in an alarming number of different ways in social work. At its most general it refers to what social workers do (social work practice), and therefore what students need to learn to do. As a result, 'practice setting' (see below) refers to the learning on placements in social work agencies. However, some social work programmes have 'practice classes', which are based in the educational setting; these are designed to prepare the student for the practical work on the placement.

As a verb, 'to practise' can mean either to be engaged in social work practice, or to be rehearsing something – as in 'practice makes perfect'. Practice is also often put in apposition to theory, with a notion that theory takes place in the educational setting and practice in the work setting. This division is being increasingly challenged.

## Practice setting

*agency; client; employer; enterprise; establishment; field; institution; organization; practitioner; public welfare department; service organization; service setting; service user; social department; social office; social welfare agency; statutory agency; user-led agency; voluntary (non-profit) agency; welfare agency; workload*

The practice setting refers to the *agency, enterprise* or *organization* where students pursue their learning about social work practice (in other words, where the student is placed). The agency's principal responsibilities are to its *clients* and *service users*, not the student. The professional staff in the agency are sometimes called *practitioners*; some of these practitioners have a student who is attached to them on their team. Such practitioners continue to work with clients or service users in addition to teaching the student about good practice and being responsible for the quality of the student's work.

Examples of types of practice setting are: residential care, group care, community work, children and family settings, hospitals, probation and correctional work and, increasingly, user-led agencies. Generic terms for these kinds of agencies include *public welfare departments, social (services) departments* and *welfare agencies;* those with specific legal responsibilities, such as child protection, are called *statutory agencies. Voluntary agencies* are those which are non-governmental and do not make a profit. Agencies are sometimes characterized as urban or rural, and described along ethnic lines (for example, a Maori agency).

The practice setting is often summarized as the *field* – a location for social work students to learn about social work practice. The field is most frequently used to distinguish from the *class* as a setting for learning.

## Practice teacher / Field instructor

*field educator; field supervisor; field teacher; long-arm supervisor; long-arm (off-site) supervisor practice assessor; specialist or semi-specialist practice teacher; student supervisor; student unit organizer*

These terms all refer to the person in a social work agency who has the responsibility for teaching a student who is placed there. The term *field instructor* is usually found in North America; in the UK and New Zealand the term has changed from *student supervisor* to *practice teacher.* Just to confuse matters, in the North American context the term 'practice teacher' is used to refer to persons in the educational setting who teach classes in social work practice! In this book the term is used as it would be in the UK – except where stated otherwise.

Some students receive teaching from a person not in direct day-to-day supervision of their work, and this person is referred to as a *long-arm (off-site) supervisor* or *teacher.* Some practitioners specialize in practice teaching / field instruction, so that – although they are employed in a social work agency – they spend a proportion of their time *(semi-specialist)* or all their time *(specialist)* teaching students. Sometimes this might be organized around a *student unit* within the agency.

The term *practice assessor* is now widely used in the UK to refer to the person who assesses practice but may not necessarily be involved in other teaching functions.

## Programme

*course; education programme; in-service training; programme provider; training course*

Together, the class-based learning (in the educational establishment) and agency-based learning (in the social work organization) make up the *training programme;* the balance of learning in the educational setting and the work setting varies, but can often be half and half, as in the UK. *Programme providers* is a collective term for all those who are responsible for the training programme.

In North America, the term *course* is used as a precise term to refer to specific elements in the programme; in the UK and Australasia it is used to mean the whole programme (though it often implicitly excludes the placement components, as in 'We haven't done that on the course yet', meaning the classroom).

There can be a tension between the training components of a programme (to produce competent agency workers) and the educative elements (to develop critical professionals). Some agencies provide *in-service training*, where their employees receive training while retaining a salary or stipend from the agency, and often the training is delivered by the agency itself.

## Social services department

This is an agency of local government in the UK with responsibility for social work and social care. Commonly, these departments are restructuring and merging with others to form, for example, a 'Housing and Social Care Department'. They are a combination of departments of public welfare and children's departments in the US, though the picture is changing daily, with some services (such as mental health services) migrating to the National Health Service. There is also talk of bringing children's services together (childcare, child protection, education, youth offending, leisure and so on) into local children's trusts. To complicate things further, the situation is becoming increasingly diverse in the four countries of the UK – England, Scotland, Wales and Northern Ireland. For many years, Scotland has had social work and probation (correction) services in the same local departments; Northern Ireland has had local boards which have brought health, social care and social work under the same roof. What we need to keep at the front of our minds is the fact that, however the services are organized, the problems and aspirations of people remain much the same throughout the UK.

## Social work degree

Curiously, the new (2003) social work qualification in the various countries that comprise the UK is often referred to as 'the new social work degree'. Unlike its predecessors, the CQSW (Certificate of Qualification in Social Work) and the DipSW (Diploma in Social Work), the new three-year degree has no recognized title. It would make sense if it were called the BSW (Bachelor of Social Work), but this is the least likely title; BA (social work) and BSc (social work) are the most common. The minimum of three years' education and training for social work qualification has been universally welcomed and seen as a vote of confidence in the future of social work in the UK.

# Bibliography

*A Child in Trust. The Report of the Panel of Inquiry into the circumstances surrounding the death of Jasmine Beckford* (1985), London: London Borough of Brent.

AASW (2000), *National Code of Ethics* at: http://www.aasw.asn.au/servicing/index.html.

Adams, A., Erath, P. and Shardlow, S.M. (eds) (2000), *Fundamentals of Social Work in Selected European Countries: present theory, practice, perspectives, historical and practice contexts*, Lyme Regis: Russell House.

Adams, A., Erath, P. and Shardlow, S.M. (eds) (2001), *Key Themes in European Social Work: theory, practice perspectives*, Lyme Regis: Russell House.

Adams, D. (2003), *The Salmon of Doubt: hitchhiking the galaxy for the last time*, New York: Harmony Books.

Adams, J. (1995), *Risk*, London: UCL Press.

Adams, R., Dominelli, L. and Payne, M. (2002), *Social Work: themes, issues and critical debates*, Basingstoke: Palgrave.

Alaszewski, A., Harrison, L. and Manthorpe, J. (1998), *Risk, Health and Welfare*, Buckingham: Open University Press.

Allen, J.V. (2000), 'Financial Abuse of Elders and Dependent Adults: the FAST (Financial Abuse Specialist Team) approach', *Journal of Elder Abuse and Neglect*, 12(2): 85–91.

Alsop, A. and Vigars, C. (1998), 'Shared Learning, Joint Training or Dual Qualification in OT and SW: a feasibility study', *British Journal of Occupational Therapy*, 61(4): 146–52.

Asch, S.E. (1952), *Social Psychology*, Englewood Cliffs, NJ: Prentice Hall.

Attlee, C. (1920), *The Social Worker*, London: Bell.

Bacon, F. (1605), *The Oxford Francis Bacon* (2000), ed. G. Rees and L. Jordine, vol. IV, *The Advancement of Learning*, ed. M. Kiernan, Oxford: Oxford University Press.

Baird, P. (1991) 'The Proof of the Pudding: a study of clients' views of student practice competence', *Issues in Social Work Education*, 10(1–2): 24–50.

Ball, C., Harris, R., Roberts, G. and Vernon, S. (1988), *The Law Report. Teaching and assessment of law in social work education, Paper 4.1*, London: Central Council for Education and Training in Social Work.

Ball, C., Roberts, G., Trench, S. and Vernon, S. (1991), *Teaching, Learning and Assessing Social Work Law*, London: Central Council for Education and Training in Social Work.

Bamford, T. (1982), *Managing Social Work*, London: Tavistock.

Bamford, T. (2001), *Commissioning and Purchasing*, London: Routledge/Community Care.

Banks, S. (1995), *Ethics and Values in Social Work*, Basingstoke: Macmillan.

Banks, S. (1998), 'Codes of Ethics and Ethical Conduct: a view from the caring professions', *Public Money and Management*, 18(1): 27–30.

Banks, S. (2002), 'Professional Values and Accountabilities', in R. Adams, L. Dominelli, and M. Payne (eds), *Critical Practice in Social Work*, Basingstoke: Macmillan, pp. 28–37.

Barclay, P.M. (1982), *Social Workers: their role and tasks* (The Barclay Report), London: Bedford Square Press.

Barr, H. (2002), *Interprofessional Education Today, Yesterday and Tomorrow*, London: LTSN for Health Sciences and Practice.

Barry, M. and Hallett, C. (2003), *Social Exclusion and Social Work*, London: Russell House Publishing.

Bartlett, H. (1970), *The Common Base of Social Work Practice*, Washington DC: National Association of Social Workers.

BASW (1975), *A Code of Ethics for Social Work*, Birmingham: British Association of Social Workers. Revised 1986 and 1996.

Beck, U. (1990), *Risk Society: towards a new modernity*, London: Sage.

Behroozi, C.S. (1992), 'Groupwork with Involuntary Clients: remotivating strategies', *Groupwork*, 5(2): 31–41.

Beresford, P. and Croft, S. (2001), 'Service Users' Knowledges and the Social Construction of Social Work', *Journal of Social Work*, 1(3): 295–316.

Bergmark, A. (1996), 'Need, Allocation and Justice – on priorities in the social services', *Scandinavian Journal of Social Welfare*, 5(1): 45–56.

Billington, J. and Roberts, S. (2002), 'Creative Practice Learning: exploring opportunities to fulfil students' requirements', *Practice*, 14(4): 29–41.

Birnbaum, M. and Wayne, J. (2000), 'Group Work Content in Foundation Generalist Education: the necessity for change', *Journal of Social Work Education*, 36: 347–56.

Blom-Cooper, L. (1985), *A Child in Trust. The Report of the Panel of Inquiry into the circumstances Surrounding the Death of Jasmine Beckford*, London: London Borough of Brent.

Bodenheimer, T. (1997), 'The Oregon Health Plan – lessons for the nation'. *New England Journal of Medicine*, 337(9): 651–56.

Bogo, M. and Vayda, E. (1987), *The Practice of Field Instruction*, Toronto: University of Toronto Press.

Bramson, R. (1981) *Coping with Difficult People*, New York: Ballantine.

Braye, S. and Preston-Shoot, M. (1990), 'On Teaching and Applying the Law in Social Work: it is not that simple', *British Journal of Social Work*, 20(4): 333–53.

Braye, S. and Preston-Shoot, M. (1992), 'Honourable Intentions: partnership and written agreements in welfare legislation', *Journal of Social Welfare and Family Law*, 6: 511–28.

Braye, S. and Preston-Shoot, M. (1995), *Empowering Practice in Social Care*, Buckingham: Open University Press.

Braye, S. and Preston-Shoot, M. (1997) *Practising Social Work Law* (2nd edn), Basingstoke: Macmillan.

Braye, S. and Preston-Shoot, M. (2002), 'Social Work and the Law', in R. Adams, L. Dominelli and M. Payne (eds), *Social Work: themes, issues and critical debates*, Basingstoke: Palgrave, pp. 62–73.

Braye, S., Lebacq, M., Mann, F. and Midwinter, E. (2003), 'Learning Social Work Law: an enquiry-based approach to developing knowledge and skills', *Social Work Education*, 22(5): 479–92.

Brayne, H. and Carr, H. (2003), *Law for Social Workers* (8th edn), Oxford: Oxford University Press.

Brearley, P. (1982), *Risk and Social Work: hazards and helping*, London: Routledge and Kegan Paul.

Breeforth, M. (1993), 'Users are People', in V. Williamson (ed.), *Users First: the real challenge for community care*, Brighton: University of Brighton, pp. 19–27.

Brewer, C. and Lait, J. (1980), *Can Social Work Survive?* London: Temple Smith.

Broadbent, G. and White, R. (2003), 'Identifying Underlying Principles in Social Work Law: a teaching and learning approach to the legal framework of decision making', *Social Work Education*, 22(5): 445–59.

Brodie, I. (1993), 'Teaching from Practice in Social Work Education: a study of the content of supervision', *Issues in Social Work Education*, 13(2): 71–91.

Brown, A. and Bourne, I. (1996), *The Social Work Supervisor*, Buckingham: Open University Press.

Bruggen, P. (1997), *Who Cares? True Stories of the NHS Reforms*, Charlebury: John Carpenter Press.

Burr, V. (1995), *An Introduction to Social Constructionism*, London: Routledge.

Butler, A. (1994), 'START (Students and Refugees Together): towards a model of practice learning as service provision', unpublished paper, Joint Social Work Education Conference, Glasgow, 2004.

Butrym, Z. (1976), *The Nature of Social Work*, Basingstoke: Macmillan.

Cabot, R.C. (1931), 'Treatment in Social Casework and the Need for Tests of its Success and Failure', *Proceedings of the National Conference of Social Work* (Fifty-eighth Annual Session), Minneapolis, MN; Chicago: University of Chicago Press, pp. 3–24.

Campbell, D.T. (1988), 'The Experimenting Society', in D.T. Campbell and E.S. Overman (eds), *Methodology and Epistemology for Social Sciences*, Chicago: University of Chicago Press.

Campbell, S., Steiner, A., Robison, J., Webb, D., Raven, A. and Roland, M. (2003), 'Is the Quality of Care in General Medical Practice Improving? Results of a longitudinal observational study', *British Journal of General Practice*, 53(489): 298–304.

Cannan, C., Berry, L. and Lyons, K. (1992), *Social Work and Europe*, Basingstoke: Macmillan.

Caspi, J. and Reid, W.J. (2002), *Educational Supervision in Social Work: a task-centred model for field instruction and staff development*, New York: Columbia University Press.

CCETSW (1991a), *Rules and Requirements for the Diploma in Social Work* (Paper 30, 2nd edn), London: Central Council for Education and Training in Social Work.

CCETSW (1991b), *Requirements and Guidance for the Approval of Agencies and the Accreditation and Training of Practice Teachers (Paper 26.3*, revised edn), London: Central Council for Education and Training in Social Work.

CCETSW (1991c), *Teaching, Learning and Assessing Social Work Law. Report of the Law Improvements Project Group*, London: Central Council for Education and Training in Social Work.

CCETSW (1995), *Assuring Quality in the Diploma in Social Work – 1*, London: Central Council for Education and Training in Social Work.

CCETSW (2000), *Working in a Multi-disciplinary Setting in Northern Ireland*, Belfast: Central Council for Education and Training in Social Work.

Chand, A., Doel, M. and Yee, J. (1999), 'Tracking Social Work Students' Understanding and Application of Anti-discriminatory Practice', *Issues in Social Work Education*, 19(1): 55–74.

Chaskin, R.J. (2003), 'Fostering Neighborhood Democracy: legitimacy and accountability within loosely coupled systems', *Nonprofit and Voluntary Sector Quarterly*, 32(2): 161–89.

Children's Rights Alliance for England (2003), *The Case for a Children's Rights Commissioner for England*, London: Children's Rights Alliance for England.

Christie, A. and Kruck, E. (1998), 'Choosing to Become a Social Worker: motives, incentives, concerns and disincentives', *Social Work Education*, 17(1): 21–34.

Christie, A. and Weeks, S. (1998), 'Life Experience: a neglected form of knowledge in social work education and practice', *Practice*, 10(1): 55–68.

Clark, C.L. (2000), *Social Work Ethics, Politics, Principles and Practice*, Basingstoke: Palgrave.

Clark, H., Dyer, S. and Hansaran, L. (1996), *Going Home: older people leaving hospital*, London: Polity Press/Joseph Rowntree Foundation/Community Care.

Clarke, C.L., Gibb, C.E. and Ramprogus, V. (2003), 'Clinical Learning Environments: an evaluation of an innovative role to support preregistration nursing placements', *Journal of Learning in Health and Social Care*, 2(2): 105–15.

Clough, R. (ed.) (1996), *Abuse in Residential Institutions*, London: Whiting and Birch.

Cochrane, A. (1972), *Random Reflections on Health Services*, London: Royal Society of Medicine Press.

Cochrane Collaboration (2003), at: http://www.cochrane.org/index0.htm.

Cohen, C.S. (1995), 'Making It Happen: building successful support group programs', *Social Work with Groups*, 18(1): 67–80.

Collins, S. (2001), 'Bullying in Social Work Organisations', *Practice*, 13(3): 29–44.

Commission for Racial Equality (2003), *Good Practice: the duty to promote racial equality*, at: www.cre.gov.uk/duty/index.html.

Cooper, A. (1994), 'A Tale of Two Cultures – race, ideology and child protection in France and England', *Social Work in Europe*, 1(3): 53–60.

Cooper, J. (ed.) (2000), *Law, Rights and Disability*, London: Jessica Kingsley.

Corby, B. (1996), 'Risk Assessment in Child Protection Work', in H. Kemshall and J. Pritchard (eds), *Good Practice in Risk Assessment and Risk Management*, London: Jessica Kingsley, pp. 13–30.

Coulshed, V. and Mullender, A. (2001), *Management in Social Work* (2nd edn), Basingstoke: Palgrave.

Coulshed, V. and Orme, J. (1998), *Social Work Practice: an introduction* (3rd edn) Basingstoke: Macmillan.

Cox, R. (2003), 'Stepping Out', *New Beacon*, June, London: RNIB.

Craig, R. (1988), 'Structured Activities with Adolescent Boys', *Groupwork*, 1(1): 48–59.

Cree, V.E. (1996), 'Why Do Men Care?' in K. Cavanagh and V.E. Cree (eds), *Working with Men*, London: Routledge.

Cree, V.E. and Macaulay, C. (2000), *Transfer of Learning in Professional and Vocational Education*, London: Routledge.

Crisp, B.R., Anderson, M.R., Orme, J. and Green Listor, P. (2003), *Learning and Teaching in Social Work Education: assessment*, London: Social Care Institute for Excellence (SCIE)/Policy Press.

Cull, L-A. and Roche, J. (2001), *The Law and Social Work: contemporary issues for practice*, Basingstoke: Palgrave.

Cullen, D. and Lane, M. (2003) *Child Care Law: a summary of the law in England and Wales* (4th edn), London: British Association for Adoption and Fostering.

Cutler, T. and Waine, B. (2003), 'Advancing Public Accountability? The social services "star" ratings', *Public Money and Management*, 23(2): 125–28.

Dalrymple, J. and Burke, B. (1998), 'Developing Anti-oppressive Practice Teaching', *Practice*, 10(20): 25–35.

Davies, M. (1994), *The Essential Social Worker: a guide to positive practice* (3rd edn), Aldershot: Arena.

Davies, M. (ed.) (2000), *The Blackwell Encyclopaedia of Social Work*, Oxford: Blackwell.

de Bono, E. (2000), *Six Hat Thinking*, London: Penguin.

Degenhardt, D. (2003), 'Teacher or Supporter? The social work tutor's role in students' professional development', *Journal of Practice Teaching in Health and Social Care*, 4(3): 54–67.

Dent, T. and Tourville, A. (2002), 'University–Community Partnerships: practicum learning for community revitalization', in S.M. Shardlow and M. Doel (eds), *Learning to Practise Social Work: International Approaches*, London: Jessica Kingsley, pp. 25–42.

Department of Health (1989), *Caring for People: Care in the Community in the next decade and beyond*. London: HMSO.

Department of Health (1990), *Community Care in the Next Decade and Beyond: policy guidance*, London: HMSO.

Department of Health (1993), *Guidance on Permissible Form of Control in Children's Residential Care*. London: HMSO.

Department of Health (2000), *National Health Service Plan*, London: HMSO.

Department of Health (2001a), *National Service Framework for Older People*, London: HMSO.

Department of Health (2001b), 'Fair Access to Care Services (FACS), General Principles of Assessment for adult social care', www.doh.gov.uk/scg/facs.

Department of Health (2002a), *Requirements for Social Work Training*, London: HMSO.

Department of Health (2002b), *Reform of Social Work Education*, retrieved 14 March 2002, from: http://www.doh.gov.uk/swgualification.

Department of Health (2003a), *Assessment in Child Care*, London: HMSO.

Department of Health (2003b), *No Secrets: Guidance on Developing and Implementing Multi-Agency Policies and Procedures to Protect Vulnerable Adults from Abuse.* London: Stationery Office.

Department of Health (2003c), *Our Inheritance, Our Future: realising the potential of genetics in the NHS*, London: Stationery Office.

Department of Health and Home Office (2003), *The Victoria Climbié Inquiry: Report of an Inquiry by Lord Laming*, London: Stationery Office.

Department of Health, Department for Education and Employment, Home Office (2000), *The Framework for the Assessment of Children in Need and their Families*, London: HMSO.

Devore, W. and Schlesinger, E.S. (1999), *Ethnic-Sensitive Social Work Practice* (5th edn), Boston, MA: Allyn and Bacon.

Dhalech, M. (1999), 'Race Equality Initiatives in South West England', in P. Henderson and R. Kaur (eds), *Rural Racism in the UK*, London: Community Development Foundation.

Doel, M. (1988), 'A Practice Curriculum to Promote Accelerated Learning', in J. Phillipson, M. Richards and D. Sawdon (eds), *Towards a Practice Led Curriculum*, London: National Institute for Social Work, pp. 45–60.

Doel, M. (2002a), 'Interprofessional Working: Berlin walls and garden fences', *Learning in Health and Social Care*, 1(3): 170–71.

Doel, M. (2002b), 'Creativity and Practice Teaching: editorial', *Practice Teaching in Health and Social Work*, 4(1): 3–7.

Doel, M. (2005), *The Groupwork Book*, London: Routledge/Community Care.

Doel, M. and Cooner, T.S. (2002), 'The Virtual Placement', interactive web-based program at: www.hcc.uce.ac.uk/virtualplacement.

Doel, M. and Lawson, B. (1986), 'Open Records: the client's right to partnership', *British Journal of Social Work*, 16(4): 407–30.

Doel, M. and Marsh, P. (1992), *Task-Centred Social Work*, Aldershot: Ashgate.

Doel, M. and Sawdon, C. (1995), 'A Strategy for Groupwork Education and Training in a Social Work Agency', *Groupwork* 8(2):189–204.

Doel, M. and Sawdon, C. (1999), *The Essential Groupworker: teaching and learning creative groupwork*, London: Jessica Kingsley.

Doel, M. and Shardlow, S.M. (1993), *Social Work Practice*, Aldershot: Gower.

Doel, M. and Shardlow, S.M. (1995), *Preparing Post-Qualifying Portfolios: a practical guide for candidates*, London: Central Council for Education and Training in Social Work.

Doel, M. and Shardlow, S.M. (1996a), 'Simulated and Live Practice Teaching: the practice teacher's craft', *Social Work Education*, 15(4): 16–33.

Doel, M. and Shardlow, S.M. (eds) (1996b), *Social Work in a Changing World: an international perspective on practice learning*, Aldershot: Arena.

Doel, M. and Shardlow, S.M. (1998), *The New Social Work Practice*, Aldershot, Arena.

Doel, M., Sawdon, C. and Morrison, D. (2002), *Learning, Practice and Assessment: signposting the portfolio*, London: Jessica Kingsley.

Doueck, H.J., English, D.J., DePanfils, D. and Moote, G.T. (1993), 'Decision-Making in Child Protection Services: a comparison of selected risk-assessment systems', *Child Welfare*, LXXII (5): 441–52.

Douglas, T. (1993), *A Theory of Groupwork Practice*, Basingstoke: Macmillan.

Duncan, T., Piper, C. and Warren-Adamson, C. (2003), 'Running Rings Round Law? An ecological approach to teaching law for child-centred practice', *Social Work Education*, 22(5): 493–503.

Durham, A. (2003), 'Young Men Living through and with Child Sexual Abuse: a practitioner research study', *British Journal of Social Work*, 33(3): 309–23.

Eadie, T. and Ward, D. (1995), 'The "Scenario Approach" to Teaching Social Work Law', *Social Work Education*, 14(2): 64–84.

Ebenstein, H. (1999), 'Single Session Groups: issues for social workers', *Social Work with Groups*, 21:(1–2): 49–60.

Ells, P. and Dehn, G. (2001), 'Whistleblowing: public concern at work', in C. Cull and J. Roche (eds), *The Law and Social Work*, Basingstoke: Palgrave.

Encarta (1999), *Dictionary*, London: Bloomsbury.

England, H. (1986), *Social Work as Art*, London: Allen and Unwin.

Evans, D., Cava, H., Gill, O. and Wallis, A. (1988), 'Helping Students Evaluate Their Own Practice', *Issues in Social Work Education*, 8(2): 113–36.

Evans, G. (1997), 'The Rationing Debate: rationing healthcare by age; the case against', *British Medical Journal*, 314: 822–25.

Fairweather, E. (1998), 'Exposing the Islington Children's Homes Scandal: a journalist's view', in G. Hunt (ed.), *Whistleblowing in the Social Services*, London: Arnold, pp. 19–40.

Fatout, M.F. (1989), 'Decision-making in a Therapeutic Group', *Groupwork*, 2(1): 70–79.

Fatout, M.F. (1998), 'Exploring Worker Responses to Critical Incidents', *Groupwork*, 10(3): 183–95.

Fieldhouse, J. (2003), 'The Impact of an Allotment Group on Mental Health Clients' Health, Wellbeing and Social Networking', *British Journal of Occupational Therapy*, 66(7): 286–96.

Fischer, J. (1976), *The Effectiveness of Social Casework*. Springfield, IL: Charles C. Thomas.

Flood, B. (1988), *Developing a Cultural Inventory*, Oregon: Division of Continuing Education, Portland State University.

Fook, J. (2002), *Social Work: critical theory and practice*, London: Sage.

Foot, P. (1997), 'Footnotes', *Private Eye*, (935): 27.

Fortune, A.E. and Abramson, J.S. (1993), 'Predictors of Satisfaction with Field Practicum among Social Work Students', *The Clinical Supervisor*, 11(1): 95–110.

Fortune, A.E., Miller, J., Rosenblum, A.F., Sanchez, B.M., Smith, C. and Reid, W.J. (1995), 'Further Explorations of the Liaison Role: a view from the field', in G.

Rogers (ed.), *Social Work Field Education: views and visions*, Dubuque, Iowa: Kendall/Hunt, pp. 273–93.

Fuller, R. and Petch, A. (1995), *Practitioner Research: the reflexive social worker*, Buckingham: Open University Press.

Fuller, R. and Tulle-Winton, E. (1996), 'Specialism, Genericism and Others: does it make a difference?', *British Journal of Social Work*, 26(5): 679–98.

Furniss, J. (1988), 'The Client Speaks Again', *Pro-file*, 3: 2–3.

Gardiner, D. (1989), *The Anatomy of Supervision*, Milton Keynes: SRHE and Open University Press.

Gelman, S.R. and Wardell, P.J. (1988), 'Who's Responsible? The field liability dilemma', *Journal of Social Work Education*, 24(1): 70–77.

Gelman, S.R., Pollack, D. and Auerbach, C. (1996), 'Liability Issues in Social Work Education', *Journal of Social Work Education*, 351(3): 351–61.

Getzel, G.S. and Mahoney, K.F. (1989), 'Confronting Human Finitude: groupwork with people with AIDS', *Groupwork*, 2(2): 95–107.

Gibbs, L. and Gambrill, E. (2002), 'Evidence-based Practice: counterarguments to objections', *Research on Social Work Practice*, 12(3): 452–76.

Glendinning, C., Coleman, A. and Rummery, K. (2002), 'Partnerships, Performance and Primary Care: developing integrated services for older people in England', *Ageing and Society*, 22(2): 185–208.

Goleman, D. (1996), *Emotional Intelligence*, London: Bloomsbury.

Gray, J.A.M. (2001), 'Evidence-based Medicine for Professionals', in A. Edwards and G. Elwyn (eds), *Evidence-based Patient Choice – inevitable or impossible*, Oxford: Oxford University Press, pp. 19–33.

GSCC (2002), *Code of Practice for Social Care Workers and Code of Practice for Employers of Social Care Workers*, London: General Social Care Council, www.gscc.org.uk.

Gurney, A. (2000), 'Risk Management', in M. Davies (ed.) *The Blackwell Encyclopaedia of Social Work*, Oxford: Blackwell, pp. 300–301.

Hadley, R. and McGrath, M. (1981), *Going Local: neighbourhood social services*. London: Bedford Square Press.

Harries, P.A. and Gilhooly, K. (2003), 'Generic and Specialist Occupational Therapy Casework in Community Mental Health Teams', *British Journal of Occupational Therapy*, 66(3): 101–109.

Harries, P.A. and Harries, C. (2001), 'Studying Clinical Reasoning, Part 2: applying social judgement theory', *British Journal of Occupational Therapy*, 64(6): 285–92.

Harrison (2003), *Typologies of Organisational Culture*, in C. Jarvis: www.sol.brunel.ac.uk/bola/culture/harrison.html.

Hawkins, P. and Shohet, R. (2000), *Supervision in the Helping Professions* (2nd edn), Buckingham: Open University Press.

Henchman, D. and Walton, S. (1993), 'Critical Incident Analysis and its Application in Groupwork', *Groupwork*, 6(3): 189–98.

Henderson, J., Scott, H. and Lloyd, P. (2003), 'In the Real World We're All Put on the Spot at Some Time or Other So You Need to be Prepared for It': an exploratory study of an oral method of assessing knowledge of mental health law', *Social Work Education*, 21(1): 91–103.

Herod, J. and Lymbery, M. (2002), 'The Social Work Role in Multi-disciplinary Teams', *Practice*, 14(4).

Heus, M. and Pincus, A. (1986), *The Creative Generalist: a guide to social work practice*, Barneveld, WI: Micamar.

Hewison, A. and Sim, J. (1998), 'Managing Interprofessional Working: using codes of ethics as a foundation', *Journal of Interprofessional Care*, 12(3): 309–21.

Hill, C. *et al.* (2002), 'The Emerging Role of the Specialist Nurse: promoting the health of looked after children', *Adoption and Fostering*, 26(4): 35–43.

Hinsliff, G. (2004), 'They Told Me to Let My Child Die', *The Guardian*, 4 January, p. 12.

Hogg, B., Kent, P. and Ward, D. (1992), *The Teaching of Law in Practice Placements*, Nottingham: School of Social Studies, University of Nottingham.

Hollis, E.V. and Taylor, A.L. (1951), *Social Work Education in the United States*, New York: Columbia University Press.

Holme, A. and Maizels, J. (1978), *Social Workers and Volunteers*, London: George Allen and Unwin.

Home, A.M. (1997), 'Enhancing Research Usefulness with Adapted Focus Groups', *Groupwork*, 9(2): 128–38.

Hopkins, G. (2003), *Plain English for Social Services: a guide to better communication*, London: Russell House Publishing.

Horn, C. (2002), *Blowing the Whistle*, retrieved 21 December 2004 from: http://www.personneltoday.com/Articles/12/03/16508/Blowing+the+whistle.htm.

Horwath, J. (ed.) (2001), *The Child's World: assessing children in need*, London: Jessica Kingsley.

Horwath, J. and Shardlow, S.M. (eds) (2003a), *Making Links Across Specialisms*, London: Russell House Publishing.

Horwath, J. and Shardlow, S.M. (2003b), 'Specialism: A Force for Change', in J. Horwath and S.M. Shardlow (eds), *Making Links Across Specialisms: understanding modern social work practice*, Lyme Regis: Russell House, pp. 1–21.

Houston-Vega, M.K., Neuhring, E.M. and Daguio, E.R. (1996), *Prudent Practice*, Annapolis, MD: NASW Press.

Howe, D. (1996), *Social Workers and their Practice in Welfare Bureaucracies*, Aldershot: Gower.

Howe, D. (2003), *An Introduction to Social Work Theory*, Aldershot: Ashgate.

Hudson, B.L. and Macdonald, G.M. (1986), *Behavioural Social Work*, Basingstoke: Macmillan.

Hugman, R. (1991), *Power in Caring Professions*, Basingstoke: Macmillan/BASW.

Hull, C. and Redfern, L. (1996), *Profiles and Portfolios: a guide for nurses and midwives*, Basingstoke: Macmillan.

Humphries, B. (2003), 'What *Else* Counts as Evidence in Evidence-based Practice?', *Social Work Education*, 22(1): 81–91.

Humphrys, J. (2003), 'Not I. It's Me', *The Guardian*, 21 October.

Hunt, G. (ed.) (1995), *Whistleblowing in the Health Service*, London: Edward Arnold.

Hunt, G. (ed.) (1998), *Whistleblowing in the Social Services: public accountability and professional practice*, London: Arnold.

IFSW (1994), *The Ethics of Social Work: principles and standards*, at: http://www.ifsw.org/Publications/4.4.pub.html.

Jayaratne, S., Croxton, T. and Mattison, D. (1997), 'Social Work Professional Standards: an exploratory study'. *Social Work*, 42(2): 187–98.

Johns, R. (2003), *Using the Law in Social Work*, Exeter: Learning Matters.

Jones, C. (2001), 'Voices from the Front Line: state social workers and New Labour', *British Journal of Social Work*, 31: 547–62.

Jones, R. (2003), *Mental Health Act Manual* (8th edn), London: Sweet and Maxwell.

Jordan, B. (2003), 'Tough Love: social work practice in UK society', in P. Stepney and D. Ford (eds) (2003), *Social Work Models, Methods and Theories*, London: Russell House Publishing.

Jovelin, E. (2001), 'Social Work as a Career: Choice or Accident? The French Example', in A. Adams, P. Erath and S.M. Shardlow (eds), *Key Themes in European Social Work*, Lyme Regis: Russell House, pp. 95–102.

JRF (2005), 'Young Turks and Kurds: a set of "invisible" disadvantaged groups', Joseph Rowntree Findings (Feb 2005 – ref 0075) at www.jrf.org.uk/knowledge/findings/.

Kadushin, A.E. (1992), *Supervision in Social Work*, New York: Columbia University Press.

Kant, I. (1785), *Groundwork of the Metaphysic of Morals*, in I. Kant, *The Moral Law*, ed. and trans. H.J. Paton, London: Routledge, pp. 53–123.

Katz, J. (1978), *White Awareness: handbook for anti-racist training*, Norman, OK: University of Oklahoma Press.

Kearney, P. (2003), *A Framework for Supporting and Assessing Practice Learning*, SCIE Position Paper No.2, London: SCIE.

Kemshall, H. (1996), 'Offender Risk and Probation Practice', in H. Kemshall and J. Pritchard (eds), *Good Practice in Risk Assessment and Risk Management*, London: Jessica Kingsley, pp. 133–45.

Kemshall, H. and Pritchard, J. (eds) (1996), *Good Practice in Risk Assessment and Risk Management*, London: Jessica Kingsley.

Khan, S. (1992), 'Culture Clash', *Young People Now*, March: 19–21.

King, C. (2003), 'A Case to Answer', *Care and Health Magazine*, (42): 10–11.

Kitwood, T. and Bredin, K. (1992), *Person to Person*, Essex: Gale Centre.

Knight, C. (1997), 'A Study of MSW and BSW Students' Involvement with Group Work in the Field Practicum', *Social Work with Groups*, 20(2): 31–49.

Knight, T. and Worsley, A. (1998), 'Creativity and Competence: reconstructing social work for the millennium', *Practice Teaching in Health and Social Work*, 1(2): 13–22.

Kronenberg, F., Algado, S.S. and Pollard, N. (2004), *Occupational Therapy Without Borders*, Elsevier: Oxford.

Kurland, R. and Salmon, R. (1993), 'Groupwork versus Casework in a Group', *Groupwork*, 6(1): 5–16.

Laming, H. (2003), *The Victoria Climbié Inquiry Report*, Cm. 5730, London: The Stationery Office.

Langan, M. and Day, L. (1992), *Women, Oppression and Social Work*, London: Routledge.

Lebacq, M. and Shah, Z. (1989), 'A Group for Black and White Sexually Abused Children', *Groupwork*, 2(2): 123–33.

Lefevre, M. (1998), 'Recognising and Addressing Imbalances of Power in the Practice Teacher/Student Dialectic: an anti-discriminatory approach', in H. Lawson (ed.) *Practice Teaching Changing Social Work*, London: Jessica Kingsley, pp. 15–31.

Levinsky, N.G. (1998), 'Can We Afford Medical Care for Alice C?', *The Lancet*, 352: 1849–51.

Lindow, V. and Morris, J. (1995), *Service User Involvement*, York: Joseph Rowntree Foundation.

Lishman, J. (1994), *Communication in Social Work*, Basingstoke: Macmillan.

Lishman, J. (2002), 'Personal and Professional Development', in R. Adams, L. Dominelli and M. Payne (eds), *Social Work: themes, issues and critical debates*, Basingstoke: Palgrave, pp. 95–108.

Littlechild, B. (1996), 'The Risk of Violence and Aggression to Social Work and Social Care Staff', in H. Kemshall and J. Pritchard (eds), *Good Practice in Risk Assessment and Risk Management*, London: Jessica Kingsley, pp. 159–75.

Loewenberg, F.M. and Dolgoff, R. (2000), *Ethical Decisions for Social Work Practice* (6th edn), Itasca, IL: Peacock.

Lordan, N. (1996), 'The Use of Sculpts in Social Groupwork Education', *Groupwork*, 9(1): 62–79.

Lorenz, W. (1994), *Social Work in a Changing Europe*, London: Routledge.

Lymbery, M. (1998), 'Care Management and Professional Autonomy: the impact of community care legislation on social work with older people', *British Journal of Social Work*, 28(6): 863–78.

Lymbery, M. (2000), 'The Retreat from Professionalism: from social worker to care manager', in N. Malin (ed.), *Professionalism, Boundaries and the Workplace*, London: Routledge.

Lymbery, M. (2001), 'Social Work at the Crossroads', *British Journal of Social Work*, 31(3): 369–84.

Lyons, K. (1999), *International Social Work: themes and perspectives*, Aldershot: Ashgate.

McDonald, A. (1999), *Understanding Community Care: a guide for social workers*, Basingstoke: Macmillan.

Macdonald, G. and Sheldon, B. with Gillespie J. (1992), 'Contemporary Studies of the Effectiveness of Social Work', *British Journal of Social Work*, 22(6): 615–43.

Macpherson, W. (1999), *Report on the Inquiry into the Stephen Lawrence Murder*, London: Home Office.

Malekoff, A. (1999), 'Expressing Our Anger: hindrance or help in groupwork with adolescents?', *Groupwork*, 11(1): 71–82.

Malks, B., Schmidt, C. and Austin, M. (2002), 'Elder Abuse Prevention: a case study of the Santa Clara County Financial Abuse Specialist Team (FAST) program', *Journal of Gerontological Social Work*, 39(3): 23–39.

Manor, O. (1988), 'Preparing the Client for Social Groupwork: an illustrated framework', *Groupwork*, 1(2): 100–14.

Manor, O. (1996), 'Storming as Transformation: a case study of group relationships', *Groupwork*, 9(3): 128–38.

Manor, O. (1999), 'Technical Errors or Missed Alternatives: an interview with Catherine Papell', *Groupwork*, 11(1): 83–93.

Manthorpe, J. (2000), 'Risk Assessment', *The Blackwell Encyclopaedia of Social Work*, ed. M. Davies, Oxford: Blackwell, pp. 298–99.

Maram, M. and Rice, S. (2002), 'To Share or Not to Share: dilemmas of facilitators who share the problem of group members', *Groupwork*, 3(2): 6–33.

Mark, R. (1996), *Research Made Simple: a handbook for social workers*, London: Sage.

Marsh, P. and Doel, M. (2005), *The Task-Centred Book*, London: Routledge/Community Care.

Martin, B. (1999), *The Whistleblower's Handbook: How to be an Effective Resister*, Charlebury: John Carpenter.

*Metro* (2003), 'Amos was "promoted on merit"', *Metro*, 13 May.

Middleton, L. (1997), *The Art of Assessment*, Birmingham: Venture Press.

Midgley, J. (2001), 'Issues in International Social Work', *Journal of Social Work*, 1(1): 21–35.

Milgram, S. (1974), *Obedience to Authority*, London: Tavistock.

Miller, C., Ross, N. and Freeman, M. (1999), *Shared Learning and Clinical Teamwork: new directions in education for multiprofessional practice*, London: English National Board for Nursing, Midwifery and Health Visiting.

Milner, J. (1986), *The Child Abuse Potential Inventory: Manual* (2nd edn), Webster, NC: Psytec.

Milner, J. and O'Byrne, P. (2002), *Assessment in Social Work* (2nd edn), Basingstoke: Macmillan.

Minuchin, S. and Fishman, C. (1981), *Family Therapy Techniques*, Cambridge, MA: Harvard University Press.

Mullen, E.J. and Dumpson, J.R. (1972), *The Evaluation of Social Intervention*, San Francisco: Jossey-Bass.

Mullender, A. (1995), 'Groups for Children Who Have Lived With Domestic Violence: learning from North America', *Groupwork*, 8(1): 79–98.

Mullender, A. and Ward, D. (1991), *Self-Directed Groupwork: users take action for empowerment*, London: Whiting and Birch.

Munro, E. (2001), *Understanding Social Work: an empirical approach*. London: Athlone Press.

Murphy, E. (2000), 'Priorities in Dementia Services: the interaction of purchasers and providers', *International Journal of Geriatric Psychiatry*, 15(8): 746–50.

Muzumdar, K. and Atthar, R. (2002), 'Social Work Placements in Police Stations: a force for change', in S.M. Shardlow and M. Doel (eds), *Learning to Practise Social Work: international approaches*, London: Jessica Kingsley, pp. 43–58.

NASW (1996), *Code of Ethics*, Silver Spring, MD: National Association of Social Workers.

*New Internationalist* (1989), 'Do You Need Treatment?', November: 10.

NOPT (1999), *Code of Practice*, London: National Organisation for Practice Teaching.

NOPT (2000), *Code of Practice*, at: www.nopt.org

Northen, H. and Kurland, R. (2001), *Social Work with Groups* (3rd edn), New York: Columbia University Press.

O'Connor, I. (1992), 'Bereaved by Suicide: setting up an "ideal" therapy group in a real world', *Groupwork*, 5(3): 74–86.

Oliver, M. (1990), *The Politics of Disablement*, Basingstoke: Macmillan.

Orme, J. (2002), 'Feminist Social Work', in R. Adams, L. Dominelli and M. Payne (eds), *Social Work: themes, issues and critical debates*, Basingstoke: Palgrave, p. 218–26.

O'Sullivan, T. (1999), *Decision Making in Social Work*, Basingstoke: Macmillan.

Øvretveit, J., Mathias, P. and Thompson, T. (eds) (1997), *Interprofessional Working for Health and Social Care*, Basingstoke: Macmillan.

Papell, C.P. (1996), 'Reflections on Issues in Social Work Education', in N. Gould and I. Taylor (eds), *Reflective Learning for Social Work*, Aldershot: Arena.

Parker, J. and Bradley, J. (2003), *Assessment, Planning, Intervention and Review*, Exeter: Learning Matters.

Parker, J. and Merrylees, S. (2002), 'Why Become a Professional? Experiences of care-giving and the decision to enter social work or nursing education', *Learning in Health and Social Care*, 1(2): 105–14.

Parsloe, P. (ed.) (1999), *Risk Assessment in Social Care*, London: Jessica Kingsley.

Parton, N. (2000), 'Some Thoughts on the Relationship between Theory and Practice in and for Social Work', *British Journal of Social Work*, 30(4): 449–63.

Payne, M. (1995), *Social Work and Community Care*, Basingstoke: Macmillan.

Payne, M. (1996), *What is Professional Social Work?*, Birmingham: Venture Press.

Payne, M. (2002), 'Social Work Theories and Reflective Practice', in R. Adams, L. Dominelli and M. Payne (eds), *Social Work: themes, issues and critical debates*, Basingstoke: Palgrave, pp. 123–38.

Payne, M. and Shardlow, S.M. (eds) (2002), *Social Work in the British Isles*, London: Jessica Kingsley.

Pearson, G. (1973), 'Social Work as the Privatised Solution of Public Ills', *British Journal of Social Work*, 3(2): 209–27.

Pelosi, A. and Birchwood, M. (2003), 'Is Early Intervention for Psychosis a Waste of Valuable Resources?', *British Journal of Psychiatry*, 182(3): 196–98.

Phillipson, J. (2002), 'Creativity and Practice Teaching', in *Practice Teaching in Health and Social Work*, 4(1): 8–26.

Pincus, A. and Minahan, A. (1973), *Social Work Practice: model and method*, Itasca, IL: F.E. Peacock.

Pithouse, A. (1998), *Social Work: the social organisation of an invisible trade* (2nd edn), Aldershot: Ashgate.

Popper, K. (1959), *The Logic of Scientific Discovery*, London: Hutchinson.

Preston-Shoot, M. (1992), 'On Empowerment, Partnership and Authority in Groupwork Practice: a training contribution', *Groupwork*, 5(2): 5–30.

Preston-Shoot, M. (1993), 'Whither Social Work Law? Future questions on the teaching and assessment of law to social workers', *Social Work Education*, 8(1): 65–77.

Preston-Shoot, M. (2001), 'A Triumph of Hope over Experience? On modernising accountability in social services – the case of complaints procedures in community care', *Social Policy and Administration*, 35(6): 701–715.

Pugh, R. (2000), *Rural Social Work*, Lyme Regis: Russell House.

QAA (2002), 'Benchmark Statement for Social Work', Quality Assurance Agency, at: http://www.qaa.ac.uk/crntwork/benchmark/socialwork.pdf.

Quinny, A. (2004), 'Supporting Practice Learning: the placements on-line project', unpublished paper, Joint Social Work Education Conference, Glasgow.

Randall, H. and Csikai, C.E. (2003), 'Issues Affecting Utilization of Hospice Services by Rural Hispanics', *Journal of Ethnic and Cultural Diversity in Social Work*, 12(2): 74–94.

Rashid, S. P., Ball, C. and McDonald, A. (2002), *Mental Health Law* (3rd edn), Norwich: University of East Anglia.

Reamer, F.G. (1994), *Social Work Practice and Liability*, New York: Columbia University Press.

Redl, F. (1966), *How Good or Bad is it to Get Angry When We Deal with Children?*, New York: Free Press.

Reed, M. (2002), 'The Practitioner's Perspective: practice focus', *Professional Social Work*, April: 16–17.

Reid, K. (1988), 'But I Don't Want to Lead a Group! Some common problems of social workers leading groups', *Groupwork*, 1(2): 124–34.

Reid, W.J. (1992), *Task Strategies: an empirical approach to clinical social work*, New York: Columbia University Press.

Reid, W.J. (2000), *The Task Planner: an intervention resource for human service planners*, New York: Columbia University Press.

Reid, W.J. (2001), 'The Role of Science in Social Work', *Journal of Social Work*, 1(3): 273–94.

Reid, W.J. and Hanrahan, P. (1980), 'The Effectiveness of Social Work: recent evidence', in E. M. Goldberg and N. Connelly (eds), *The Effectiveness of Social Care for the Elderly*, London: Heinemann.

*Report of the Committee of Inquiry into the Care and Supervision Provided in Relation to Maria Colwell* (1974), London: HMSO.

Roberts, H., Smith, S.J. and Bryce, C. (1995), *Children at Risk*, Buckingham: Open University Press.

Sacco, T. (1996), 'Towards an Inclusive Paradigm for Social Work', in M. Doel and S.M. Shardlow (eds), *Social Work in a Changing World*, Aldershot: Arena, pp. 31–42.

Sackett, D.L., Richardson, W., Rosenberg, W. and Haynes, R.B. (1997), *Evidence-based Medicine. How to practice and teach evidence-based medicine*, New York: Churchill Livingstone.

Sackett, D.L., Rosenberg, W.M., Gray, J.A.M., Haynes, R.B. and Richardson, W.S. (1996), 'Evidence-based Medicine – what it is and what it isn't', *British Medical Journal*, 312(7023): 71–72.

Salmon, D., Hook, G. and Hayward, M. (2003), 'The Specialist Health Visitor Post: a parental perspective', *Community Practitioner*, 76(9): 334–38.

Schön, D.A. (1987), *Educating the Reflective Practitioner*, San Francisco: Jossey-Bass.

Schwartz, W. (1976), 'Between Client and System: the mediating function', in R.W. Roberts and H. Northen (eds), *Theories of Social Work with Groups*, New York: Columbia University Press.

Seebohm, F.C. (1968), *Report of the Committee on Local Authority and Allied Personal Social Services* (Seebohm Report), Cmnd 3703, London: HMSO.

Seebohm, F.C. (1989), *Seebohm Twenty Years On: three stages in the development of the personal social services*, London: PSI.

Senge, P.M. (1990), *The Fifth Discipline: the art and practice of the learning organization*, New York: Doubleday.

Shannon, G. (1998), 'Are We Asking the Experts? Practice teachers' use of client views in assessing student competence', *Social Work Education* 17(4): 407–18.

Shardlow, S.M. (1988), 'The Economics of Student Help', *Insight*, 3(23): 24–25.

Shardlow, S.M. (ed.) (1989), *The Values of Change in Social Work*, London: Routledge.

Shardlow, S.M. (1995), 'Confidentiality, Accountability and the Boundaries of Client–Worker Relationships', in R. Hugman and D. Smith (eds), *Ethical Issues in Social Work*, London: Routledge, pp. 65–83.

Shardlow, S.M. (2000), 'Legal Responsibility and Liability in Fieldwork', in L. Cooper and L. Briggs (eds), *Fieldwork in the Human Services*, Sydney: Allen & Unwin, pp. 117–30.

Shardlow, S.M. and Doel, M. (eds) (2002), *Learning to Practise Social Work: international approaches*. London: Jessica Kingsley.

Shardlow, S.M. and Doel, M. (forthcoming), *Practice Learning and Teaching* (2nd edn), Basingstoke: Macmillan.

Shardlow, S.M., Nixon, S. and Rogers, J. (2002), 'The Motivation of Practice Teachers: decisions relating to involvement in practice learning provision', *Learning in Health and Social Care*, 1(2): 67–74.

Shardlow, S.M., Davis, C., Johnson, M., Murphy, M., Long, T. and Race, D. (2004), *Standards and Inter-professional Education in Child Protection*, Salford: Salford Centre for Social Work Research.

Sharkey, P. (2000), *The Essentials of Community Care: a guide for practitioners*, Basingstoke: Macmillan.

Sharry, J. (1999), 'Building Solutions in Groupwork with Parents', *Groupwork*, 11(2): 68–89.

Sharry, J. (2001), *Solution-Focused Groupwork*, London: Sage.

Shaw, I. and Shaw, A. (1997), 'Game Plans, Buzzes and Sheer Luck', *Social Work Research*, 21(2): 69–79.

Sheldon, B. (1998), 'Evidence based Social Services: prospects and problems', *Research Policy and Planning*, 16(2):16–18.

Sheldon, B. and Chilvers, R. (2000), *Evidence-Based Social Care: a study of the prospects and problems*, Lyme Regis: Russell House.

Sheldon, B. and Macdonald, G. (1999), *Research and Practice in Social Care: mind the gap*, Exeter: Centre for Evidence-Based Social Services.

Shepherd, J. (2001), 'Where Do You Go When It's 40 Below? Domestic violence among rural Alaska native women', *AFFILIA – Journal of Women and Social Work*, 16(4): 488–510.

Sheppard, M. (1995a), *Care Management and the New Social Work: a critical analysis*, London: Whiting and Birch.

Sheppard, M. (1995b), 'Social Work, Social Science and Practice Wisdom', *British Journal of Social Work*, 25(3): 265–93.

Shulman, L. (1999), *The Skills of Helping Individuals, Families, Groups and Communities* (4th edn), Itasca, IL: Peacock Publishers.

Singleton, W.T. and Holden, J. (eds) (1994), *Risk and Decisions*, London: John Wiley and Sons.

Skinner, B.F. (1969), *Contingencies of Reinforcement*, New York: Appleton-Century-Crofts.

Smale, G., Tuson, G., Ahmad, B., Davill, G., Domoney, L. and Sainsbury, E. (1994), *Negotiating Care in the Community: the implications of research findings on community based practice for the implementation of Community Care and Children Acts*, London: HMSO.

Social Services Inspectorate (1999), *Care in the Community – inspection of Community Care services in rural areas*, London: Department of Health.

Solas, J. (1994), 'Why Enter Social Work? Why on earth do they want to do it? Recruits' ulterior motives for entering social work', *Issues in Social Work Education*, 14(2): 51–63.

SSI (1991a), *Care Management and Assessment: Practitioner's Guide*, London: HMSO.

SSI (1991b), *Care Management and Assessment: Manager's Guide*, London: HMSO.

Stalker, K. (2003), 'Managing Risk and Uncertainty in Social Work', *Journal of Social Work*, 3(3): 211–33.

Stepney, P. and Ford, D. (eds) (2003), *Social Work Models, Methods and Theories*, London: Russell House Publishing.

Stevenson, O. (1988), 'Law and Social Work Education: a commentary on The Law Report', *Issues in Social Work Education*, 8(1): 37–45.

Stevenson, O. and Parsloe, P. (1993), *Community Care and Empowerment*, York: Rowntree Foundation with Community Care.

Sullivan, H. (2003), 'New Forms of Local Accountability: coming to terms with "many hands"?', *Policy and Politics*, 31(3): 353–69.

Szymkiewicz-Kowalska, B. (1999), 'Working with Polarities, Roles and Timespirits: a process oriented approach to emotions in the group', *Groupwork*, 11(1): 24–40.

Tajfel, H. (1981), *Human Groups and Social Categories*, Cambridge: Cambridge University Press.

Tan, N-T. (ed.) (2004) *Social Work Around the World III*. Berne: International Federation of Social Workers.

Tan, N-T. and Dodds, I. (eds) (2002), *Social Work Around the World II*, Berne: International Federation of Social Workers.

Tan, N-T. and Envall, E. (eds) (2000), *Social Work Around the World*, Berne: International Federation of Social Workers.

Taylor, A. (1998), 'Hostages to Fortune: the abuse of children in care', in G. Hunt (ed.), *Whistleblowing in the Social Services*, London: Arnold, pp. 41–64.

Taylor, P. (1994), 'The Linguistic and Cultural Barriers to Cross-national Groupwork', *Groupwork*, 7(1): 7–22.

Thomlison, B. and Collins, D. (1995), 'Use of Structured Consultation for Learning Issues in Field Education', in G. Rogers (ed.), *Social Work Field Education: views and visions*, Dubuque, IA: Kendall/Hunt, pp. 233–38.

Thompson, N. (2000a) *Understanding Social Work: preparing for practice*, Basingstoke: Macmillan.

Thompson, N. (2000b) *Tackling Bullying and Harassment in the Workplace*, Birmingham: Pepar Publications.

Thompson, N. (2002), 'Developing Anti-discriminatory Practice', in D. Tomlinson and W. Threw (eds), *Equalising Opportunities, Minimising Oppression*, London: Routledge.

Thompson, N. (2003), *Promoting Equality*, London: Palgrave Macmillan.

Thompson, N., Murphy, M., Straddling, S. with O'Neill, P. (2003), *Meeting the Stress Challenge*, London: Russell House Publishing.

Tidd, J., Bessant, J. and Pavitt, K. (2001), *Managing Innovation: integrating technological, market and organisational change*, Chichester: Wiley.

Tisdal, K., Lavery, R. and McCrystal, P. (1997), *Child Care Law: a comparative review of new legislation in Northern Ireland and Scotland; the Children (Northern Ireland) Order 1995 and the Children (Scotland) Act 1995*, Belfast: Queens University Belfast, Centre for Child Care Research.

Tolson, E.R., Reid, W. and Garvin, C.D. (1994), *Generalist Practice: a task-centred approach*, New York: Columbia University Press.

TOPSS (2002), *National Occupational Standards for Social Work*, London: Training Organisation for Personal Social Services.

Toren, N. (1969), 'Semi-Professions and Social Work', in A. Etzioni (ed.), *The Semi-Professions and Their Organisation*, New York: Free Press, pp. 141–96.

Trevithick, P. (1995), ' "Cycling over Everest": groupwork with depressed women', *Groupwork*, 8(1): 15–33.

Trevithick, P. (2005), *Social Work Skills* (3rd edn), Buckingham: Open University Press.

Trinder, L. (ed.) (2000), *Evidence-based Practice: a critical appraisal*, Oxford: Blackwell.

Trotter, C. (1999), *Working with Involuntary Clients: a guide to practice*, London: Sage.

Tuckman, B. (1965), 'Developmental Sequences in Small Groups', *Psychological Bulletin*, 6(3): 384–99.

Turkie, A. (1995), 'Dialogue and Reparation in the Large, Whole Group', *Groupwork*, 8(2): 152–65.

Underhill, D. with Betteridge, C., Harvey, B. and Patient, K. (2002), 'Learning Opportunities and Placements with Asylum Seekers', in S.M. Shardlow and M. Doel (eds), *Learning to Practise Social Work: international approaches*, London: Jessica Kingsley, pp. 77–90.

Uttley, S. (1981), 'Why Social Work? A comparison of British and New Zealand studies', *British Journal of Social Work*, 11(3): 329–40.

Vernon, S. (1998), 'Legal Aspects of Whistleblowing in the Social Services', in G. Hunt (ed.), *Whistleblowing in the Social Services*, London: Arnold, pp. 222–39.

Ward, D. (2000), 'Totem Not Token: groupwork as a vehicle for user participation', in H. Kemshall and R. Littlechild (eds), *User Involvement and Participation in Social Care*, London: Jessica Kingsley.

Ward, D. (2002), 'Groupwork', in R. Adams, L. Dominelli and M. Payne (eds), *Social Work: themes, issues and critical debates*, Basingstoke: Macmillan.

Wayne, J. and Cohen, C.S. (2001), *Group Work Education in the Field*, Alexandria, VA: Council on Social Work Education.

Webb, S. (2002), 'Evidence-based Practice and Decision Analysis', *Journal of Social Work*, 2(1): 45–63.

Weinstein, J. (1997), 'The Development of Shared Learning: Conspiracy or Constructive Development?', in J. Øvretveit, P. Mathias and T. Thompson (eds) (1997), *Interprofessional Working for Health and Social Care*, Basingstoke: Macmillan.

Weinstein, J., Whittington, C. and Leiba, T. (2003), *Collaboration in Social Work Practice*, London: Jessica Kingsley.

Wenger, N.S. *et al.* (1999), 'Reporting Unethical Research Behaviour', *Evaluation Review*, 23(5): 553–70.

West, J. and Watson, D. (2002), 'Preparing for Practice: the use of personal learning audits in social work education', *Practice*, 14(4): 43–52.

Whitaker, D. and Archer, J.L. (1989), *Research by Social Workers: capitalizing on experience.* London: Central Council for Education and Training in Social Work.

White, I.A. and Hart, K. (1995), *Report of the Inquiry into the Management of Child Care in the London Borough of Islington*, London: London Borough of Islington.

Whittington, C. (2003), *Learning for Collaborative Practice*, London: Department of Health.

Wilcox, R., Smith, D., Moore, J., Hewitt, A., Allan, G., Walker, H., Ropata, M., Monu, L. and Featherstone, T. (1991), *Family Decision Making, Family Group Conferences*, available from Practitioners' Publishing, PO Box 30–430, Lower Hutt, New Zealand.

Williams, A. (1997), 'The Rationing Debate: rationing health care by age: the case for', *British Medical Journal* 314 (7038): 820–822.

Younghusband, E. (1981), *The Newest Profession: a short history of social work*, Sutton: Community Care/IPC Business Press.

# Index